Troubleshooting Microsoft® Outlook® 2002

Microsoft Office XP Application

Don Gilbert and Julia Kelly

PUBLISHED BY
Microsoft Press
A Division of Microsoft Corporation
One Microsoft Way
Redmond, Washington 98052-6399

Library of Congress Cataloging-in-Publication Data
Gilbert, Don, 1948-
Troubleshooting Microsoft Outlook 2002 / Don Gilbert.
p. cm.
Includes index.
ISBN 0-7356-1487-3
1. Microsoft Outlook. 2. Business--Computer programs. 3. Time management--Computer programs. 4. Personal information management--Computer programs. I. Title.

HF5548.4.M5255 G55 2002
005.369-dc21 2001059086

Printed and bound in the United States of America.

1 2 3 4 5 6 7 8 9 QWT 7 6 5 4 3 2

Distributed in Canada by Penguin Books Canada Limited.

A CIP catalogue record for this book is available from the British Library.

Microsoft Press books are available through booksellers and distributors worldwide. For further information about international editions, contact your local Microsoft Corporation office or contact Microsoft Press International directly at fax (425) 936-7329. Visit our Web site at www.microsoft.com/mspress. Send comments to *mspinput@microsoft.com*.

Acquisitions Editor: Alex Blanton
Project Editor: Aileen Wrothwell
Technical Editor: Aaron L'Heureux

Body Part No. X08-41919

Acknowledgements

This book, in its second edition now, has benefited from the help of many people in its lifetime. In particular, this edition owes a great deal to its Project Editor, Aileen Wrothwell; while juggling several projects at once she somehow managed to appear totally focused on just this book. Alex Blanton, Acquisitions Editor, deserves special thanks for getting the ball rolling on this edition and coordinating many necessary details.

Thank you also to the Technical Editor, Aaron L'Heureux, for methodically testing every procedure and providing valuable insights, to Nancy Depper for her excellent job as Manuscript Editor, and to the team at Online Training Solutions, Inc. (OTSI) for making the words and images used in this book look far better than I ever imagined at their creation.

Finally, a heartfelt thank you goes to everyone not mentioned here who contributed to this book from its inception and provided the groundwork for this edition of the book.

Quick contents

Contents

Contents

Contents

Contents

About this book

Troubleshooting Microsoft Outlook 2002 presents a fast and direct way to diagnose and solve the problems you've encountered with Microsoft Outlook 2002. Whether you're a beginning user of Outlook or have upgraded from an earlier version, chances are you bought this book because you want to fix those problems as quickly and easily as possible, without having to read pages of technical background information. We've written this book with three goals in mind: ease, simplicity, and speed. We know you'd like to figure out why your e-mail is stuck in the Outbox or why Outlook won't import your Microsoft Excel Contacts list, so we'll show you how to locate your problem, describe what might be causing it without going into too many specifics, and then lead you right to the solution so that you can get back to what you were doing.

This book is an update of *Troubleshooting Microsoft Outlook*. Unlike the first edition, it does not contain solutions for Microsoft Outlook Express. Targeting the solutions to a single program leaves more room to cover troubleshooting topics that are unique to Outlook 2002 and helps make the solutions more straightforward.

How to use this book

This book isn't meant to be read in any particular order or even from cover to cover. It's designed so that you can jump in, quickly diagnose your problem, and get the information you need to fix it—whether you've just begun to learn about computers and programs or you're knowledgeable enough to get right to the source of the problem. Common problems are grouped into chapters that are listed alphabetically; the chapter titles are kept simple so that you know at a glance what kinds of topics are included in the chapter. Each chapter is broken down into two specific elements: the flowchart and the solution spread.

Flowcharts

The first thing you'll see when you go to a chapter is a dynamic, easy-to-use flowchart. It starts by posing a general question about a common problem and then, as you answer a series of yes-or-no questions, it helps you diagnose your problem. If the solution to your problem is a simple one involving only one or two steps, you'll find a Quick Fix right there on the flowchart. Take a few minutes to work through the steps, and presto—your problem is solved and you're back to work (or play) with a minimum of downtime. If the solution to your problem requires a little more explanation and a few more steps, you'll find the page number of the solution spread and the statement of the problem it addresses. And if your problem isn't shown on the flowchart, you'll find a list of related chapters where your problem might be addressed.

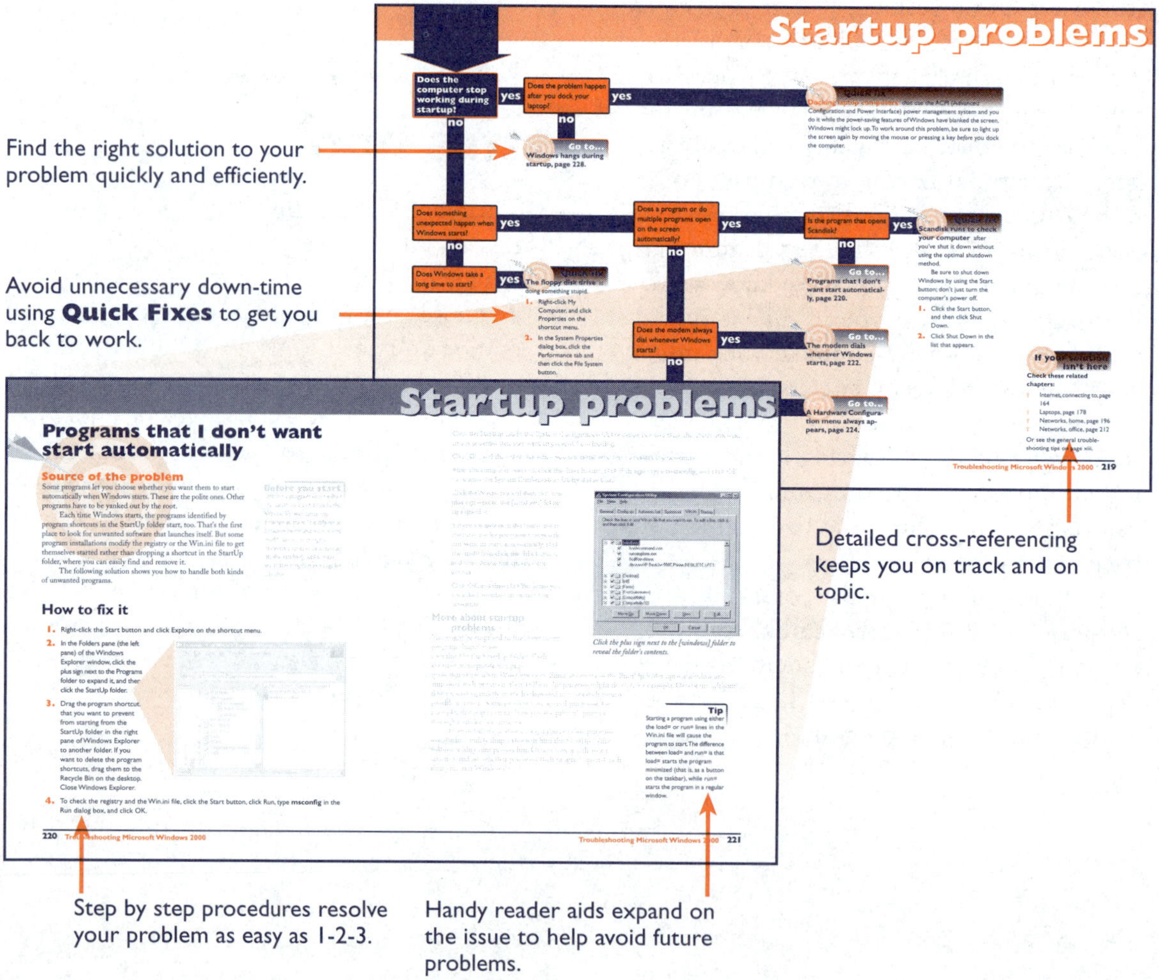

Solution spreads

The solution spreads are where the real troubleshooting takes place. We briefly explain the source of the problem you're experiencing and then tell you how to fix it with clear, step-by-step instructions. The solutions contain screen shots and illustrations that show you what you'll be seeing as you move through the steps. Although our goal is to give you just the facts so that you quickly get back to what you were doing, in some cases we've also provided some background information for a deeper understanding of why you might have encountered your problem. Also scattered throughout the solution spread are tips that contain additional, related material you might find interesting, and a few warnings that tell you what you should or shouldn't do in a given situation.

Assumptions about operating system versions

Outlook 2002 runs on several versions of the Microsoft Windows operating system, including Windows 95, Windows 98, Windows Me, Windows 2000 Professional, and Windows XP. To simplify the procedure descriptions and allow more room for troubleshooting Outlook problems, only one operating system—Windows 2000 Professional—is used when describing interactions between Outlook and the operating system. All screen shots in this book were captured in Windows 2000 Professional as well. If you use a version of Windows other than Windows 2000 Professional, pay attention to the tips when encountering steps involving Windows interaction.

Troubleshooting tips

To troubleshoot, as defined by the *Microsoft Press Computer Dictionary*, is to "isolate the source of a problem in a program, computer system, or network and remedy it." But how do you go about isolating the source of the problem in the first place? The source can be difficult to identify even for those well versed in the intricacies of an e-mail program such as Outlook. When the symptoms can be caused by a variety of problems, how do you isolate the real problem? And what if what you think is the source of the problem is only a symptom of another problem whose source lies deeper than you realize? If you can't immediately identify what's wrong, you might be tempted to quote the hardware engineer ("It's a software problem!") or the software engineer ("It's a hardware problem!"). However, blame won't get your computer working properly—information and persistence will. So put on your detective hat, strap on your virtual tool belt, and get ready to solve the problem.

How to troubleshoot

Your primary objective is to isolate the problem. As soon as you encounter the problem, write down your observations in the greatest detail possible. (After you start trying to fix the problem, you probably won't be able to reexamine the symptoms.) Then ask yourself questions; start with the broadest, and gradually narrow down the scope of the problem. For example, if you can't start Windows, first make sure the computer is plugged in and the monitor is turned on—you can't get much broader than that! If you pass that test, move on to a more specific question. For example, does Windows begin to start up, and then fail?

Now you can start closing in. (This is where you'll appreciate your notes.) Go to the chapter that looks like it covers your problem. Follow the questions in the flowchart until you see one that sounds like your problem, and follow the steps in the Quick Fix or go to the solution spread that the question points you to. If you don't see a question that sounds like your problem, look in the other chapters that are recommended in the flowchart. (Your problem might be covered by a different chapter topic.)

Your troubleshooting might take you down a few dead ends before it leads you to the source of your problem. You're going to need patience and determination to get to the bottom of some problems. If your main method of fixing things is to experiment, be aware that sometimes your "fixes" can cause a second problem, and then you'll have two problems to troubleshoot. Keep detailed notes about what you've done so you don't travel down the same dead end again, and so you can, if necessary, reverse any actions you took that might have caused more problems.

If you're still stuck

This book addresses the most common problems you're likely to run into as you use Outlook, but, obviously, it can't address every problem. If the solutions here haven't addressed your problem, make sure that what you've encountered is a real problem rather than just a misconception. If you're looking for a comprehensive book on Outlook 2002 for intermediate to advanced topics, take a look at *Microsoft Outlook Version 2002 Inside Out* (Microsoft Press) by Jim Boyce.

If you do run into a dead end, you can turn to the Help file; your company's help desk; the manufacturer of your computer, hardware device, or software program; or Microsoft product support. Be cautious, however, about turning to your co-workers for help unless you're certain they know what they're doing.

If you want to try to search out the information you need yourself, try the following Web sites:

- Microsoft Support Knowledge Base: *http://search.support.microsoft.com/kb/*
- Microsoft Outlook Frequently Asked Questions at SlipStick Systems: *http://www.slipstick.com/outlook/faq.htm*
- Microsoft Office Assistance Center: *http://office.microsoft.com/Assistance /default.aspx*

Backing up

Do you need to back up your Outlook data? — yes

no

Do you need to restore your backed-up data? — yes

Go to...
I don't know how to restore my backup data, page 6.

no

Do you need to move your data to a different computer? — yes

no

Do you need to change AutoArchive settings for several folders? — yes

no

Do you need to find the largest files or folders to archive or delete? — yes

Go to...
I don't know what's taking up the room in my storage file, page 12.

Are you using Outlook on Microsoft Exchange Server?

yes

Quick fix

I'm on Microsoft Exchange Server, and I don't know if I need to back up my data Your Outlook data is most likely stored in a mailbox on the server, and your network administrator will make regular backups of your Outlook data. You might also have data stored in your Contacts folder, which is stored in your Outlook *.pst* file. Follow the steps in "I don't know how to back up my data" on page 4 to back up any local *.pst* file.

If you are also using a Personal Address Book (a file with a *.pab* extension), Microsoft recommends that you convert it to a Contacts folder. (This is done automatically at setup.) See "Convert your Personal Address Book to a Contacts folder" in Help to learn how to do this.

no

Go to...
I don't know how to back up my data, page 4.

Go to...
I don't know how to move my data to a different computer, page 8.

Go to...
I don't know how to change AutoArchive settings for several folders at once, page 10.

If your solution isn't here, see the general troubleshooting tips on page xvii.

I don't know how to back up my data

Source of the problem

Suppose that you live in a region of frequent power fluctuations (as many of us do these days), and over time, the power surges have scrambled your hard disk. Or perhaps a virus wiped out all your data—it can happen. Less dramatically, you might get a new computer and need to move all your existing Microsoft Outlook data into the new copy of Outlook. For whatever reason, you'll need to have a backup copy of all your Outlook data so that you can transfer it to a new location.

Before you start

If you use Outlook on a network with Microsoft Exchange Server, your Outlook data is most likely stored in a mailbox on the server, and your network administrator makes regular backups of your Outlook data. If you use Outlook without Microsoft Exchange Server, your data is stored in Personal Folders on your hard disk, and you can use this backup procedure.

How to fix it

1. On the File menu, click Import And Export.
2. On the first page of the Import And Export Wizard, click Export To A File, and then click Next.
3. Click Personal Folder File (*.pst*), and then click Next.
4. Click the files you want to back up. To back up all your data, click Personal Folders, and then select the Include Subfolders check box. To back up specific folders, click the folder you want to back up. (You need to run this procedure for each folder you want to back up.)

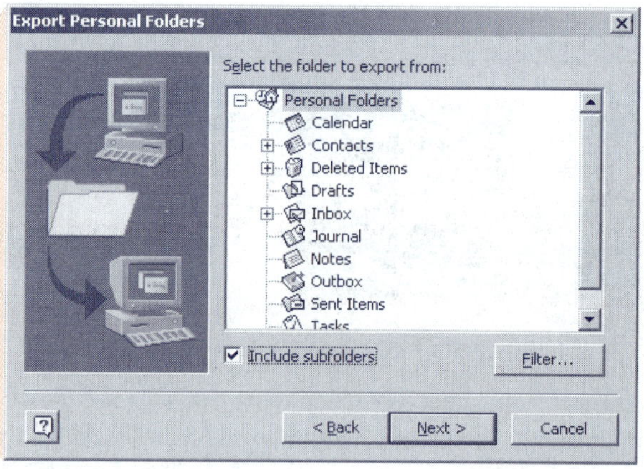

5. Click Next. The final page displays the path where your backup file will be saved, with the name *backup.pst*. Feel free to click the Browse button to browse to a different folder, create a new folder in which to store the backup file, or give the file a different name.

6. Select the duplicates option you want in the Options area. Selecting Do Not Export Duplicate Items speeds up the backup process because items that were previously in this backup file won't be backed up again.

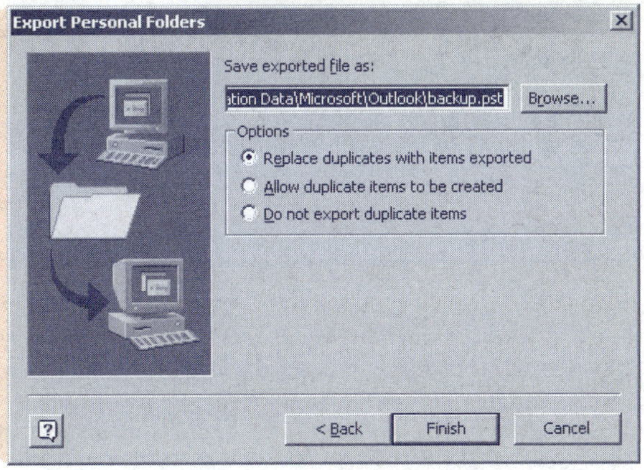

7. Click Finish. You can accept the default name or type a new one. Click one of the encryption options, and if you want to password protect the file, type a password and verify it. Click OK to complete the backup.

Tip

Storing copies of your backup data on removable media, such as floppy or zip disks, is the best way to save the data in the event that your hard disk crashes completely. If you choose to do this, you must close Outlook before copying the backup file to the removable media.

Tip

You can also use the Outlook 2000 Personal Folders Backup utility, which can be downloaded free from this Microsoft Web site: *http://office.microsoft.com/downloads/2000/Pfbackup.aspx*. Although the utility was written for Outlook 2000, it also works with Outlook 2002.

I don't know how to restore my backup data

Source of the problem

You've dutifully backed up your data, and of course you remember (or wrote down) where you stored those backup files. Now some unforeseen event has wiped out your data—perhaps someone else somehow deleted your *outlook.pst* file while playing with your computer. All your Outlook data has disappeared, and you need to restore it from the backup.

Relax—because you've made a backup file, your data is safe. First, if it's a major catastrophe, get your hard disk fixed and reformatted at your local computer repair shop and then re-install all your programs. After Outlook is up and running, you can restore the data from your backup files.

Tip

The Import Personal Folders dialog box is also used to import archived data, and in that case you'd want to make a decision about importing duplicates. But if you're restoring data, there won't be any duplicates, so it doesn't matter which duplicates option you select.

How to fix it

1. On the File menu, click Import And Export.
2. On the first page of the Import And Export Wizard, click Import From Another Program Or File, and then click Next.
3. Click Personal Folder File (*.pst*), and then click Next.
4. Verify that the path and folder name in the File To Import box is pointing to your backup file. (Click the Browse button if you need to locate your *.pst* file.) Select an option for importing duplicates, and then click Next.
5. If you've specified a password for the backup file, type the password in the Personal Folders Password dialog box, and click OK.

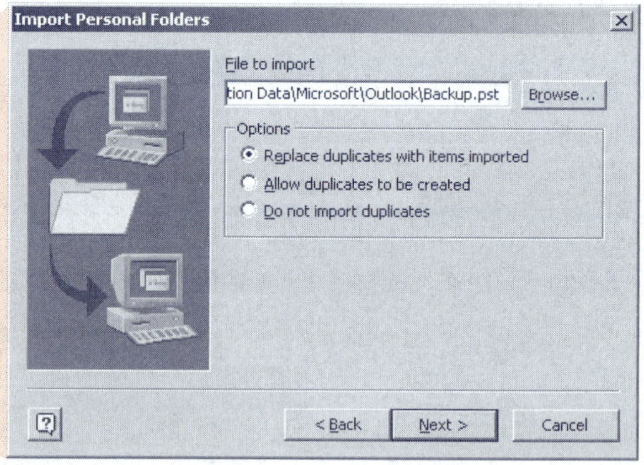

6. Click the folder from which you want to retrieve backup data. If you want to include subfolders, make sure Include Subfolders is selected. By default, the data you retrieve will be copied into the same folder from which it was backed up.

7. Click Finish.

More about Outlook data

Unless you are using Outlook on a network with Exchange Server, all your Outlook data is stored in a Personal Folder file called *outlook.pst*. Within that one file, the data is separated into Inbox, Calendar, Tasks, and so forth, and can be retrieved only by Outlook. The backup *.pst* file that you create is a copy of the *outlook.pst* data that includes only the folders you choose to back up. This file can be stored anywhere on your hard disk. (You should save copies of backup files off your hard disk, too, to fully protect the data.) Your toolbar and menu settings are stored in a file called *outcmd.dat,* which can also be backed up, restored, and moved. Your Outlook Bar settings are stored in a file with the *.fav* extension, and although it can be backed up and restored, it can't be moved to another machine because those links and shortcuts are unique to the Outlook mailbox where they were created.

Tip

You can learn more about archiving in the Outlook help files. Also, see "I don't know how to change Auto-Archive settings for several folders at once" later in this chapter for more about the AutoArchive feature and how it has changed in Outlook 2002.

You can also archive your older Outlook data on a regular basis by scheduling Outlook's AutoArchive feature for the specific folders you want to archive.

Archived data is stored in a file called *archive.pst,* and can be restored using the same procedures as those for restoring backup files. Because Outlook automatically opens *archive.pst* when it is created, you'll also see the archive folder in the Folder List. You can access archived data directly from the Folder List by opening the archive folder. Archived data won't be included in a backup file, though, because it's already in its own file.

I don't know how to move my data to a different computer

Source of the problem

When you get a new computer and want to move your existing Outlook data to it, the best way to transfer the data is to create backup files, move the files to the new computer, and then import copies of the backup files into the new installation of Outlook.

The files can be transferred to the new computer on a floppy disk if you have a relatively small *.pst* file, or by moving or copying the files over the network (if your old and new computer are on the same network). After you place the files in an easy-to-find folder on the new computer, you can bring the data into Outlook either by using the Import Wizard, as shown in the first method below, or by manually moving or copying items from the backup folder to your Outlook Today folder, as shown in the second method.

Tip

If you've archived Outlook data, the archived data and backup data are in separate files. You'll need to move both files to transfer a complete set of data to the new computer.

How to fix it

Use the Import And Export Wizard

1. Copy the backup file to an easy-to-find folder on the new computer (perhaps a newly-created Backups folder).
2. On the File menu, click Import And Export.
3. On the first page of the Import and Export Wizard, click Import From Another Program Or File, and then click Next.
4. Click Personal Folder File (*.pst*), and then click Next.
5. Click the Browse button to locate your backup *.pst* file.
6. In the Open Personal Folders dialog box, click the name of the backup or archive file, and then click Open. The path to the backup or archive file appears in the wizard's File To Import box.
7. In the Options section, select a duplicates option, and then click Next.
8. Click the folders you want to import:

   To import all the backed up data, click Personal Folders in the list box.

To import a single folder or subfolder, click that folder name to select it. ▶

To import a subset of the data in a folder (for example, just the data accumulated during the current month), click the Filter button, and create filter criteria to specify the data you want to import.

9. Click Finish. The data you specified in Step 8 is imported into Outlook on the new computer.

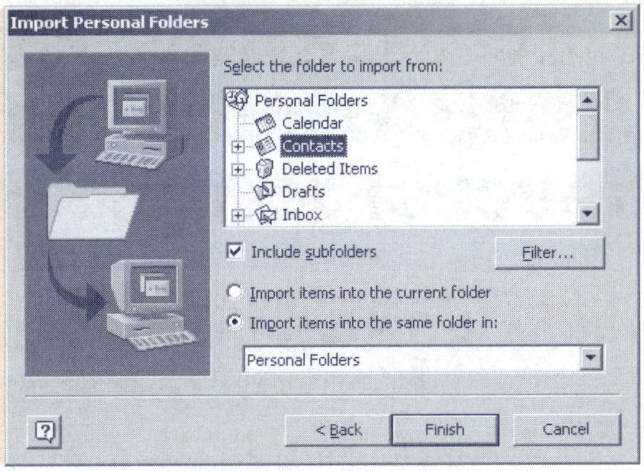

Move the data manually

Another way to import your data from your backup *.pst* file is to open the file and copy or move folders from that file to your mailbox by hand—that is, without using a wizard. (You can also move individual items, but you can't copy them). The advantage of this method is that it's straightforward—you can quickly grab a folder or a few items. Also, you can search for items if you can't remember which folder they're in, which you can't do using the Import And Export Wizard. In fact, moving them by hand is the only way to move individual items to another file.

1. On the File menu, click Open, click Outlook Data File, select the backup *.pst* file, and click OK. The folder will appear in your Folder List, probably called Personal Folders, unless you've renamed it.
2. Click the Personal Folders folder to expand it, and select the folder or items you want.
3. If you want to move an entire folder, click the folder, hold down the right mouse button, and drag the folder to where you want it. Then release the mouse button, and click Move or Copy on the shortcut menu.
4. If you're moving an item or a group of items, just drag the item or items where you want them to go.
5. If you don't want the items removed from their original file, copy the entire folder they're in to your Folder List, move the items from the copied folder to where you want them, and then delete the copied folder when you're done.

Tip

You can't copy or move folders if there's already a folder with the same name in your Folder List. For example, if you copy or move the Contacts folder from your backup file to the top level of your Folder List (where you want it) it will be renamed Contacts1. You can, however, copy or move individual items from a folder in your backup file to a folder in your Folder List.

I don't know how to change AutoArchive settings for several folders at once

Source of the problem

The AutoArchive utility runs periodically, sweeping old items into an archive file if you click Yes when prompted. But suppose you want to keep data around for some length of time other than the default?

Archiving is handled in two places: at the global level and on a per-folder basis. Outlook 2002 provides default settings for AutoArchive, such as the interval of time between archiving the folder, how old data must be to be archived, and where to put the archived data. Each folder can use these settings. To change them, you need to do three things: make sure each folder you want to archive uses the default settings, adjust the defaults in the AutoArchive dialog box, and test your settings.

How to fix it

Perform these steps on each folder you want to archive.

1. In the Folder List, right-click the folder you want to archive (such as Inbox), and click Properties on the shortcut menu.
2. In the Inbox Properties dialog box, click the AutoArchive tab.
3. Select Archive Items In This Folder Using The Default Settings. ▶

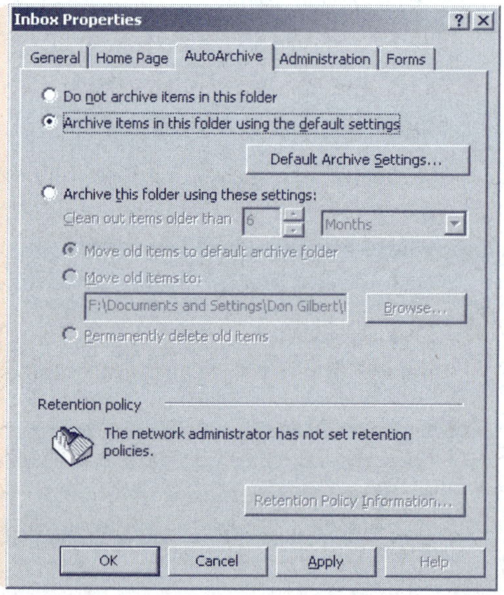

Tip

Don't try to set Auto-Archive on the Contacts folder—you can't archive Contacts.

4. Click the Default Archive Settings button to open the AutoArchive dialog box.

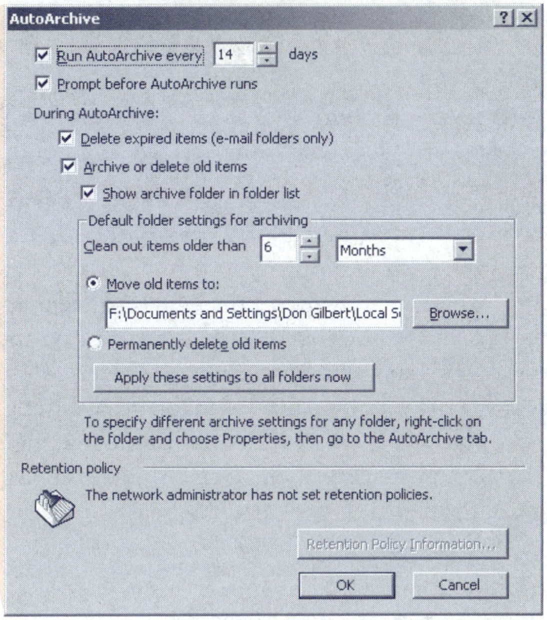

5. Select Run AutoArchive Every __ Days, and set the interval you want.
6. In the During AutoArchive area, select the Archive Or Delete Old Items check box. When this box is checked, all of the remaining options on the dialog box become accessible. This is the key to enabling default settings at the global level.
7. Set your default folder settings, and click the Apply These Settings To All Folders Now button.
8. Click OK twice to close the dialog boxes.
9. To test your archive solution, on the File menu, click Archive.
10. In the Archive dialog box, select Archive All Folders According To Their AutoArchive Settings.
11. Click OK.

Tip

It's possible that you've upgraded from another version of Outlook and, because the global settings are new to this version, you already have archive settings at the folder level that you want to keep. In this case, you don't need to do anything—the upgrade will have picked up these settings for you.

Tip

You can also open the AutoArchive dialog box by clicking Options on the Tools menu, clicking the Other tab, and clicking the AutoArchive button.

I don't know what's taking up the room in my storage file

Source of the problem

Your personal storage file has grown too large and you want to trim it down, but you don't know exactly where to start. With the Mailbox Cleanup tool, you can see which folders are taking up the most room and which items are the oldest, so it is easy to weed out e-mail items that have hung around too long in your mailbox or are making it bigger than it needs to be. Using this feature can make managing your e-mail a lot easier!

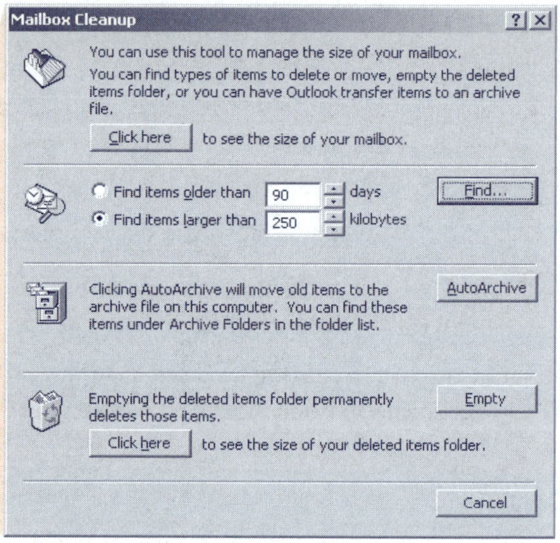

How to fix it

1. On the Tools menu, click Mailbox Cleanup to open the Mailbox Cleanup dialog box. ▶
2. To view the size of all folders in your mailbox, click the Click Here button at the top of the dialog box. The Folder Size dialog box displays the size of each folder in your mailbox as well as the total combined size of all your folders. ▶

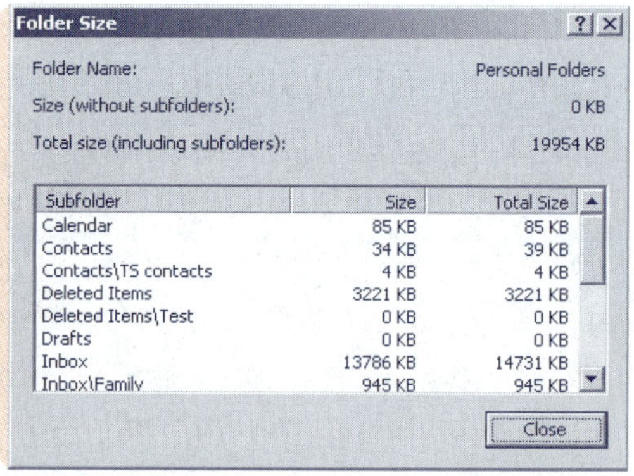

Tip

In addition to locating the largest and oldest folders and items, you can also use the Mailbox Cleanup dialog box to quickly perform the two most suitable activities for reducing the size of your mailbox—archiving and emptying the Deleted Items folder. Just click the Auto-Archive button to archive your older items, and click the Empty button to get rid of the deleted items permanently.

3. To find data in all folders that matches an age criteria, in the Mailbox Cleanup dialog box, select Find Items Older Than, set the number of days, and click Find. The Advanced Find dialog box appears, showing all files older than the number of days you set.

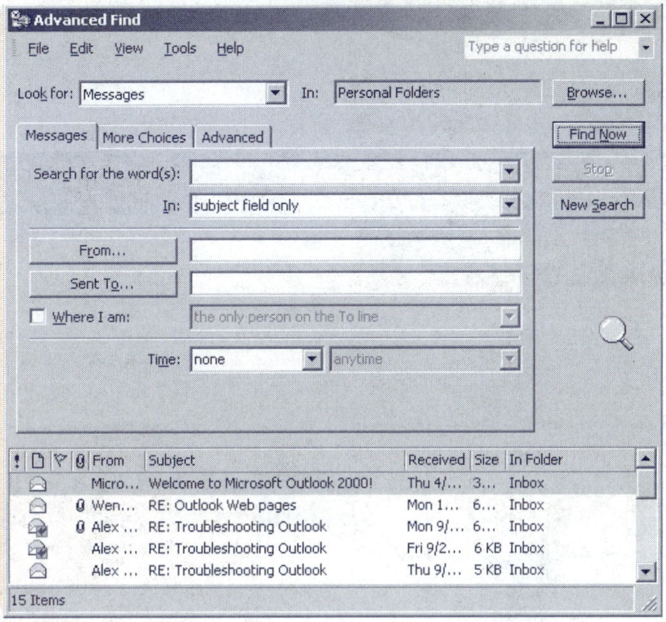

4. To find data in all folders that matches a size criterion, in the Mailbox Cleanup dialog box, select Find Items Larger Than, set the number of kilobytes, and click Find. The Advanced Find dialog box appears, showing all files larger than the size you set.

5. If you've opened the Advanced Find dialog box, on the File menu, click Close.

6. Click Cancel to close the Mailbox Cleanup dialog box when you're done.

More about using the Advanced Find dialog box

When the Advanced Find dialog box displays your results, you can perform further searches to narrow the set of results, by using the comprehensive set of options included in the Advanced Find dialog box. For example, if you searched for all files older than 90 days, you can find the subset of those files that have attachments by clicking the More tab, selecting the Only Items With check box, clicking One Or More Attachments from the drop-down list, and then clicking Find Now.

If, while you are looking over a set of files listed in the Advanced Find dialog box, you spot a file you want to delete, right-click the file, click Delete on the shortcut menu, and then click Yes when you are asked if you are sure you want to permanently delete the file (it will not be placed in the Deleted Items folder). You can also use any of the other commands on the shortcut menu.

Are you having problems setting appointment times or durations?

yes

no

Do you need to create appointments from your tasks?

yes

Quick fix

I want my tasks to show up as appointments Although tasks are like appointments in many ways, they don't appear as appointments in your calendar. However, that's easily remedied.

1. On the Outlook Bar, click Calendar.
2. On the View menu, point to Current View, and click Day/Week/Month.
3. Click the Day button on the toolbar (or any other view except Month) so that the TaskPad is displayed.
4. Drag your task from the TaskPad to the day on which you want your task to appear as an appointment.
5. Set the Start and End times, or select All Day Event if you don't want a specific time.
6. Click Save And Close.

no

Are there too many holidays in your calendar?

yes

no

Do you need to identify your appointments without opening them?

yes

Go to...

I can't identify my appointments at a glance, page 18.

Does an error message appear when you try to set a recurring daily event shorter than 24 hours?

yes

Go to...
When I try to set the time on a recurring event, I get an error message, page 16.

no

Do you want to change your time zone without changing your appointment times?

yes

Go to...
I can't change the time zone without changing appointment times, page 20.

Go to...
There are too many holidays in my calendar, page 23.

If your solution isn't here, check these related chapters:

- Calendar, layout, page 24
- Calendar, scheduling meetings, page 32

Or see the general troubleshooting tips on page xvii.

When I try to set the time on a recurring event, I get an error message

Source of the problem

You want to create a daily recurring event with unique start and end times in the Calendar, or perhaps modify these times for an existing daily recurring event. (For example, you've set the Start time to 8:00 A.M. and the End time to 10:00 A.M. in the Appointment Recurrence dialog box, where the recurrence pattern is Daily.) But when you click OK to close the dialog box, you get an error message that starts with these words: "The duration of the appointment must be shorter than how frequently it occurs…."

This is one of those error messages that can leave you staring blankly at the screen in bewilderment. You distinctly remember setting the End time to 10:00 A.M., which is only two hours later than 8:00 A.M., right? Well, not exactly. In the Calendar, events have a duration of 24 hours by default, and when you set the End time to something later than the Start time, you're really setting it to 24 hours plus that difference. So in this example, you've actually set the duration to 26 hours, which runs this instance of the event into the recurring event for the next day! That's what Outlook is complaining about.

The solution is pretty simple: either change the duration of the event to something less than 24 hours or create a new recurring appointment instead of a recurring event. The default duration of a recurring appointment is 30 minutes, so you'll avoid this kind of confusion. You can also easily turn a recurring event into a recurring appointment.

How to fix it

1. If the error message is still displayed, click OK to close it.

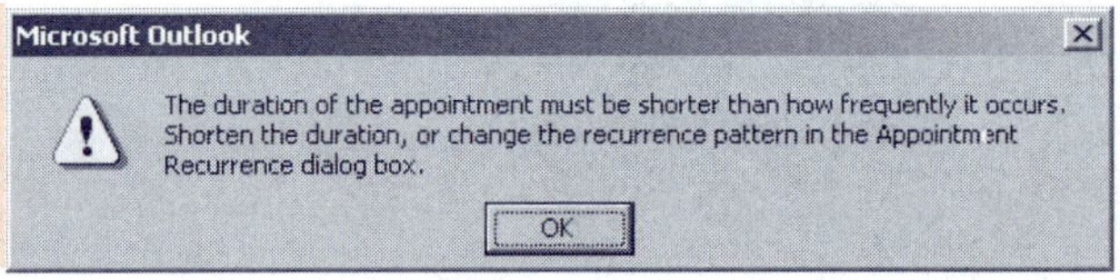

2. Close the Appointment Recurrence dialog box, right-click the Calendar, and click Create New Recurring Event on the shortcut menu.

3. In the Appointment Recurrence dialog box, click the down arrow to the right of the Start box, scroll through the list of possible start times, and click the time you want.

4. Click the down arrow to the right of the Duration box, scroll through the selections, and then choose a duration. ▶

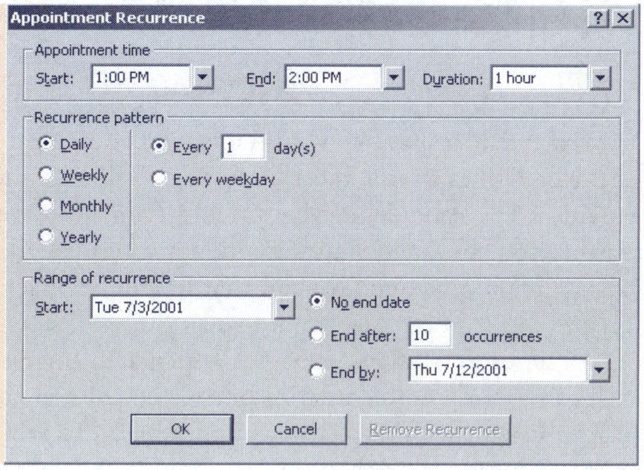

5. Select your range of recurrence (when you want to start and end this series of appointments), and then click OK.

6. If a message appears stating that you'll lose any exceptions associated with the recurring appointment, click OK if you don't mind losing them.

7. Click Save And Close in the Recurring Appointment form.

Tip

When you change the duration setting in a recurring event to less than 24 hours, you are actually changing it to a recurring appointment. The duration is the only difference between events and appointments.

I can't identify my appointments at a glance

Source of the problem

Your calendar is full of appointments, and you might find that it's not always easy to quickly discern which ones are the most important. You might accidentally overlook an appointment you shouldn't. For example, maybe you added an appointment to your calendar for an important meeting that you absolutely must attend, but when you glance at your schedule, there's nothing in the subject line of that appointment that immediately lets you know your presence is required. If you forget, there's nothing to remind you.

Microsoft Outlook 2002 has anticipated this problem and now gives you the ability to tag each of your appointments with one of ten colored labels. Each color corresponds to a category, such as Personal, Must Attend, Important, and so on. Here are the steps for setting a label, followed by information about how to modify the categories associated with the colors.

How to fix it

If the Appointment form is open:

- Click the down arrow to the right of the Label box, and select one of the labels.

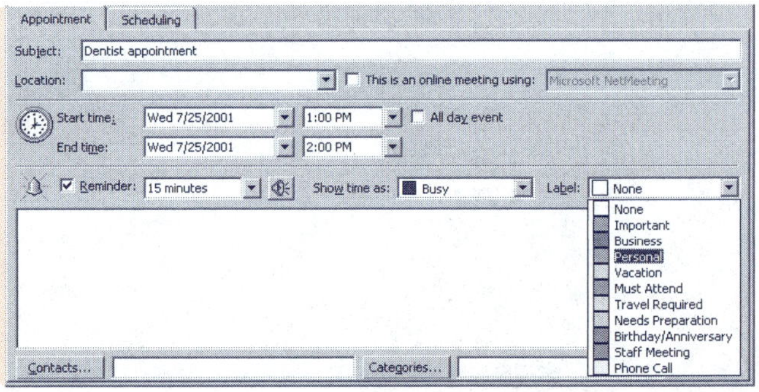

If the Appointment form is not open:

- Right-click the appointment in the Calendar, and on the shortcut menu, point to Label, and then click one of the labels.

If the label text doesn't fit

Outlook provides ten colors, each with its own label text describing the label. You can use this label text, or you can create your own.

> **Tip**
> On the shortcut menu, the current color and category selection appears with a square around the appropriate item in the list. If you've forgotten what text label is associated with the tag color, just open this menu to view the label.

To edit the list of labels, on the Calendar's Edit menu, point to Label, and click Edit Labels. Then, in the Edit Calendar Labels dialog box, select the text of the label you want to change, and type a new label.

There is a maximum of ten labels; if you find that you run out, combine some existing categories to free up a slot. For example, instead of using one label for birthdays and another for anniversaries, create a Birthday/Anniversary label with the Birthday color and assign the former Anniversary label to the new category (for example, Staff Meeting).

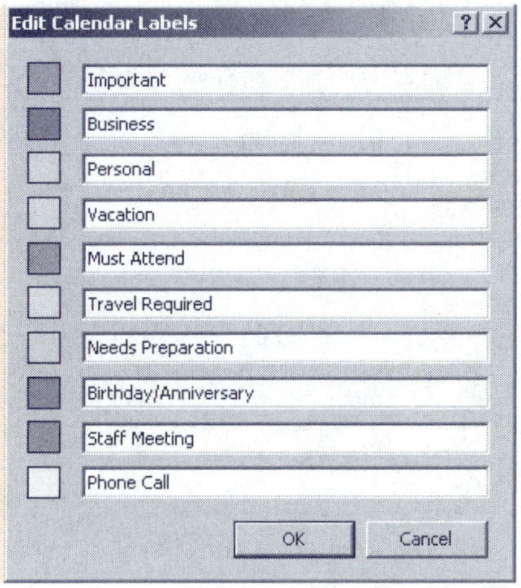

Automatic appointment labels

In Outlook 2002, you can set up rules for your appointment labels to automatically tag appointments based on a set of criteria. These criteria can be based on certain words in the subject or body of the appointment, or on a meeting's organizer or attendees. For example, you can create a rule to automatically mark as Important all appointments organized by a certain person. To create appointment label rules, on the Calendar's Edit menu, click Automatic Formatting. In the Automatic Formatting dialog box, click Add to create a rule, select a label you want to apply, and click Condition to set the criteria.

See Outlook's Help menu or consult an in-depth book on Outlook 2002 for more information on setting rules for appointment colors.

Tip
There is no way to change the colors provided by Outlook for the labels. You can change only the text associated with each color.

I can't change the time zone without changing appointment times

Source of the problem

You've had to change the time zone on your computer because you've moved to a different geographical location, or maybe it was set incorrectly when you installed Outlook and set up your appointments. But now you've noticed that all your appointment times have changed. For example, if you moved the time zone from Pacific Time to Mountain Time, your 1:00 P.M. appointments are now scheduled for 2:00 P.M.

Unfortunately, Outlook doesn't have a quick fix for this problem. If you have just a few appointments, it might be easiest to simply delete the old ones and create new ones. If you have many appointments, you can avoid the problem by exporting the appointments, changing the time zone, and then importing the appointments back into Outlook.

Before you start

This solution won't export recurring appointments but will, instead, convert recurring appointments to individual appointments. If most of your appointments are recurring and you don't want them converted, it might be faster to change the time in each of these appointments individually rather than performing the following procedure to export and import the appointments. Alternately, you could use this procedure to export the recurring appointments, let Outlook convert them to individual appointments, and then, after importing them, open the last individual appointment of each series and make it into a recurring appointment that starts from there.

How to fix it

1. Make sure your time zone is set to the old time zone so that the appointments appear at the correct time.
2. On the File menu, click Import And Export.
3. On the first page of the Import And Export Wizard, select Export To A File, and then click Next.
4. In the Export dialog box, select Comma Separated Values (Windows), and then click Next.
5. Select the Calendar folder that contains the appointments you want to move, and click Next. ▶

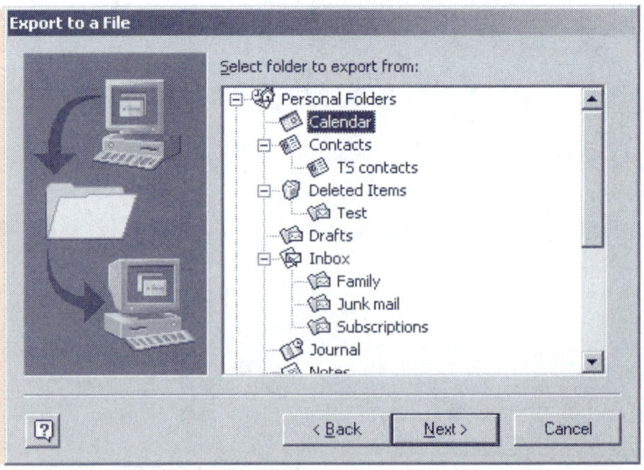

6. Click the Browse button, navigate to an easy-to-find folder, and type a name for the file, such as *appointments*. Click OK.

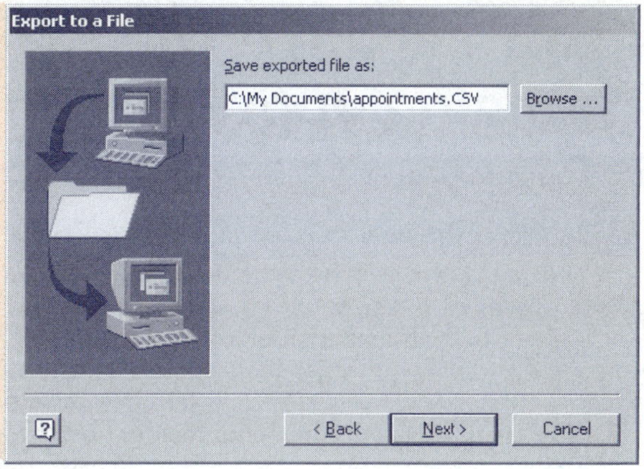

7. Click Next.
8. Click Finish to close the Export dialog box.
9. In the Set Date Range dialog box, set the range of appointment dates you want to export. Write down the date range—you'll need it later.
10. Click OK to begin the export process.

Now you need to delete all appointments that fall within the date range you set in step 9.

1. On the View menu, point to Current View, and click Active Appointments.
2. On the View menu, point to Current View again, and click Customize Current View.
3. In the View Summary dialog box, click Filter, click Clear All, and click OK twice to close the dialog boxes. This causes all appointments to be listed according to their start times.

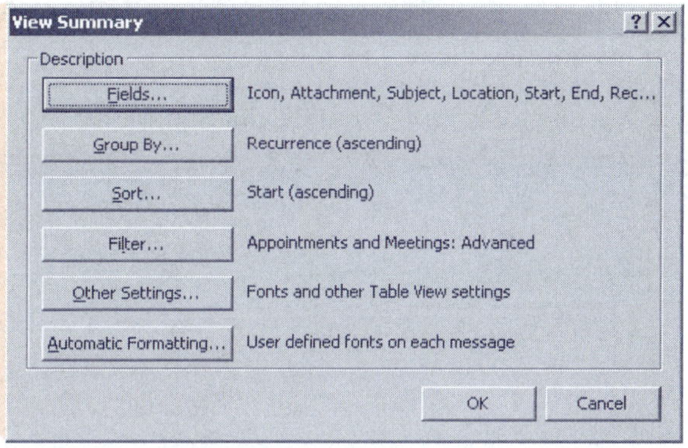

4. Select all the appointments in the date range you've chosen, right-click the selection, and click Delete on the shortcut menu.
5. On the View menu, point to Current View, and click Define Views to display the Define Views For "Calendar" dialog box.
6. In the View Name column, click Active Appointments, and click Reset.
7. Click OK to confirm that you're sure you want to do this.
8. Click Close.
9. On the View menu, point to Current View, and click Day, Week, Month, or whatever view you generally use in the Calendar.

This solution is continued on the next page.

I can't change the time zone without changing appointment times

(continued from page 21)

10. To reset the time zone, double-click the clock in the system tray at the right end of the Windows taskbar, switch to the new time zone, and click OK.

Now you will import the appointment data that you exported earlier.

1. On the Calendar's File menu, click Import And Export.
2. On the first page of the Import And Export Wizard, select Import From Another Program Or File, and then click Next.
3. Select Comma Separated Values (Windows), and then click Next.
4. Browse to the file that you exported, and then click Next.

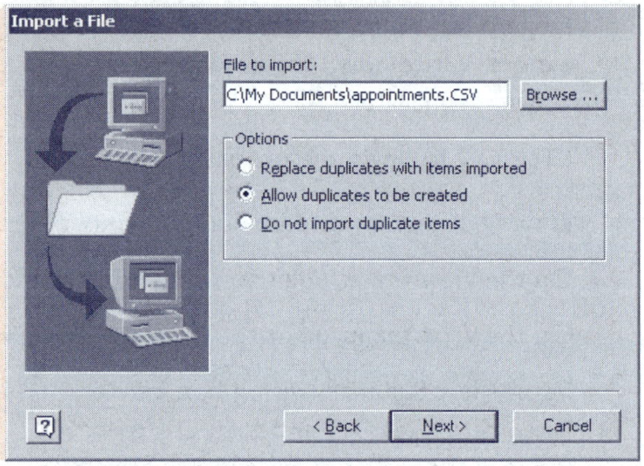

5. Select Calendar as the destination folder, and click Next.

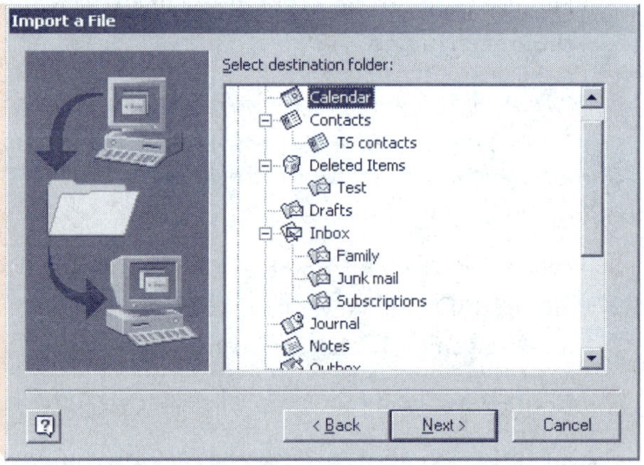

6. Click Finish.

There are too many holidays in my calendar

Source of the problem

You've recently learned how to add holidays to your calendar. It was fun looking up when National Day is in Switzerland and helpful to know when Father's Day is in the U.S. next year. But now you've got so many holidays in your calendar that there's barely room for your appointments. You need to remove some holidays, but removing them one-by-one is tedious and time consuming.

How to fix it

1. In the Calendar, on the View menu, point to Current View, and then click Events. Your calendar switches to a table-type view.
2. Click the Location header to sort all the events (and holidays) by location. Each set of holidays is sorted together as a group according to the country of origin.
3. Drag down the left side to select all the holidays in the group you want to remove.
4. Click the Delete button on the toolbar. The selected holidays are removed, and you can switch back to the view you like best.

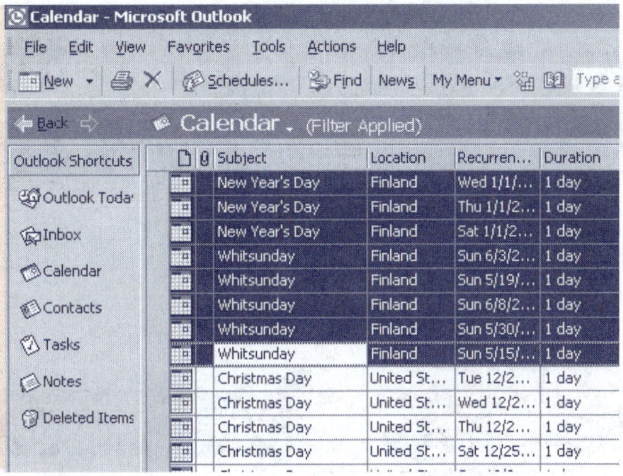

Does your calendar show incorrect work week days or hours?

yes

Go to... My workweek days and hours are wrong, page 26.

no

Do you want to move to distant dates more quickly?

yes

no

Is your Saturday/Sunday layout wrong?

yes

Go to... My Saturday/Sunday layout is wrong, page 27.

no

Can you read your appointment easily?

yes

Is your TaskPad missing?

yes

no

Go to... I can't read my appointments easily, page 30.

Calendar, layout

Quick fix

I need to jump several months ahead or behind You can move quickly to months that are far in the future or past.

1. Switch to a Daily or Weekly view so that the Date Navigator is visible in the upper-right corner of the Calendar window.
2. Point to the month in the Date Navigator, and then hold down the mouse button. A list of seven months appears, including three before and three after the month you're pointing to. Point to the month you want; when it's highlighted, release the mouse button.
3. If you want to jump forward or backward more than three months, point to the name of a month in the Date Navigator, and hold down the mouse button. Move the mouse pointer slightly above the list of months to scroll backward or slightly below the list to scroll forward. Point to the month you want; when it's highlighted, release the mouse button.

Go to...
The Calendar is not showing the TaskPad, page 28.

If your solution isn't here, check these related chapters:

- Printing, page 228
- Backing up and moving data, page 2

Or see the general troubleshooting tips on page xvii.

My workweek days and hours are wrong

Source of the problem

The Calendar was designed to be your *personal* calendar, to record activities and appointments for your own workdays and work hours, and when you click the Work Week button on the Calendar toolbar, it would sure be nice if it showed *your* workweek.

But the default workweek that Microsoft Outlook comes with isn't everyone's workweek. It's becoming more common for people to work four 10-hour days each week, or to work a swing or night shift. The Calendar's default setting assumes, however, that you work the same shift on all your workdays. For the Calendar to be truly useful, you need to alter the workdays and hours to show your real schedule.

How to fix it

1. On the Tools menu, click Options.
2. In the Options dialog box, click the Preferences tab, and then click the Calendar Options button.
3. In the Calendar Work Week area, select the check boxes for your workweek days (and clear the check boxes for your days off).
4. Set your workday start time in the Start Time box, and set your workday end time in the End Time box.
5. Click OK to close each dialog box.

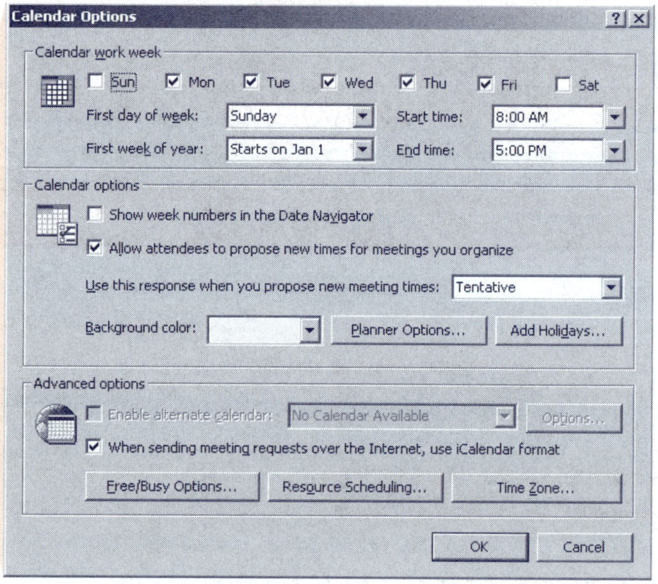

My Saturday/Sunday layout is wrong

Source of the problem

When you look at a monthly calendar, do you like to see Saturday and Sunday as smaller spaces that share a single column so that your weekday spaces are larger and can record more events? Or would you rather show every day of the week in its own full-size space so that there's room for several events on Saturday and Sunday? If the Calendar doesn't display the days the way you find them most useful, you need to change them. After all, it's *your* calendar.

How to fix it

1. Open the Calendar.
2. On the View menu, point to Current View, and then click Day/Week/Month view. (It doesn't matter whether you have the Daily, Weekly, or Monthly view displayed.)
3. On the View menu, point to Current View, and then click Customize Current View.
4. In the View Summary dialog box, click the Other Settings button.
5. In the Format Day/Week/Month View dialog box, select the Compress Weekend Days check box.
6. Click OK to close each dialog box.

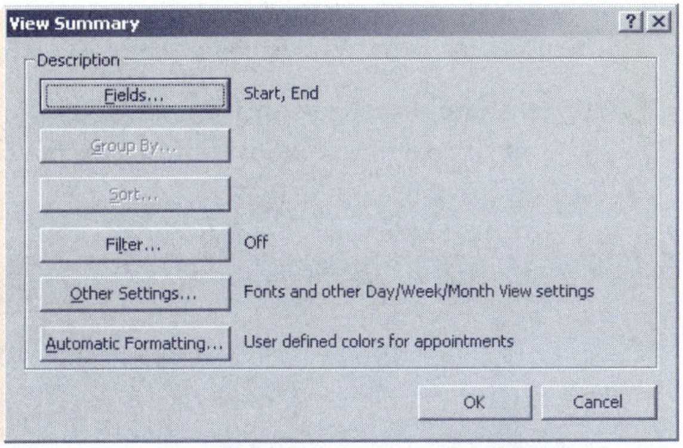

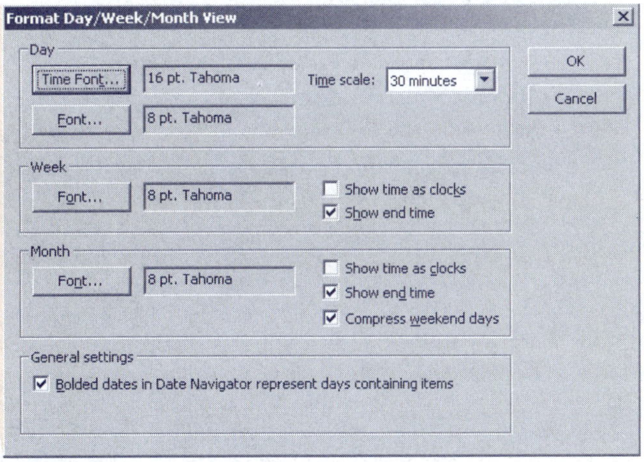

Tip

If you want to know what a particular check box does, right-click its label to read a short description.

The Calendar is not showing the TaskPad

Source of the problem

The TaskPad is a useful little feature in Outlook; it provides an abbreviated list of tasks that you can review while you look at your calendar and try to decide where to fit each task into your schedule. But your TaskPad can disappear if you're clicking and dragging randomly while you learn to use Outlook. You need to find it and get it back in position.

How to fix it

1. Open the Calendar.
2. Click the Daily or Weekly view. (The TaskPad doesn't appear in the Monthly view.)
3. Any of these maneuvers might bring your TaskPad back into view:

   Maximize the Outlook window by double-clicking the Outlook title bar.

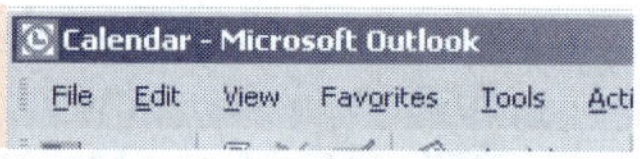

   If the Folder List is visible, hide it by clicking the Close button in its upper-right corner, or resize it by pointing to its right border, and when the pointer changes to a double-headed arrow, dragging the border to the left to make the Folder List narrower.

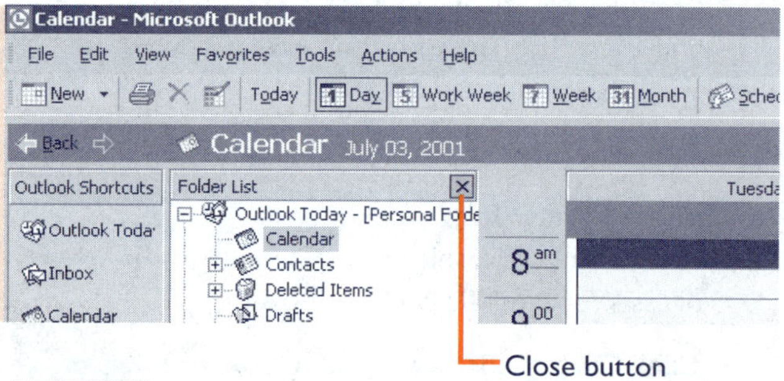

   If the Date Navigator isn't visible, point to the right border of the Outlook window, and when the pointer changes to a double-headed arrow, drag the border to the left.

If the Date Navigator is visible on the right side of the Outlook window, point to the bottom border of the Date Navigator column, and when the pointer changes to a double-headed arrow, drag the border upward at least two inches.

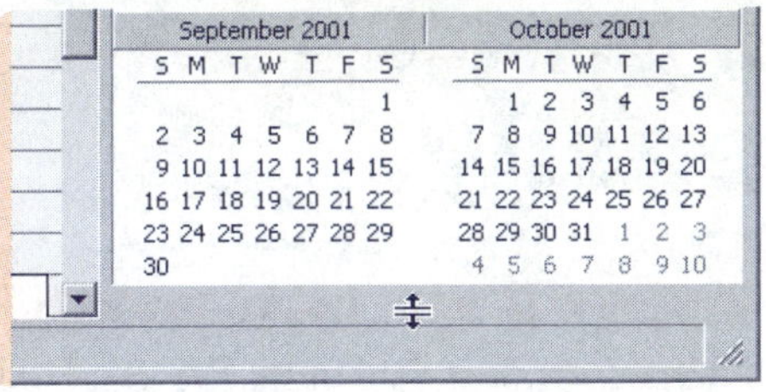

Other reasons why your TaskPad might be missing

The TaskPad might be missing for reasons other than inadvertent clicking and dragging.

If no Tasks folder is available, there won't be a TaskPad. For example, if you're looking at a Calendar folder in a backup or archive Personal Folders file that doesn't include a Tasks folder, there won't be a TaskPad in that Calendar.

If you're looking at someone else's shared Calendar but you haven't been granted access to the Tasks folder, you won't see the TaskPad. If you need to see the TaskPad, ask that person to grant you permission to view the Tasks folder on his or her computer.

I can't read my appointments easily

Source of the problem

The default font size in all the Calendar views (Daily, Weekly, and Monthly) is 8 points, which is a mere one-ninth of an inch. For some of us, that's awfully small type to read. If you find it too small for comfort, you need to resize the font to be larger and more readable.

How to fix it

1. On the View menu, point to Current View, and then click Day/Week/Month view.
2. On the View menu, point to Current View again, and then click Customize Current View.
3. In the View Summary dialog box, click the Other Settings button.
4. In the Format Day/Week/Month View dialog box, click the Font button under the view (Day, Week, or Month) you want to resize.

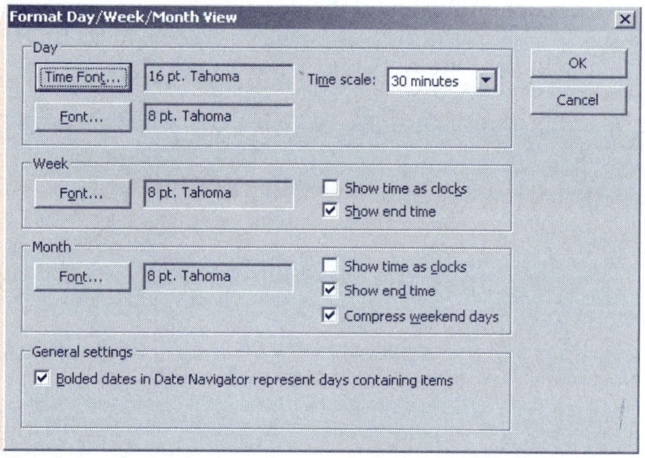

> **Tip**
>
> While you have the Font dialog box open, you can also change the font (typeface) for that view.

5. In the Size area of the Font dialog box, click a larger font size. ▶

6. Click OK to close each dialog box.

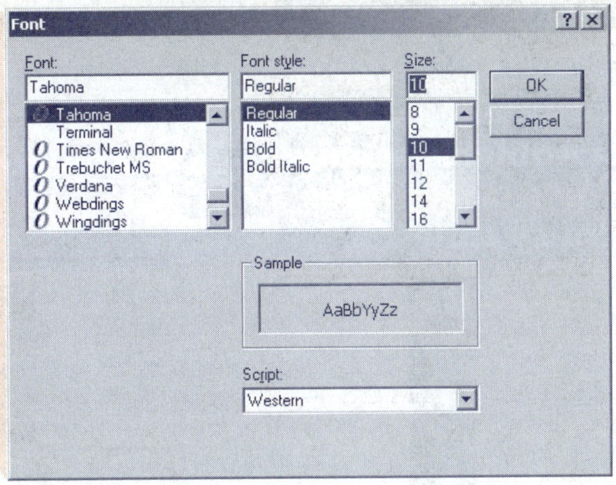

Calendar, sc

Are you having problems seeing or sharing free/busy times?

yes → Do you want to use Group Scheduling to set up meetings?

yes → **Go to...**

I don't want to re-create the attendee list every time I schedule a meeting, page 36.

no → Are the free/busy times for some people not available more than two months ahead?

yes →

no → Are you on a Microsoft Exchange server?

yes → Are the free/busy times not appearing where they should?

yes → **Quick fix**

I can't see free/busy times for people on my Exchange network Contact your network admistrator to see why free/busy times for others are not showing up.

no → Are you having problems sharing your schedules with others?

yes →

Quick fix

I can't see free/busy times in the future Anyone sharing their free/busy information can set the block of time that Outlook posts. Meeting participants who use Outlook 2002 can increase this period.

1. On the Tools menu, click Options.
2. In the Options dialog box, click Calendar Options.
3. In the Calendar Options dialog box, click Free/Busy Options.
4. In the Free/Busy Options dialog box, in the Publish box, enter a number greater than 2.
5. Click OK three times to close the dialog boxes.

Go to...
I'm having problems sharing my schedule over the Internet, page 34.

If your solution isn't here, see the general troubleshooting tips on page xvii.

I'm having problems sharing my schedule over the Internet

Source of the problem

You hold meetings with people who use Microsoft Outlook and have an Internet connection, but who aren't on a Microsoft Exchange network with you. You've set up an account with the Microsoft Office Internet Free/Busy service to share your schedule, but you get e-mail from someone who is trying to schedule a meeting, telling you that your schedule is listed as not available (or that it is available but not showing any information). Or maybe you didn't even know that you could share your schedule information over the Internet and would like to know how to set this up.

To share schedule information using this service, you must have a Microsoft Passport account, have signed up for the Microsoft Office Internet Free/Busy service, have authorized others to view your schedule information, and have Outlook configured to post your free/busy times to this Web site. If you have an account with this service but your schedule isn't available to someone else trying to view it, it's possible you've forgotten to give that person access. If your schedule is available to them but contains no information (even though you have appointments in your calendar), it could be that Outlook isn't set up to post your schedule information. The following solution shows you how to set up this service in Outlook. If you've never set this service up, this will get you up to speed; if you've set it up but are having problems, read this solution to make sure the service is set up correctly.

Tip

It's quite possible that the person attempting to view your schedule is not signed up with Microsoft Office Internet Free/Busy service, which is a requirement. Outlook automatically presents a dialog box with a link to the Microsoft Office Internet Free/Busy Web site when it detects that an unregistered user is trying to view the schedule of a registered user. However, this only occurs the first time, so if the registered user fails to register at that time, they'll need to register later. You can send them this information so that they'll know how.

How to fix it

1. On the Tools menu, click Options.
2. In the Options dialog box, click the Preferences tab, and then click Calendar Options.
3. In the Calendar Options dialog box, click Free/Busy Options.
4. Select Publish And Search Using Microsoft Office Internet Free/Busy Service.
5. In the Free/Busy dialog box, click the Manage button. A Web page appears in your browser asking you to sign in using a Microsoft Passport login.

6. Sign in using a Microsoft Passport name that matches the e-mail address you use in Outlook. If you don't have a Microsoft Passport, create a new one by clicking Get One Here at the bottom of the Web page. After you have a valid Microsoft Passport, click the Manage button again to bring up the login page.

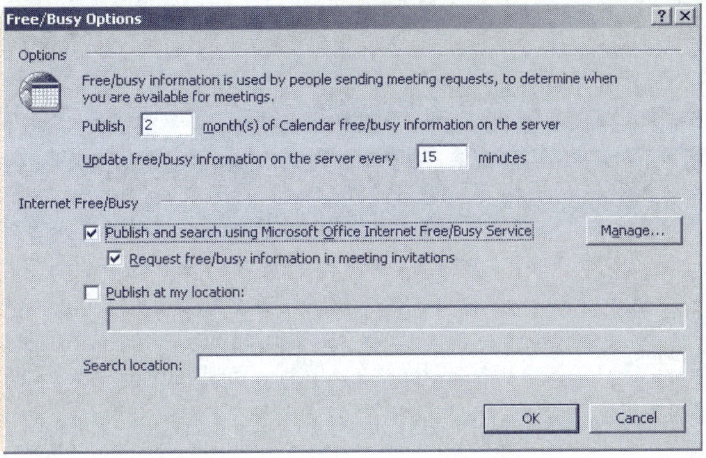

7. If you're new to the service, read the agreement on the Microsoft Office Internet Free/Busy Web site, and, if you agree, click Yes, I Agree. If you've already signed up, you won't see this page, so jump to step 9.

8. Because you have already manually configured Outlook to work with this service in the preceding steps, you don't have to do anything else to enable Outlook; just click Continue.

9. In the Authorize Additional Users box on the Internet Free/Busy Web page, type the addresses of everyone you want to have access to your free/busy information, separating the addresses with semi-colons. Click OK. People you add here who are not currently signed up with this Microsoft service will receive an e-mail message that will provide a link for them to sign up.

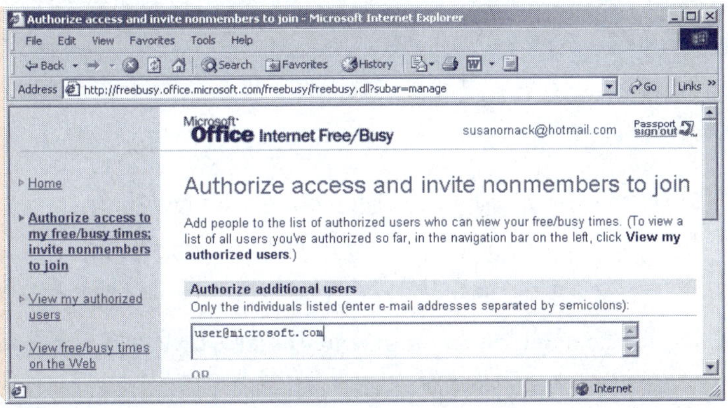

10. Click View My Authorized Users to see who is authorized. If you find you've forgotten to add someone, click the Authorize Access To My Free/Busy Times; Invite Nonmembers To Join link.

11. Click OK to close each open dialog box.

Tip

Click the Address Book link on the Internet Free/Busy Web page to add users from your Address Book to the authorization list.

I don't want to re-create the attendee list every time I schedule a meeting

Source of the problem

You have a few groups of people that you meet with on a regular basis; but every time you create a new meeting request, you find yourself creating a new list of attendees from scratch—a time consuming process. In fact, quite often you just want to see who's available at a certain time before even bothering to schedule a meeting.

Outlook 2002 has solved this problem by introducing Group Scheduling—a means of enabling you to create groups of people and resources that you often schedule for meetings. Each group is sort of like a distribution list, but in addition to the e-mail addresses, it also shows the availability of everyone who shares their free/busy information with you. Any time after you have created the group you can open the group, see who's available, and quickly book a meeting with members of the group.

The following solution shows you how to create a group using the Group Schedules feature, and how to use it to create a meeting request.

How to fix it

1. In the Folder List, click Calendar to open it.
2. On the toolbar, click the Schedules button.

3. In the Group Schedule dialog box, click New.
4. In the New dialog box, type the name of the group you want to create, and then click OK. A Group Schedule dialog box for the name you just typed appears.
5. To add a person to the group schedule, click Add Others, click Add From Address Book, select each person you want to add in the Name list, and click To, which adds them to the list. Click OK when you have finished adding members in the Select Members dialog box. You'll see these members added to your group schedule.
6. If any group members are not in your Address Book, add them to your list by typing the e-mail address of each person you want to add in the Group Members list and then pressing Enter.

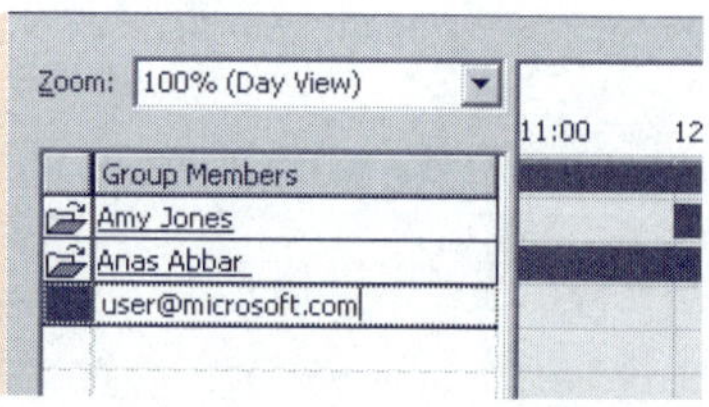

7. If any of the people in your Group Members list have not shared their free/busy information with you, a message box might appear, enabling you to send them a link to the Microsoft Office Internet Free/Busy website. If this box appears, click Link to generate a message (you'll need to then send it), or click Cancel to dismiss the message box.

8. Click Save And Close when you've finished adding your list of attendees.

Scheduling a meeting with a group

The quickest way to schedule a one-hour meeting with everyone in the group is to open the group, click the down arrow to the right of the Go To box, select a day, and then find a time when no one is busy. Right-click that available hour block in the schedule, and click New Meeting With All on the shortcut menu.

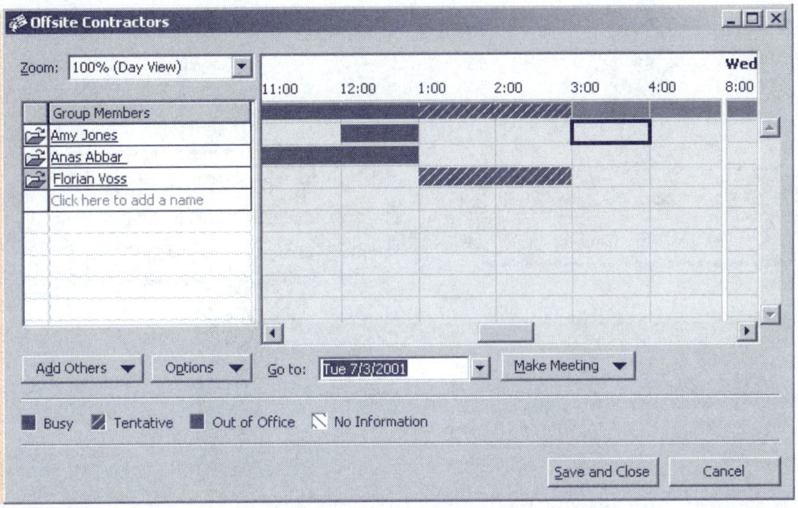

A Meeting Request form opens, listing everyone in the group as attendees. Before you send the invitation, be sure to check the start and end times; you'll need to reset the end time if the duration isn't one hour.

Although you can select blocks longer than one hour by dragging the selected hour to the left or right, this tends to be a bit clumsy—and there's an easier way. Instead of choosing the time block in the Group Schedule dialog box, you can wait until you've opened the meeting request form and then click the Scheduling tab. The Scheduling tab has the advantage of easy-to-move edges on the time block. It also has the AutoPick feature, which enables you to click the AutoPick Next button to find the next available open time for everyone in the group. You can keep clicking this button to select the next available time until you find a time you like. You can also manually scroll until you find a non-conflicting time, and drag the green start marker on the left to the start time of the meeting and the red end marker to the end time.

Tip

If you're picking a meeting time during working hours, click Options on the Meeting Request form, click the Scheduling tab, and then make sure that Show Only Working Hours is selected. This is particularly helpful when you're using AutoPick and want to jump to the next day—you don't want to click your way through the off-hours!

Con

Do you need to enter data for which there's no field?

yes

Go to...
There's no field for the data I need to enter, page 40.

no

Do you need to display your custom data?

yes

Do you need to display your custom data in a table or card view?

yes

no

Do you want to find your custom data in the Contacts form?

yes

Go to...
I don't see my custom data field, page 42.

Quick fix

I can't find my custom data in the Contact form You've created a custom field in the Contacts folder but can't find it when you open the Contact form. You need to tell Outlook to display user-defined fields.

1. Open any Contact form.
2. Click the All Fields tab.
3. Click the down arrow to the right of the Select From box, and select User-Defined Fields In Folder in the drop-down list.

If your solution isn't here, check these related chapters:

- Contacts, folder display, page 44
- Contacts, general, page 48

Or see the general troubleshooting tips on page xvii.

There's no field for the data I need to enter

Source of the problem

You might find that you need to keep track of contact information for which there's no built-in field in Microsoft Outlook. For example, you might need to record employee ID numbers, or perhaps you need a yes/no field to track active membership in an organization. If you can record data such as this, it's easier to filter contacts for a mail merge or to organize a long list of contacts. If there's no built-in field for the data you need to record, you can create your own field.

How to fix it

1. Open the folder or subfolder in which you want to create a custom field. (In this example, the Contacts folder is opened.)
2. On the View menu, point to Current View, and then click Customize Current View.
3. In the View Summary dialog box, click the Fields button.
4. In the Show Fields dialog box, click the New Field button.
5. In the Name box of the New Field dialog box, type a name for the new field.
6. Click the down arrow to the right of the Type list box, and select the type of data the field will contain from the drop-down menu. For most data, the appropriate type is Text.
7. In the Format list box, select a display format for your data. (If you selected Text in the Type box, the only Format option is Text.)

Tip

You can show the Show Fields dialog box more quickly if you right-click an empty space in the Contacts window and then click Show Fields on the shortcut menu.

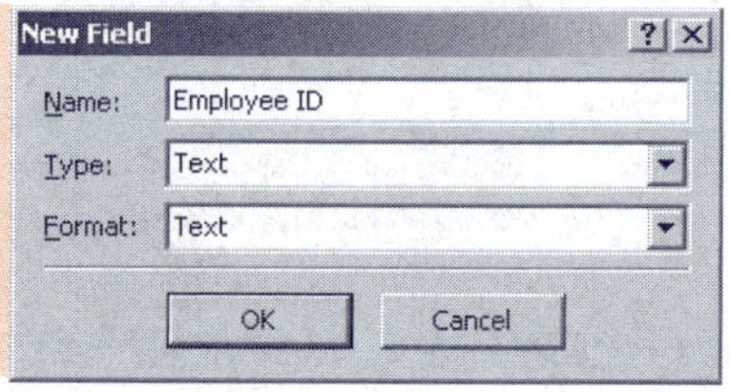

8. Click OK. In the Show Fields dialog box, the new custom field appears in the Show These Fields In This Order box. You can click Add or Remove to set up the fields you want to display. ▶

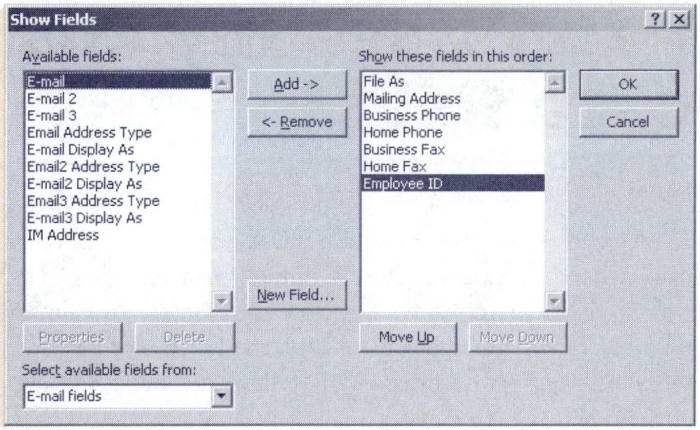

9. Click OK to close the Show Fields dialog box, and in the View Summary dialog box, click Other Settings.

10. In the Format Card View dialog box, select Show Empty Fields.

11. Click OK twice to close the dialog boxes. Whichever view is displayed in your folder, the new custom field is also displayed. You can click an empty field to select it and then type an appropriate entry. ▶

More about custom fields

You might not really need a custom field. There are many more built-in Contacts fields than are displayed in any default view. To find a field you want displayed, open the Show Fields dialog box (shown in step 8) and select different field categories in the Select Available Fields From box. In each category you select, look at the fields in the Available Fields list above the box. You can add or remove fields from this list to modify what's displayed.

There are four generic text-type fields in the Miscellaneous Fields category: User Field 1, User Field 2, User Field 3, and User Field 4. You can't rename these fields, but they're ready to use if you need them. (You should record what kind of data the field holds—perhaps in an Outlook note.)

I don't see my custom data field

Source of the problem

If you've created a custom data field, it won't be displayed on the built-in Contact form. Although it's possible to create a custom Contact form that displays custom fields, you don't need a custom form to display and use your custom data fields. You can display custom fields in a table-type view of your Contacts folder, such as a phone list, as well as in the Card view of your Contacts folder. Table-type views often make data entry and sorting easier, and the Card view makes it easier to see all the data for each contact.

This solution shows you how to display and use a custom field in both a table-type view and in Card view.

How to fix it

You can add a custom field to a table-type view.

1. Open the folder in which you created the custom field.
2. On the View menu, point to Current View, and select a table-type view. In a Contacts folder, the Phone List view is a simple table-type view.
3. Right-click the column heading row, and then click Field Chooser on the shortcut menu.
4. In the Field Chooser dialog box, click the down arrow to the right of the box at the top of the dialog box, and click User-Defined Fields In Folder in the drop-down list.
5. Drag the custom field from the Field Chooser dialog box to the column heading row.
6. Close the Field Chooser dialog box by clicking its Close button.

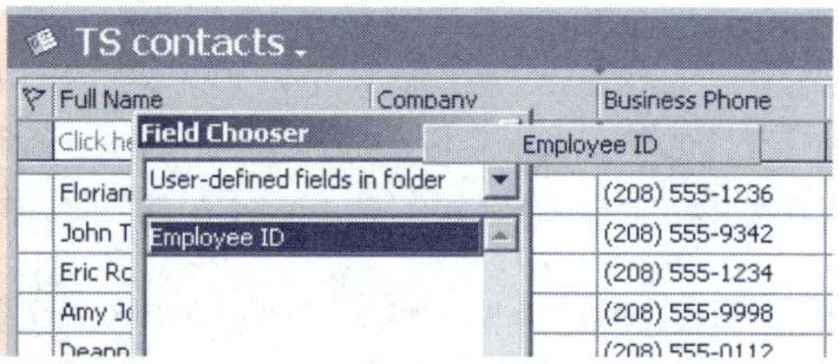

With your custom field displayed, you can enter or edit data, and you can use the custom field to sort and filter the list.

You can also use a custom field in the Card view.

1. On the View menu, point to Current View, and then click Address Cards.
2. Right-click any empty space in the Contacts window, and then click Show Empty Fields on the shortcut menu.

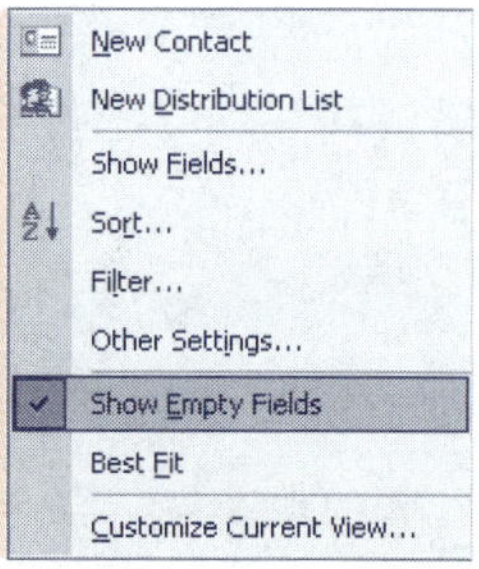

3. If the field you need to edit doesn't appear, right-click an empty space in the Contacts window, and then click Show Fields on the shortcut menu.

4. If the field you want to display is a custom field that you created, in the Show Fields dialog box, select User-Defined Fields In Folder in the Select Available Fields From box.

5. In the Available Fields list, double-click each field you want to add to the view.

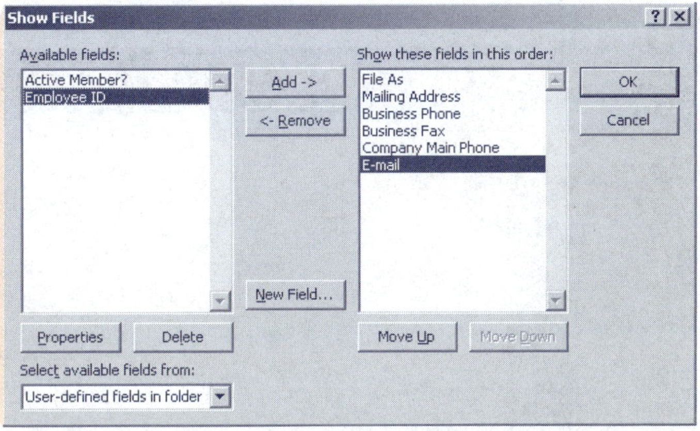

6. To move a field to a different position in the Card view, drag it up or down in the Show These Fields In This Order list.

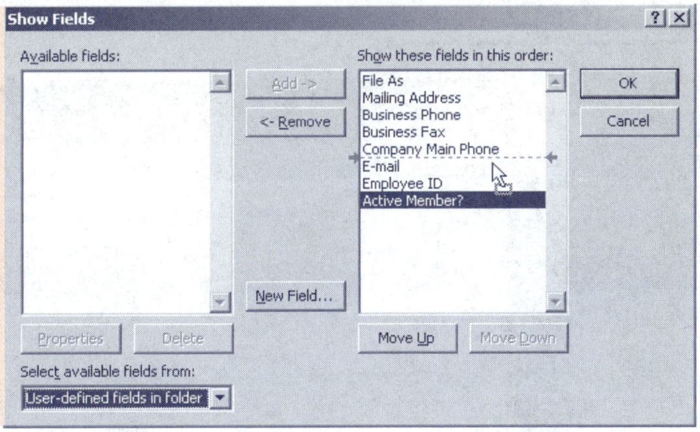

7. Click OK to close the Show Fields dialog box.

Tip

You can also select the field and click the Move Up or Move Down button below the Show These Fields In This Order list box.

8. If you need to enter or edit data in a contact's custom field, simply click the custom field, and type or edit the entry.

Do you need to sort the Contacts Card view by a field other than "File As"?

yes → **Go to...** I don't know how to sort the Contacts Card view, page 46.

no

Are letter buttons missing from your Contacts window?

yes

no

Do you need to separate a group of contact entries from the rest of the list on a regular schedule?

yes → **Go to...** I don't know how to filter contact entries, page 47.

Quick fix

Letter buttons are missing from my Contacts window Check your sort order—if your Contacts cards are sorted by a non-text field (such as birthday or anniversary, which are date fields), there won't be any letter buttons.

If your solution isn't here, check these related chapters:

- Contacts, custom data, page 38
- Contacts, general, page 48

Or see the general troubleshooting tips on page xvii.

I don't know how to sort the Contacts Card view

Source of the problem

The Contacts Card view is sorted by the File As field. This provides an easy way to locate a contact's phone number—simply click a letter button on the right side of the Contact form to jump to the correct part of the alphabetical list, and then scroll to the contact entry you want to see. But what if you have a Contacts list that's hundreds of entries long, and the only thing you remember about a contact is the company name? You can sort the Card view by the Company field and scan the contact names in the company to locate the person you need to find.

How to fix it

1. On the View menu, point to Current View, and then click Customize Current View.
2. In the View Summary dialog box, click the Sort button. ▶
3. Click the down arrow to the right of the Sort Items By box, and click Company in the drop-down list. ▶
4. Click OK.
5. If you see a prompt telling you that the field named Company is not shown and asking whether you want to show it, click Yes. (If you click No, the cards will be sorted by company, but you won't know which contacts belong to which company.)

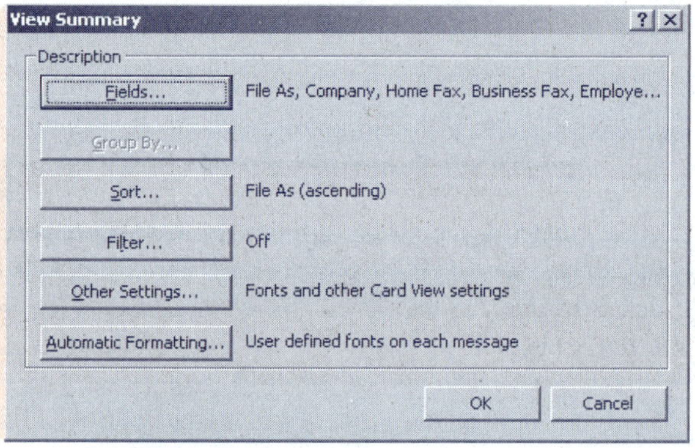

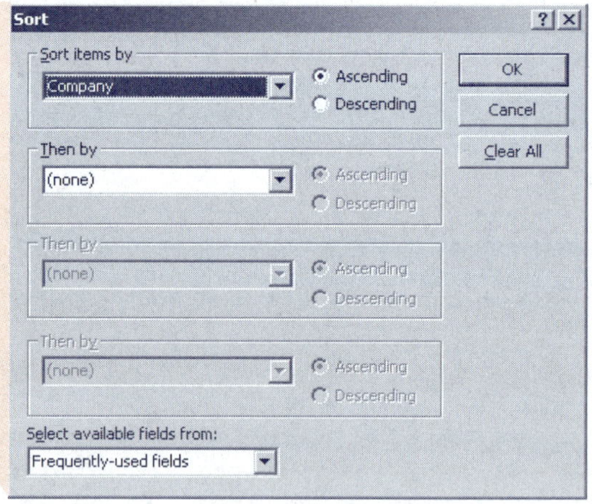

I don't know how to filter contact entries

Source of the problem

Part of your job requires that you send a weekly update fax to all your contacts, which you know you can do using the mail-merge capabilities of Microsoft Outlook. Filtering your contacts by fax number, and doing so quickly, would make your job much easier. The solution is to define a new view of your Contacts list that filters those entries that have business fax numbers; then all you have to do each week is select that view and run your mail merge.

How to fix it

1. On the View menu, point to Current View, and then click Define Views.
2. In the Define Views dialog box, click the New button.
3. In the Create A New View dialog box, type a name for the view (something easy to recognize, such as Fax Merge), and select Card from the Type Of View list. ▶
4. Click OK.
5. In the View Summary dialog box, click the Filter button.
6. In the Filter dialog box, set up the filter for the view. In this Fax Merge view example, a criterion is set in the Advanced tab that specifies the field as Business Fax and the condition as Is Not Empty.
7. Click the Add To List button to add the filter to the Find Items That Match These Criteria list. ▶
8. Click OK twice, and then click Close to close each of the dialog boxes.

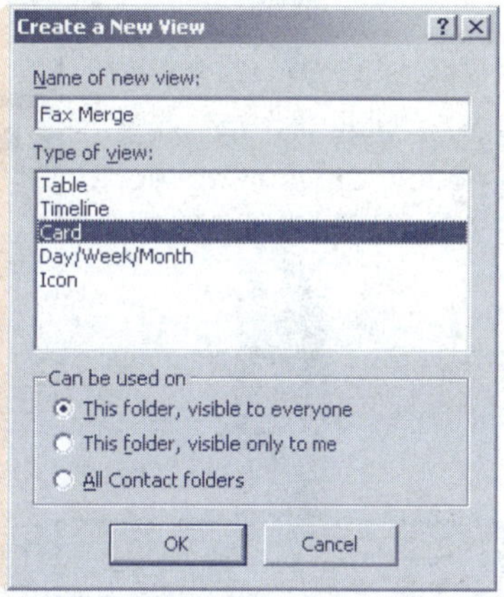

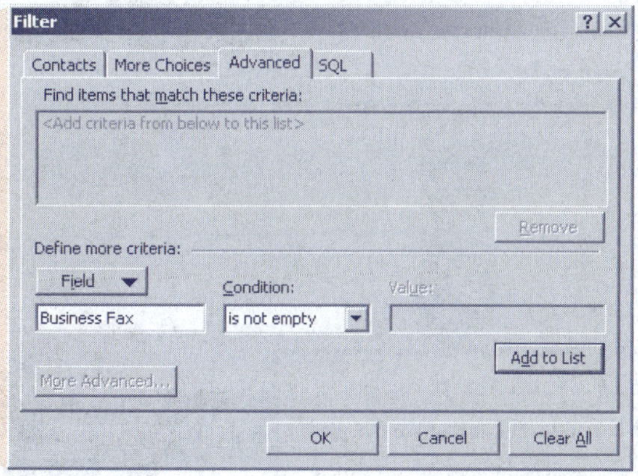

Do you need a quick way to change the same company address for many contacts?

yes → **Go to...** It takes too long to edit the address of contacts at the same company, page 50.

no

Is your Contacts folder accessible to too many people on your network?

yes

no

Does your search for a contact containing a specific word come up empty?

yes → **Quick fix**

My search for a contact based on a specific word is not working In the Find Items In Contacts page, be sure the Search All Text In The Contact check box is selected.

no

Do you have problems importing a contacts list from Excel?

yes → **Go to...** I can't import a list of contacts from Excel, page 55.

Does your Contacts folder have to be in a Public Folders file?

yes

Go to...

Too many people can access my Contacts folder, page 54.

no

Quick fix

I want my contacts to be available only to me on my computer Place the Contacts folder in the Personal Folders file, rather than a Public Folders file.

1. On the View menu, click Folder List.
2. Open both the Public Folders file and the Personal Folders file by clicking the small plus symbols next to each one.
3. Drag your Contacts folder from the Public Folders file to the Personal Folders file. (If you drop it on the Personal Folders folder, it will become a first level folder under Personal Folders, called Contacts1.)

Alternately, select all the individual contacts in your Public Folders Contacts folder and drag them into the Contacts folder in your Personal Folders file.

If your solution isn't here, check these related chapters:

- Contacts, folder display, page 44
- Contacts, custom data, page 38

Or see the general troubleshooting tips on page xvii.

It takes too long to edit the address of contacts at the same company

Source of the problem

You've got several business associates at the same company—perhaps 10, perhaps 200—and the company they work for has moved to a new location across town. You need to update the business address for all these contacts. You can copy and paste the changed address into each individual contact, but what a tedious waste of time! There are faster ways to change an identical address (or any other data) for a group of contacts, and the method that's best for you depends both on the size of the group of contacts that needs to be changed and your skills in other software programs (such as Microsoft Excel).

There are a couple of good ways to make the same change to several contacts. For a small group of contacts—up to about 30—you can use the "group and move" technique in Microsoft Outlook. For a larger group of contacts, export the entire group to Excel, edit the data, and then import the changed contacts back into Outlook.

Note

The second method requires that you have Excel installed on your computer.

How to fix it

For a small number of contacts

This method is useful for changing up to about 30 contacts, but for more than that, it becomes unwieldy.

1. Open the Contact folder, and double-click a contact whose address you want to change.
2. In the Contact dialog box, click Address, type the new address, and save and close the contact.
3. On the View menu, point to Current View, and then click By Company.
4. Right-click the arrow next to Microsoft Outlook Help, click Advanced to display the Advanced toolbar, and then click the Group By Box button.

5. If the Business Address field is not displayed, add it to the view.

Tip

To add a field to a view, right-click the row of column headings, and click Field Chooser on the shortcut menu. Then drag the field from the Field Chooser to the row of column headings.

6. Drag the Business Address column heading into the Group By box, and place it to the right of the Company column heading. ▶

The contacts are now grouped first by Company and then by Business Address.

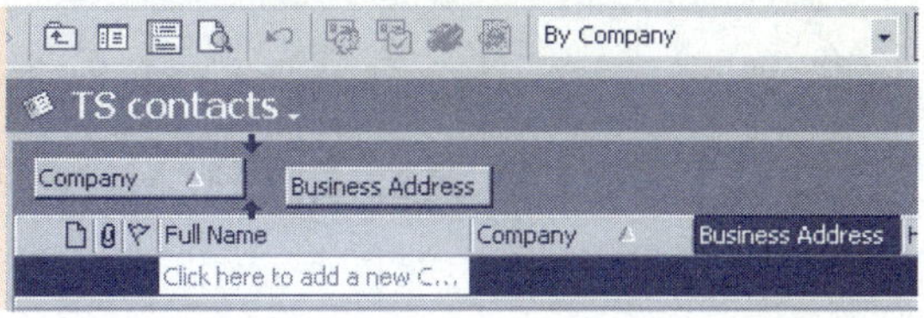

7. Now create a filter for the list that hides all contacts except those in the company whose address you want to change. On the Contact's View menu, point to Current View, and click Customize Current View.

8. In the View Summary dialog box, click Filter.

9. In the Filter dialog box, click the Contacts tab, and type the company name in the Search For The Words box. In the In List box, select Company Field Only, and then click OK to close the Filter dialog box.

10. Click OK again to run the filter. When the filter is finished, you should have two groups displayed—one with the company name and the old address, and one with the company name and the new address (which you entered in step 1). ▶

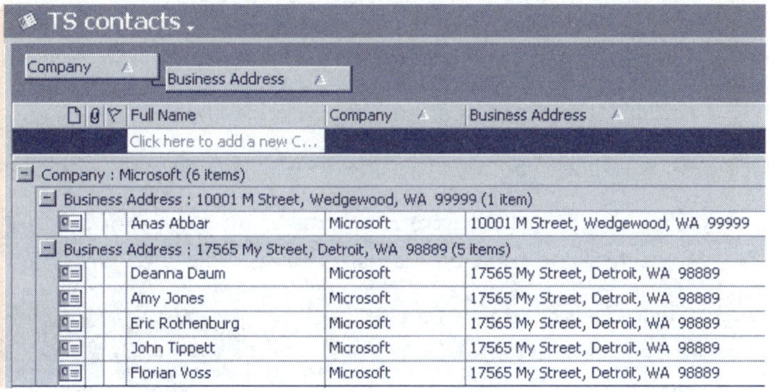

11. Select all the items in the old address group, and drag them to the group with the new address. When the screen tip next to the mouse pointer reads Change Company To (followed by the company name and the new business address), release the mouse button to place the items in their new location. ▶

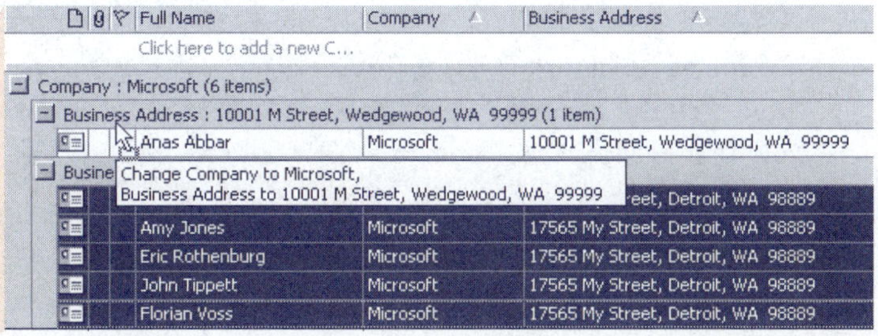

12. To remove the filter, on the View menu, point to Current View, click Customize Current View, and then click Filter.

13. In the Filter dialog box, click the Clear All button, and then click OK twice to close all dialog boxes.

If this solution didn't solve your problem, go to the next page.

It takes too long to edit the address of contacts at the same company

(continued from page 51)

For a large number of contacts

Using Excel to change larger quantities of data is quicker than the method just outlined because Excel is adept at handling a lot of data. With this technique, you export your contacts to Excel, change the addresses that need changing (using one of Excel's data-manipulation features, such as Search and Replace or AutoFill), and then import the contacts back into Outlook.

1. Open the Contacts folder in any view.
2. On the File menu, click Import And Export.
3. On the first page of the Import And Export Wizard, select Export To A File, and then click Next.
4. Select Microsoft Excel, and then click Next.
5. Be sure the Contacts folder you want to export is selected, and then click Next.
6. Click the Browse button, navigate to an easy-to-locate folder where you can store the new Excel file, and then type a name for the file into which you will export the contacts.
7. Click OK to return to the Export To A File Wizard, and then click Next.
8. Click the Map Custom Fields button.
9. In the Map Custom Fields dialog box, click the Default Map button, and then click OK to return to the Export To A File Wizard.

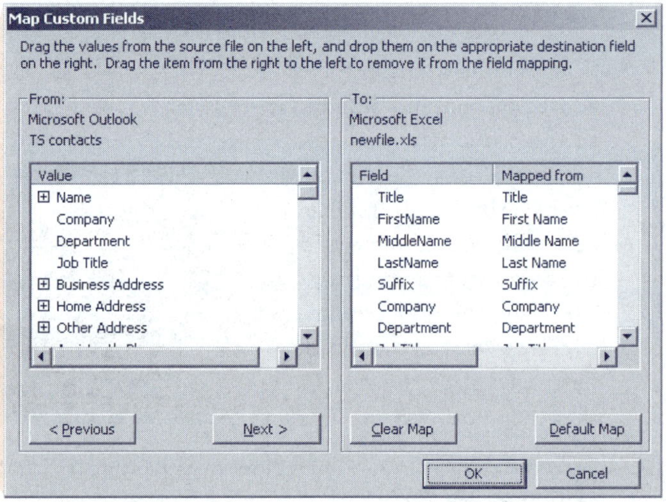

Tip

It's important to click the Default Map button and export *all* your contact fields, because any data you don't export won't be available when you re-import.

10. Click Finish. Copies of your contact data are exported to the Excel workbook.
11. To change the data in Excel, open the Excel workbook.

12. Use any of Excel's features, such as Search And Replace, copy and paste, AutoFill, or any technique you're comfortable with, to change all the data at once.

13. Save and close the Excel file.

14. To import the updated contacts back into Outlook, on the File menu, click Import And Export.

15. On the Import And Export Wizard's first page, click Import From Another Program Or File, and then click Next.

16. Click Microsoft Excel, and then click Next.

17. Make sure the path and file name in the File To Import box are correct, select the Replace Duplicates With Items Imported option, and then click Next.

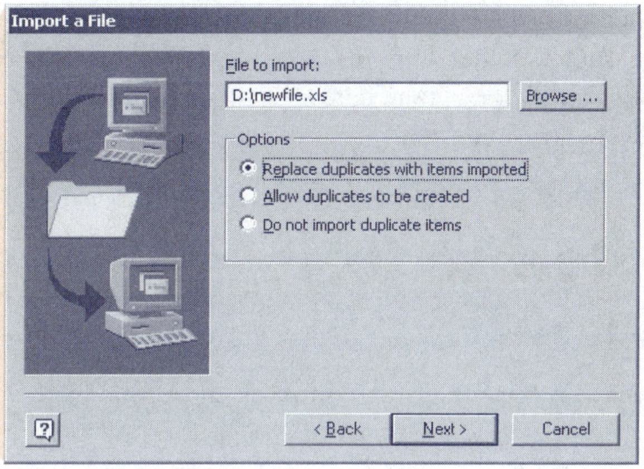

18. Make sure the correct Contacts folder is selected, and then click Next.

19. Click Finish.

All the existing contacts in your folder are replaced with the updated contact information imported from Excel.

More about changing your data in Excel

Here are several easy ways to change data in an Excel workbook:

- Change the data in a single cell (for example, a street address), and then click away from the cell. Select that cell, and press Ctrl+C to copy it. Select all the cells where you want to paste the copied data, and press Enter to paste the copied data into all the cells at once (Copy and Paste).
- Change the data in a single cell at the top of a column, and then click away from the cell. Select the cell you changed and all the cells below it where you want to paste the changed data. Press Ctrl+D to copy the data in the top cell to the selected cells below (Fill Down).
- Change the data in a single cell at the top of a column, and then click away from the cell. Select the cell with the changed data, and drag the small black box in the lower-right corner of the selected cell (the *fill handle*) to copy the data in the selected cell to the cells below. This works well with text, but not with numbers—you could end up pasting a number series instead of copying the same number (AutoFill).
- Copy the top cells in several adjacent columns, and use any of the techniques in this list to paste the data in the cells of several columns at once.

Too many people can access my Contacts folder

Source of the problem

You use Outlook in a network environment, and your Contacts folder is public, which means it's open to everyone on the network. Some of your networked associates need to have access to your Contacts folder, but you don't want *everyone* to have access to your confidential contact data. The solution is to change permissions for your public Contacts folder so that you can decide who has access to your data.

How to fix it

1. On the View menu, click Folder List.
2. In the Folder list, right-click the Contacts folder you want to set permissions for, and click Properties on the shortcut menu.
3. In the Properties dialog box, click the Permissions tab. In the Name list, the names of all the people who should have access to your Contacts folder are listed.
4. In the Name list, select one or more names.
5. In the Permission Level list box, select a role that grants the selected name(s) only the permissions you want them to have. For example, if you want a person to have no access, select None.
6. Below the Permission Level list box is a set of options and check boxes for specific activities that the selected names can be granted or denied permission for. Make sure that (at least) the Read Items and Folder Visible check boxes are selected for people you want to be able to view your contacts.
7. Click OK.

Tip

You can apply the same permissions to several names at once by selecting several names in step 4. Use the Ctrl or Shift key to select multiple names.

Tip

You can mark individual contacts as Private by selecting the Private check box in the lower-right corner of the Contact form. Private contacts won't appear to others who open your public Contacts folder, regardless of their permission level.

I can't import a list of contacts from Excel

Source of the problem

You've got a list of contacts in an Excel workbook and you need to get that list into your Contacts folder in Outlook, but every time you try to import the list, you get an error message. It's very frustrating—but it's easy to fix. The problem is that the Excel worksheet from which you're importing must be set up correctly, with column headings and a named range, so that Outlook can identify the data you want to import.

Tip

This solution is *not* for importing a list that you previously exported from Outlook, as covered earlier in this chapter in "It takes too long to edit the address of contacts at the same company." This solution is for importing a fresh list from Excel that's never been in Outlook.

How to fix it

1. In the Excel worksheet from which you are importing, make sure that all your contact data is in a neat, rectangular table, with no blank rows or columns.
2. In the row immediately above the table, give each column a heading (such as FirstName, LastName, Street, City, and so forth).
3. Select the entire table (not the entire workbook), including the headings row.
4. Click the worksheet's Name box, type a single-word name that's not identical to any column headings (the example uses Contax as the name), and press Enter. Don't click away or press Tab—just press Enter.

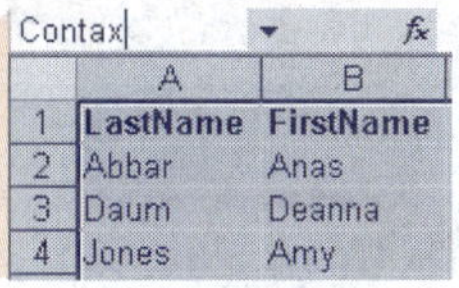

   You can tell the data range has been correctly named by clicking the arrow to the right of the Name box—the range name you created appears in the drop-down list, and when you click the range name, your data table is selected.
5. Save and close the Excel workbook.
6. Import the data from the worksheet into Outlook. (See step 14 on page 53 for information about how to do this.) Outlook recognizes the range name, and in the fifth page of the Import A File Wizard, you can map the Excel column headings to match Outlook's field names.

Are you trying to set up a Web-based e-mail account (such as Hotmail or Yahoo!)?

yes → **Go to...** I can't set up my Web-based e-mail account, page 64.

no

Are you trying to set up an e-mail account with Microsoft Network, AOL, or CompuServe?

yes

no

Is the Find tool not searching all your e-mail accounts?

yes

no

Does it take a long time to connect to your ISP?

yes → **Go to...** Getting connected takes a long time, page 62.

no

Is there a Send button for e-mail messages you create?

yes

no

Quick fix

There's no Send button for my messages and I've never set up an account If there's no Send button in the upper-left corner of the new message's window, you don't have any accounts set up from which Outlook can send e-mail. To set up an e-mail account, find a local Internet service provider (ISP) and set up an Internet account with them. They'll tell you exactly what you need to do to set up Outlook so that you can send e-mail using the new account (and if they can't tell you how to set up Outlook, find another ISP).

You can locate ISPs in the Yellow Pages, but a better way is to get recommendations from friends or look at associates' business cards to see where they have their e-mail accounts.

E-mail, accounts

Go to...
I can't set up my MSN, AOL, or CompuServe e-mail account, page 68.

Go to...
The Find tool doesn't find messages in my Hotmail account, page 67.

Is your e-mail account with a local ISP working properly?

no

Go to...
My e-mail account doesn't work, page 58.

If your solution isn't here, check these related chapters:

- E-mail, sending, page 120
- Multiple users, page 204

Or see the general troubleshooting tips on page xvii.

My e-mail account doesn't work

Source of the problem

You've set up an Internet e-mail account with a local Internet service provider (ISP), and you have all the account information that you need to create the account in Microsoft Outlook. But for some reason, your new e-mail account isn't working.

Or perhaps your ISP changed some of the information for your account, such as the name of the incoming mail server or outgoing mail server, and you don't know where to make those changes.

Tip

Record all the account information your ISP gives you in an Outlook note so that you can find it easily when you need it.

How to fix it

The E-mail Accounts Wizard stores all your ISP account information, and you can check it and change it if you need to.

1. On the Tools menu, click E-mail Accounts.
2. On the E-mail Accounts Wizard's first page, select the View Or Change Existing E-mail Accounts option, and click Next.
3. In the Outlook Processes E-mail For These Accounts In The Following Order list, click your account name, and then click the Change button.
4. On the Internet E-mail Settings (POP3) page of the E-mail Accounts Wizard, in the User Information area, make sure you have a name and the correct e-mail address entered.
5. In the Server Information area, make sure the addresses in the Incoming Mail Server (POP3) and Outgoing Mail Server (SMTP) boxes are correct, with no typing errors. (There are never any spaces in server names.)

Tip

This procedure assumes that you are using an Internet e-mail account. If you have a non-POP3 account, the wizard will look different than described in these steps. If you are connected to a Microsoft Exchange server, contact your administrator before troubleshooting your e-mail account.

6. In the Logon Information area, delete and retype your user name and password. (Some accounts have case-sensitive account names and passwords—if yours does, be sure you type the correct uppercase and lowercase letters.) ►

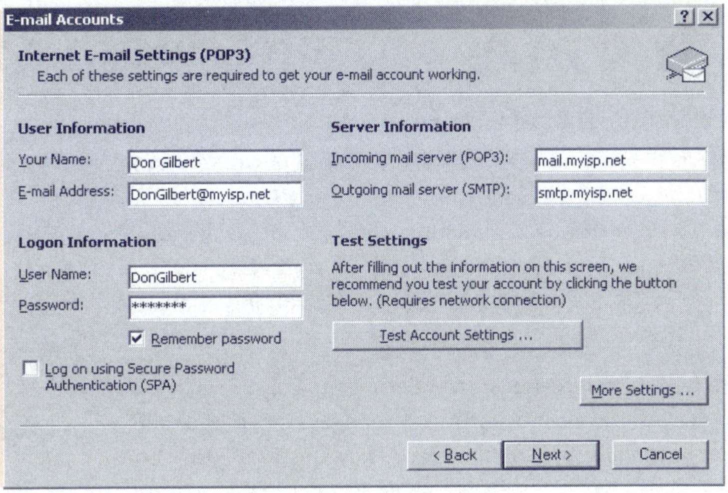

7. If your e-mail account requires that you log on using secure password authentication, be sure to select the Log On Using Secure Password Authentication (SPA) check box.

8. Click More Settings. If your ISP told you that you need to log on to your outgoing mail server, in the Internet E-mail Settings dialog box, click the Outgoing Server tab, select the My Outgoing Server (SMTP) Requires Authentication check box, and then check that your outgoing mail server settings are correct.

9. Click the Connection tab, and make sure you have the correct connection option selected. If you connect through your computer's modem, select the Connect Using My Phone Line option. If you use a cable or DSL modem or are connected through your office network, select the Connect Using My Local Area Network (LAN) option. ►

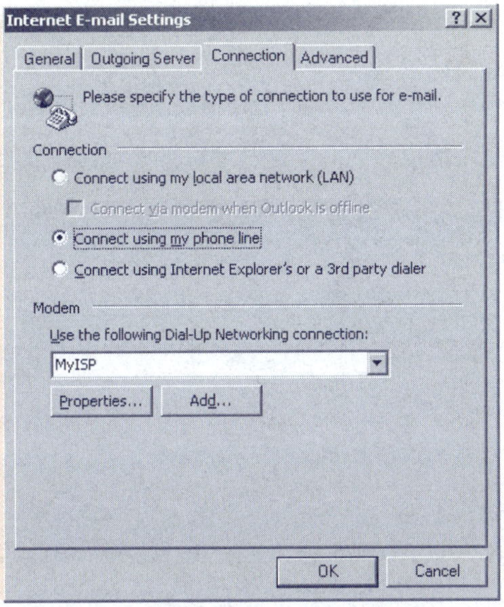

This solution is continued on the next page.

My e-mail account doesn't work

(continued from page 59)

10. If you connect using a phone line, in the Modem area, click Properties. In the dialog box named for your dial-up connection, click the General tab, and check the phone number. If it's correct, click Cancel; if it's wrong, type the correct phone number, and click OK.

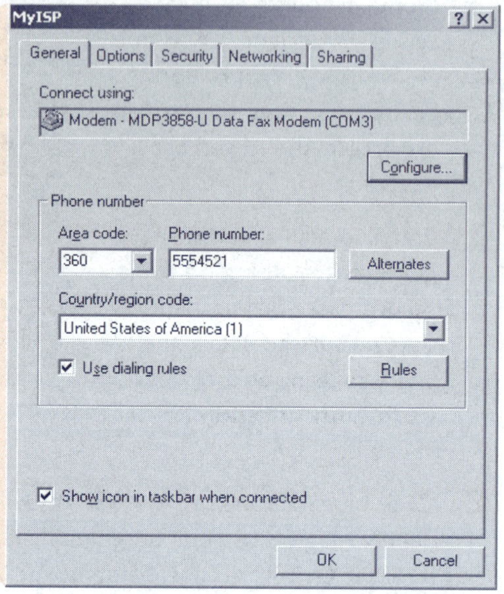

11. In the Internet E-mail Settings dialog box, click the Advanced tab, but make changes only if your ISP or network administrator has specifically directed you to do so. (The default settings are fine in most cases.)
12. Click OK to close the Internet E-mail Settings dialog box.
13. On the Internet E-mail Settings page of the E-mail Accounts Wizard, click Test Account Settings. If there are no errors, you've fixed your problem. Click Close, click Next, and then on the final page of the E-mail Accounts Wizard, click Finish to exit the wizard.

If your account still doesn't work after you've checked and corrected the account information as described here, call your ISP, and ask someone to walk you through the Outlook setup, step by step.

E-mail, accounts

Getting connected takes a long time

Source of the problem

Outlook dials in to your ISP, but it seems to take a long time to get connected. There are a few settings that might be slowing down your connection time. You can check (and change, if you need to) these connection settings.

How to fix it

1. On the Tools menu, click E-mail Accounts.
2. On the first page of the E-mail Accounts Wizard, select the View Or Change Existing E-mail Accounts option, and click Next.
3. On the wizard's second page, in the Outlook Processes E-mail For These Accounts In The Following Order list, click your account name, and then click the Change button.
4. Click More Settings.
5. In the Internet E-mail Settings dialog box, click the Connection tab.
6. In the Modem area, click the down arrow next to the Use The Following Dial-Up Connection box, click your account name in the drop-down list, and then click the Properties button. ▶

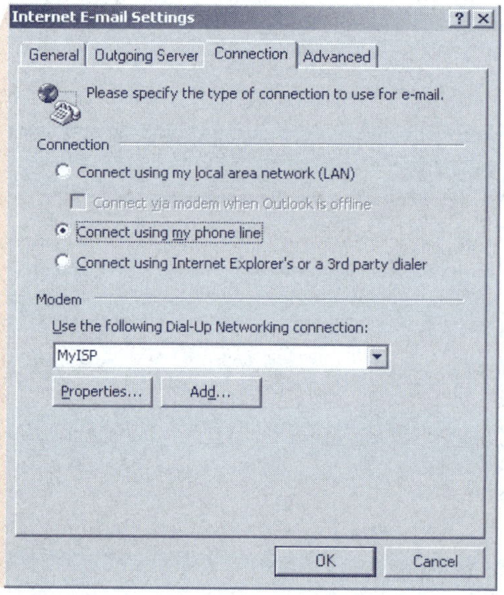

7. In the dialog box for your account, on the Networking tab, clear the NetBEUI check box, as well as any other protocols except Internet Protocol (TCP/IP). ▶

8. Click OK twice to close all the dialog boxes.

9. Click Next, and then click Finish to close the E-mail Accounts Wizard.

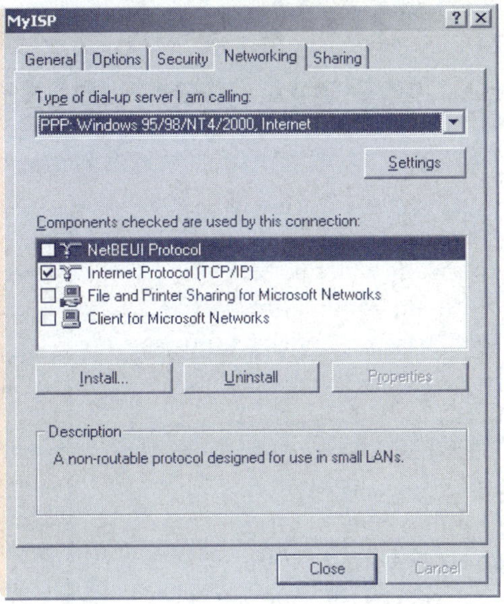

I can't set up my Web-based e-mail account

Source of the problem

You want to set up a Hotmail, Yahoo!, or other Web-based e-mail account (because it's free—what a deal!) or you already have a Web-based e-mail account, and you want to use it with Outlook. But you don't know how to set it up, or you tried to set it up but it didn't work.

Before you start

The way you access a Web-based e-mail account in Outlook depends on the Web-based e-mail service provider you use. Hotmail and MSN support Outlook's ability to host your Web-based e-mail as a fully integrated part of Outlook. Other Web-based e-mail service providers can also integrate with Outlook 2002 if they provide an appropriate server URL. Even if your Web-based e-mail service provider doesn't support integration with Outlook, you can still access it from Outlook in the same way that you can open a Web page in Outlook. If you're unsure whether a service provider supports Outlook 2002 integration, contact the service. In either case, the Web-based e-mail account must be established before you can set it up in Outlook. You typically set this up through the service provider's Web page. For example, to set up a Hotmail account, visit *www.msn.com*, click Hotmail, and then click Sign Up.

How to fix it

Tip

Although Web-based e-mail accounts are free, you must still have a dial-up, cable, or DSL connection to access a Web-based e-mail program.

Set up an integrated Web-based account

1. On the Tools menu, click E-mail Accounts.
2. On the first page of the E-mail Accounts Wizard, select the Add A New E-mail Account option, and click Next.
3. On the wizard's second page, select the HTTP option, and click Next.

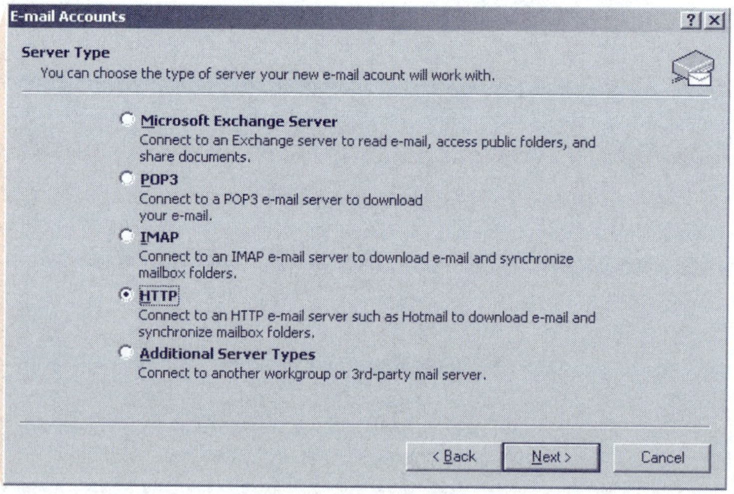

4. On the wizard's third page, in the Server Information area, click the down arrow next to the HTTP Mail Service Provider box, and click your Web server in the drop-down list. If it's not Hotmail or MSN, select Other, and type the URL address of the server. (This is not the same URL you use to access your Web-based e-mail using a browser.)

5. In the User Information area of the wizard's third page, type your name and e-mail address. In the Logon Information area, type your user name and password.

   The name you type in the Your Name box should be the name that is displayed outside the parentheses in the From box of an e-mail message when recipients see your e-mail. (For example, if your e-mail messages show From: John Tippett (jp_tippett@hotmail.com), type *John Tippett*.) The name you type in the User Name box should be the part of your e-mail address that appears before the @ symbol (jp_tippett in this example).

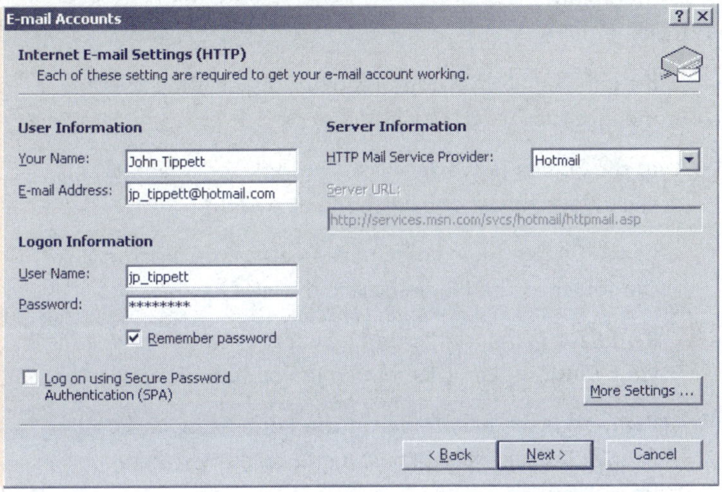

6. When you are finished, click More Settings.

7. In the Internet E-mail Settings dialog box, click the Connection tab. Select the Connect Using My Phone Line option if you are using a dial-up connection, or the Connect Using My Local Area Network (LAN) option if you're using a cable or DSL modem.

8. Click OK to close the Internet E-mail Settings dialog box, click Next in the E-mail Accounts Wizard, and click Finish to complete the wizard.

You should now see a new folder in the Folder List, named for your e-mail service (for example, Hotmail, if you chose that service) and containing an Inbox folder with your Web-based e-mail.

If this solution didn't solve your problem, go to the next page.

I can't set up my Web-based e-mail account

(continued from page 65)

Set up a stand-alone Web-based account

Because you can set any folder's home page in Outlook to display a Web address, if your Web-based e-mail account doesn't support integration with Outlook, you can create a new folder and associate it with your Web-based e-mail address.

1. If the Folder List is not already displayed, on the View menu, click Folder List.
2. In the Folder List, right-click Outlook Today, and then click New Folder on the shortcut menu.
3. In the Create New Folder dialog box, type a name for the folder in the Name box, and click OK.

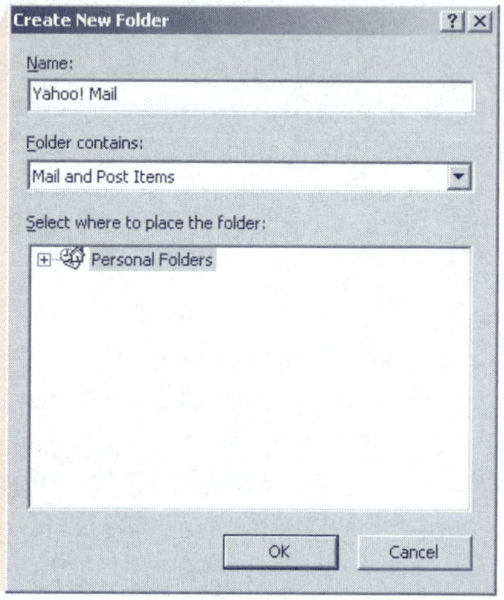

4. If you are prompted to add a shortcut to this folder to your Outlook Bar, click either Yes or No.
5. Right-click the new folder in the Folder List, and click Properties on the shortcut menu to display the Properties dialog box.
6. Click the Home Page tab, and in the Address box, type the URL for the account's Web page.
7. Select the Show Home Page By Default For This Folder check box, and click OK.

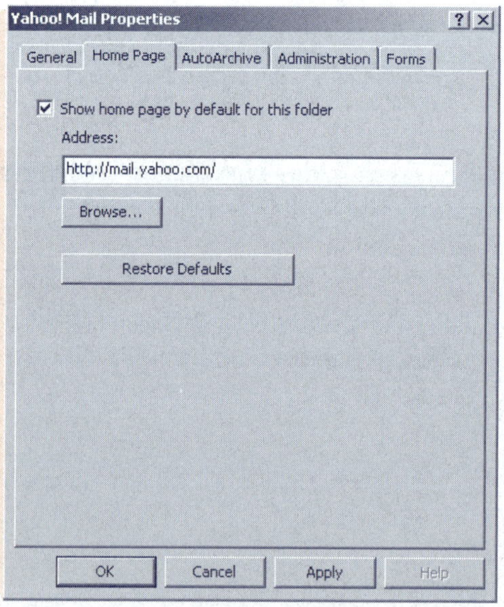

Tip

If there's an option for automatically logging you in on this computer, select it before signing in the first time and you'll always go directly to your e-mail when you open this folder in Outlook.

The Find tool doesn't find messages in my Hotmail account

Source of the problem

You've added Hotmail, Microsoft Network (MSN), or another Web-based e-mail account to Outlook, and your Web account folders appear in the Folder List with those of other e-mail accounts. But when you click Find on the Tools menu and search all folders for messages containing specific words, Outlook doesn't find the ones in your Web-based folders. You know they're there—you can see them!

The problem is that unlike your other accounts, which deliver messages to the Inbox folder and store sent messages in the Send Items folder, Hotmail has its own Inbox and Sent Items folders. (This is true for any Web-based account that integrates into Outlook.) The Find feature can search one set of folders or the other, but not both at the same time. You need to tell Find to specifically search the folders in your Web-based e-mail account.

How to fix it

1. If the Search Bar isn't currently displayed, on the Tools menu, click Find.
2. In the Search Bar, type the word or words you want to search for in the Look For box.
3. Click Search In, and click Choose Folders in the drop-down list.
4. In the Select Folder(s) dialog box, clear the Inbox check box, and then click Hotmail.
5. At the bottom of the dialog box, select the Search Subfolders check box.

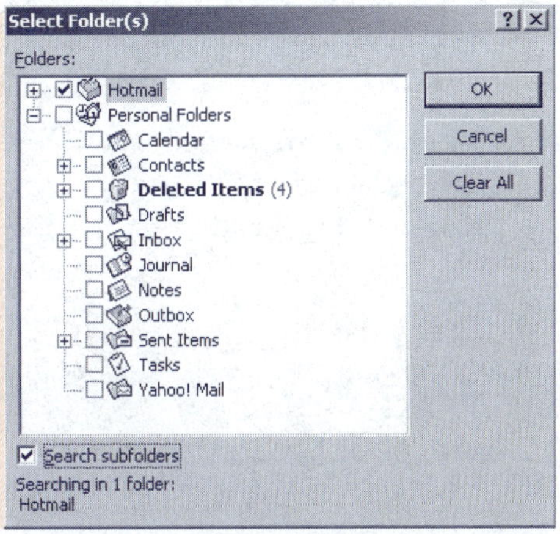

6. Click OK.
7. In the Search Bar, click Find Now.

I can't set up my MSN, AOL, or CompuServe e-mail account

Source of the problem

You've got a Microsoft Network (MSN), America Online (AOL), or CompuServe account, and you're having difficulty getting Outlook to send and receive e-mail through that account. The following solution might fix the problem, depending on which of these programs you're trying to use.

How to fix it

MSN

To use Outlook with MSN, you must be using Microsoft Network 2.5 or later. To set up your Microsoft Network 2.5 account in Outlook, you follow normal account setup procedures, but you must be sure to set a few specific settings.

1. On the Tools menu, click E-mail Accounts.
2. In the E-mail Accounts Wizard, click the Add A New E-mail Account option, and then click Next.
3. On the wizard's second page, select the POP3 option, and click Next. ▶

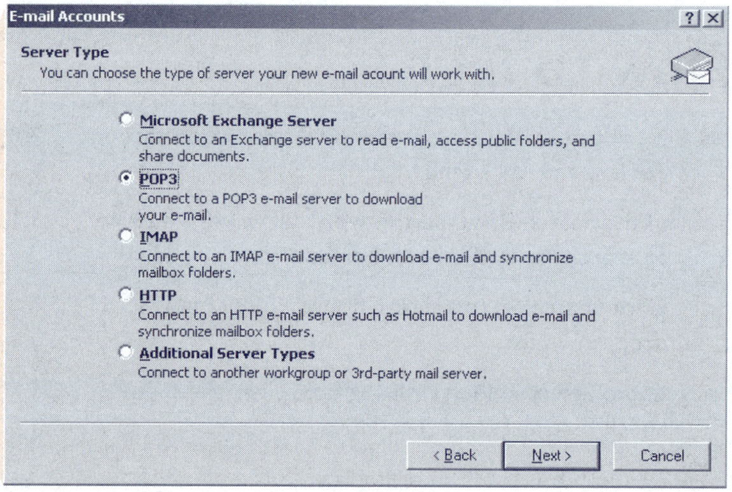

4. On the wizard's third page, complete the boxes in the User Information and Logon Information areas. In the Server Information area, type *pop3.email.msn.com* in the Incoming Mail Server (IMAP) box, type *secure.smtp.email.msn.com* in the Outgoing Mail Server (SMTP) box, and then select the Log On Using Secure Password Authorization (SPA) check box.

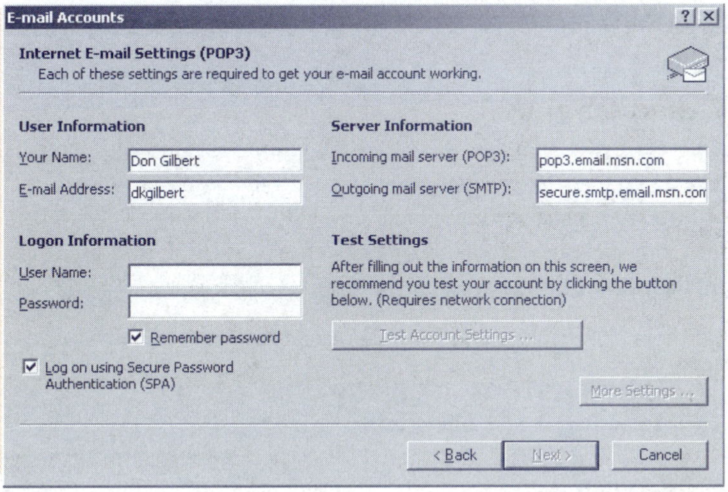

5. Click More Settings, and in the Internet E-mail Settings dialog box, click the Connection tab.
6. Select the Connect Using My Phone Line option if you are using a dial-up connection, or the Connect Using My Local Area Network (LAN) option if you're using a cable or DSL modem.
7. Click OK to close the Internet E-mail Settings dialog box.
8. Click Next, and then click Finish to complete the E-mail Accounts Wizard.

> **Tip**
> For more information about your MSN e-mail account, contact Microsoft Network technical support.

AOL

If your e-mail account is with AOL, there's no way to fix it. As of the writing of this book, AOL uses its own e-mail system, which isn't compatible with the Internet standards supported by independent e-mail programs, such as Outlook and Microsoft Outlook Express. In other words, you can get your AOL e-mail only through the AOL software.

If this solution didn't solve your problem, go to the next page.

I can't set up my MSN, AOL, or CompuServe e-mail account

(continued from page 69)

CompuServe

To set up your CompuServe 2000 account in Outlook, you follow normal account setup procedures, but you must be sure to set a few specific settings. This procedure describes how to set up CompuServe 2000 5.0 (or later) with Outlook and assumes the last part of your e-mail address is @cs.com.

> **Tip**
> If you have an earlier version of CompuServe, you can still use Outlook to send and receive e-mail on your account. The Microsoft Knowledge Base article Q299325 describes how to do this.

1. On the Tools menu, click E-mail Accounts.
2. In the E-mail Accounts Wizard, select the Add A New E-mail Account option, and then click Next.
3. On the wizard's second page, select the IMAP option, and click Next.

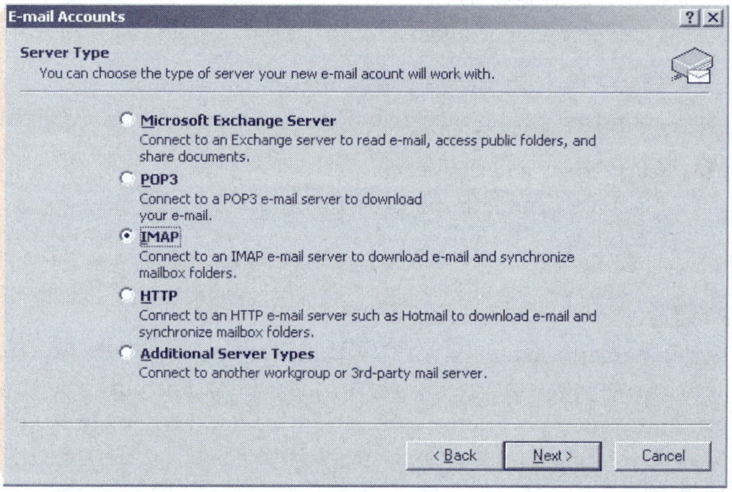

4. On the wizard's third page, in the Server Information area, type *imap.cs.com* in the Incoming Mail Server (IMAP) box, and *smtp.cs.com* in the Outgoing Mail Server (SMTP) box (unless CompuServe tells you otherwise).
5. Click More Settings, and in the Internet E-mail Settings dialog box, click the Outgoing Server tab.

6. Select the My Outgoing Server (SMTP) Requires Authentication check box.
7. Select the Use Same Settings As My Incoming Mail Server option.
8. Click the Connection tab, and in the Connection area, select the Connect Using My Phone Line option if you are using a dial-up connection, or the Connect Using My Local Area Network (LAN) option if you're using a cable or DSL modem.
9. Click OK to close the Internet E-mail Settings dialog box.
10. Click Next, and then click Finish to complete the E-mail Accounts Wizard.

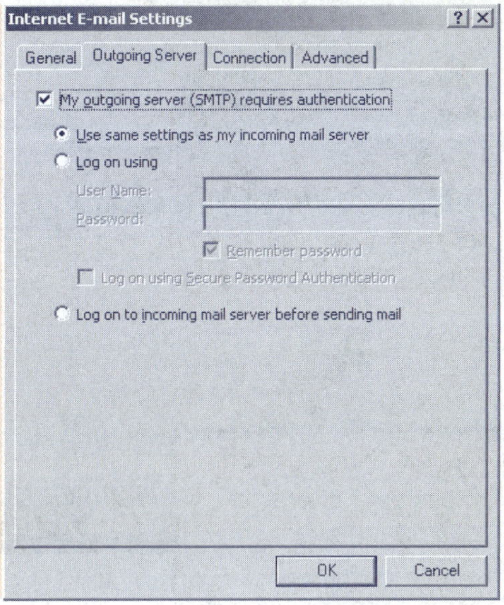

Tip

For more information about your CompuServe 2000 e-mail account, contact CompuServe technical support.

E-mail, ad

Can you easily find the addresses of people you want to e-mail?

yes → Are you unable to create a long distribution list? yes →

no

Are you having trouble finding your contact's name in the Select Names dialog box?

yes →

no

Are you trying to type nicknames to cause Outlook to automatically complete the address?

yes → **Go to…** My nicknames no longer distinguish between my contacts, page 76.

no

Is your Personal Address Book missing?

yes → **Go to…** I can't find my Personal Address Book, page 74.

no

Do you want Outlook to generate a new contact when you send a reply to someone?

yes →

Quick fix

I can't create long distribution lists Distribution lists have a limit of 107 names. Also, some mail servers won't send a message to more than perhaps 50 names in an attempt to prevent spamming and virus threats from traveling through the server. Rather than creating one very long distribution list, create multiple shorter distribution lists, and send each a separate copy of the message so that you don't run into any server limits.

Quick fix

I can't find a contact in the Select Names dialog box Make sure you're looking in the correct Contacts folder or subfolder. (Click the down arrow to the right of the Show Names From The box, and click the folder name in the drop-down list.)

Go to...

I can't automatically create contacts anymore, page 78.

If your solution isn't here, check these related chapters:

- E-mail, importing addresses, page 98
- E-mail, sending, page 120

Or see the general troubleshooting tips on page xvii.

I can't find my Personal Address Book

Source of the problem

Before upgrading to Outlook 2002, you stored your e-mail addresses in the Personal Address Book (PAB), but now you can't find the PAB in Outlook 2002. The reason for this likely goes back to setup. If the Outlook Setup program encountered a PAB in your profile, it recommended that you import it and asked if you wanted to do so. If you clicked Yes at that point, Outlook imported the contents of the Personal Address Book into your Contacts folder and removed the Personal Address Book service from your computer. If you clicked No, the Personal Address Book was not imported. It should still be on your computer, and you can import it now.

Importing your PAB requires that you find it and then run the Outlook Import Wizard.

How to fix it

1. On the taskbar, click the Start button, point to Search, and click Files Or Folders.
2. In the Named box, type **.pab*. This will find all files with an extension of *.pab*.
3. Click Search Now. Your PAB file will be displayed if it is on your computer. Leave the results window open so you can refer to the path where the file is located, or write down the path—you'll need it soon.
4. To import the PAB, on the File menu, click Import And Export.
5. On the first page of the Outlook Import And Export Wizard, click Import From Another Program Or File, and then click Next.
6. Select Personal Address Book, and then click Next. ▶
7. Click Browse, and navigate to the location of the PAB file.

Tip

Be sure to look in your Contacts folder first before looking for a PAB. It's possible the PAB information was already imported, and you just haven't looked in the right place.

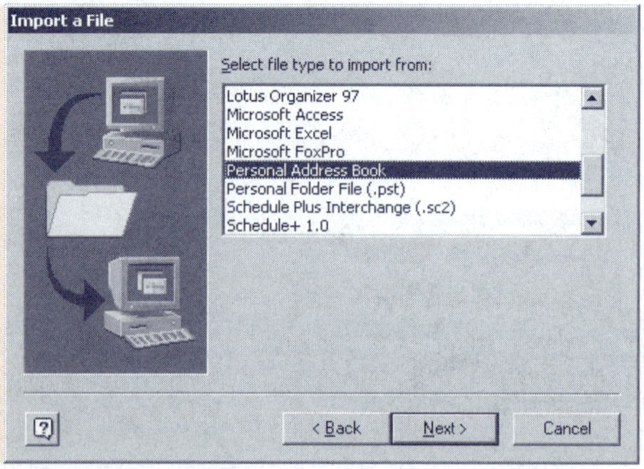

8. Click Change Destination if you want your Personal Address Book imported into a folder other than the main Contacts folder. If you want to make mapping changes (to specify that only certain fields be imported, for example), click the Map Custom Fields button, and make any necessary changes. ▶

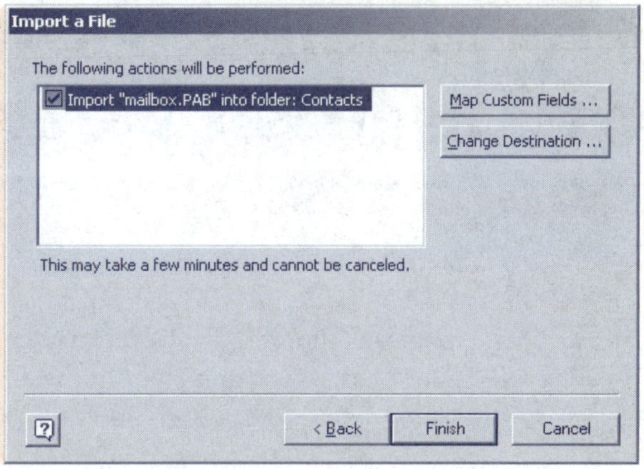

9. Click Finish.

More about using a Personal Address Book in Outlook

Although Outlook recommends that you convert your PAB to the Contacts folder, you can still view an existing PAB without converting it. For example, you might want to do this if you want to open a PAB to look for an address but not necessarily import all the information.

To view a PAB, you need to add the Personal Address Book service to your profile.

1. On the Tools menu, click E-mail Accounts.
2. On the E-mail Accounts Wizard's first page, select Add A New Directory Or Address Book.
3. Click Additional Address Books.
4. Click Personal Address Book.
5. When the Personal Address Book dialog box appears, browse to the location of your PAB, or type the path name, and click OK. ▶

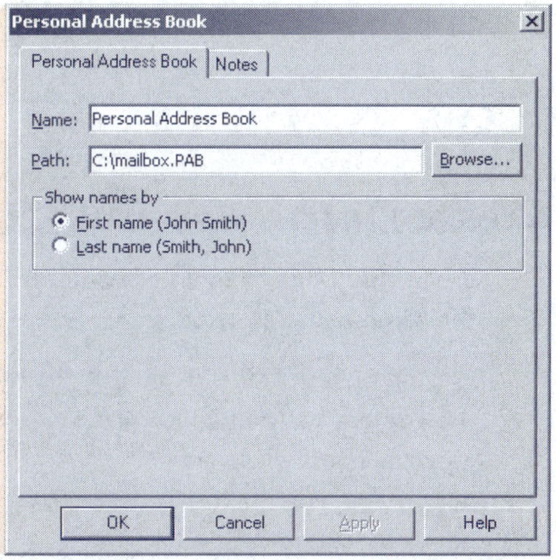

Tip

Because the Personal Address Book exists outside your personal storage (*.pst*) file, it is not archived with other parts of Outlook, it will not work with AutoName, and you can't search it for entries using Outlook's search tools. Consider this if you decide to add rather than import your PAB.

My nicknames no longer distinguish between my contacts

Source of the problem

In previous versions of Outlook, you could type a nickname (from a contact's Nickname field) on the To or Cc line of a message, and Outlook would distinguish between contacts with the same name. But since upgrading to Outlook 2002, this no longer works. The reason is that the way the AutoName feature works has changed—and it doesn't recognize the Nickname field. Instead, it uses a new field called Display As. One advantage of the Display As field is that when a contact has more than one e-mail address, you can have different Display As names for each one. And, as with nicknames, the Display As name can be used to distinguish between two contacts with the same name. By default, Outlook creates a Display As name that uses the full name followed by the e-mail address in parentheses, but you can set up unique Display As names for contacts with multiple addresses and use them to distinguish between contacts.

How to fix it

Create Display As names for your contacts

1. Open the Contact form of someone who either uses more than one e-mail address or who has the same name as another contact.
2. On the General tab, if the contact has multiple e-mail address, click the down arrow to the left of the E-mail box to select from E-mail, E-mail 2, or E-mail 3.
3. Below the e-mail address, in the Display As box, type a name that you can remember for the e-mail address that's entered above, and then click Save And Close. ▶

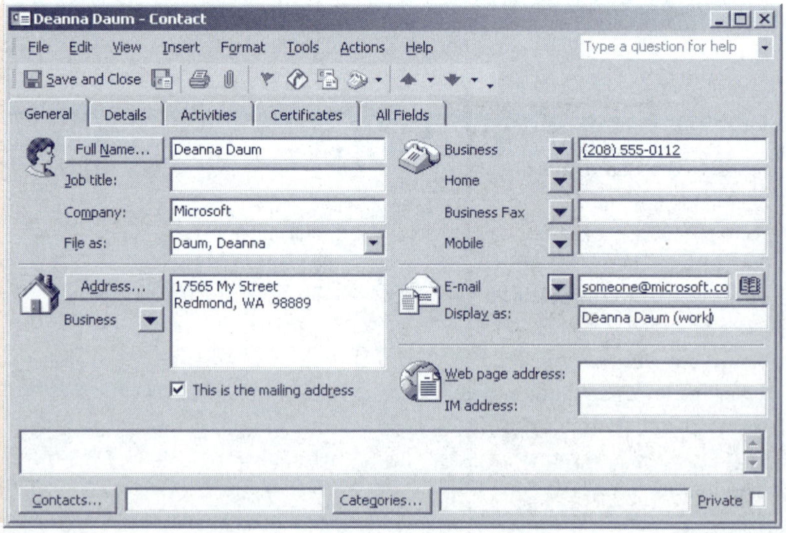

4. Repeat steps 2 and 3 to create a memorable nickname for each of the contact's e-mail addresses. (Display names such as Eric Work and Eric Home are memorable and functional.)

5. Repeat steps 1 and 3 for two or more contacts who share the same name. Then click Save And Close.

Tip

Unlike nicknames, your correspondents will see the Display As name you use, so be aware of this when you choose the Display As name.

Use the Display As names when addressing

1. To address a message, type all or part of the Display As name or the full name of the contact in the To or Cc box of the Message form.

2. If the name isn't immediately recognized, click the Check Names button, or move the cursor out of the box in which you typed the name. If you have a unique contact (that is, a contact with only one e-mail address) who matches the name, the contact's name will be entered in the box and underlined with a solid line. (After a while name recognition will occur quickly, without your interaction.)

3. If AutoName doesn't find a unique name, the Check Names dialog box appears when you click the Check Names button. ►

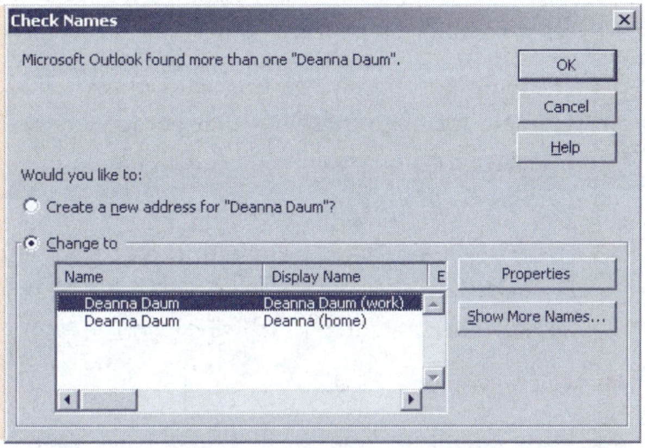

4. Select the display name that corresponds to the e-mail address you want, and click OK.

Tip

If you are using Outlook with Microsoft Exchange Server and the names in your personal Contacts folder are not recognized by AutoName, right-click Contacts in the Folder List, and click Properties; then click the Outlook Address Book tab, select Show This Folder As An E-mail Address Book, and click OK.

I can't automatically create contacts anymore

Source of the problem

Before upgrading to Microsoft Outlook 2002, you set your older version of Outlook to generate a new contact whenever you sent a reply to someone who was not already in your contacts list. But now you can't figure out how to enable this feature in Outlook 2002. Well, you can stop looking because it isn't there—it was dropped in Outlook 2002. However, if you want an easy way to generate new contacts based on your correspondence, you can generate contacts from messages in your Inbox.

How to fix it

1. Open your Inbox or any folder in which you've stored e-mail messages, and find a message from someone you want to add as a contact.
2. Drag the e-mail message to your Contacts folder. A new Contact form appears with that person's e-mail address displayed in the E-mail box, the Full Name box, and the Display As box.
3. Replace the e-mail address with the correct information for each box. (You might want to do this later, in case you already have an entry for this person.)
4. Click Save And Close.
5. If the Duplicate Contact Detected dialog box appears, click Cancel, or select the option to update the existing contact or add a duplicate. Then click OK.

Tip

If you see text other than the e-mail address in any boxes except File As, you probably already have a contact entry for this person.

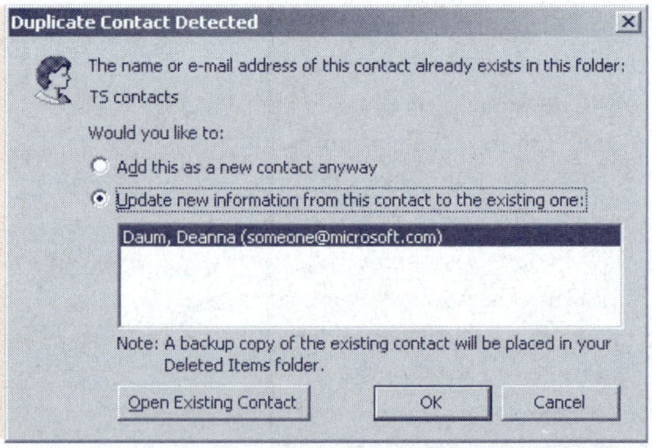

dressing messages

Can you send and receive e-mail messages?

yes

Do you get disconnected after you receive e-mail?

yes

no

Go to...

I can't send and receive e-mail messages, page 82.

no

Do you want to automatically dial in to retrieve e-mail messages?

yes

Go to...

I don't know how to schedule a regular time for Outlook to automatically dial in and retrieve messages, page 86.

no

Did Outlook stop sending and receiving when you installed a cable or DSL modem?

yes

Go to...

After I send or receive e-mail, I get disconnected, page 85.

Quick fix

I can't get Outlook to work with my new cable or DSL modem The key to switching from a dial-up connection to a cable or DSL modem connection is reconfiguring your connection in Outlook.

1. On the Tools menu, click E-mail Accounts.
2. On the first page of the E-mail Accounts Wizard, select the View Or Change Existing E-mail Connections option, and click Next.
3. On the wizard's second page, select the e-mail connection you want to reconfigure, and click Change.
4. Click More Settings, and in the Microsoft Exchange Server dialog box, click the Connection tab.
5. Select the Connect Using My Local Area Network (LAN) option, and click OK.
6. Click Next, and then click Finish.

If your solution isn't here, check **these related chapters:**

- E-mail, accounts, page 56
- Error messages, page 130

Or see the general troubleshooting tips on page xvii.

I can't send and receive e-mail messages

Source of the problem

You write new messages and send them to the Outbox, but nothing happens. Or you might get connected to your ISP and then receive any of several error messages. All you know for sure is that your e-mail is not going out or coming in.

One possibility is that your Internet account settings have been altered for some reason—installing or upgrading an anti-virus program can sometimes have this effect. You might also want to test all accounts to see which of them work. If you find an account that doesn't work, you can re-enter the information.

How to fix it

Check and restore settings

If you recently installed or upgraded an anti-virus program, that new program might have changed some of your Internet account settings. You need to restore the correct settings.

1. On the Tools menu, click E-mail Accounts.
2. On the first page of the E-mail Accounts Wizard, click the View Or Change Existing E-mail Accounts option, and then click Next.
3. On the second page of the E-mail Accounts Wizard, if you have more than one account listed (which is the case after installing some anti-virus programs), click the name of the original account in the Name list, and click the Move Up button to move it to the top of the list so that it will be your default account.
4. Click the original account name, and then click the Change button.

E-mail, connecting

5. In the Server Information area of the wizard page, delete any existing server names, and retype the correct server names. (If you don't have this information, your ISP can give it to you.) ▶

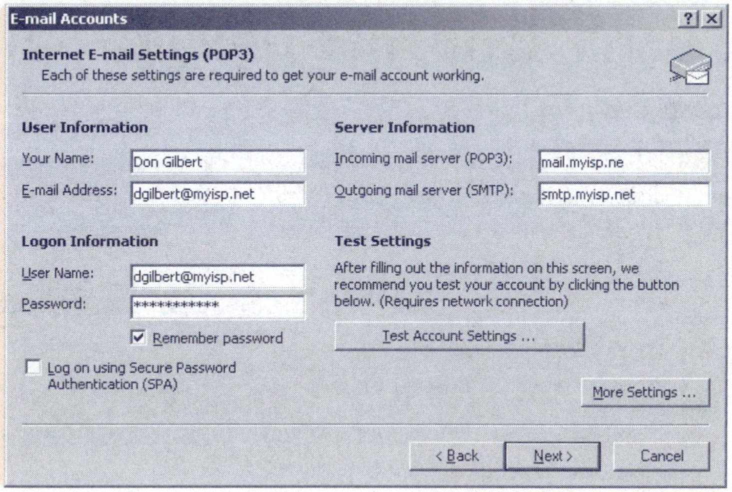

6. Click Next, and then click Finish to close the E-mail Accounts Wizard.
7. Quit Outlook, and then start it again.

Test accounts

You can test your accounts to find which one isn't working.

1. On the Tools menu, click E-mail Accounts.
2. On the first page of the E-mail Accounts Wizard, click View Or Change Existing E-mail Accounts, and then click Next.
3. On the wizard's second page, click the account name you want to test, and click Change.
4. On the third page of the wizard, if you are currently connected to your network (for Exchange users) or to the Internet, click Test Account Settings. ▶

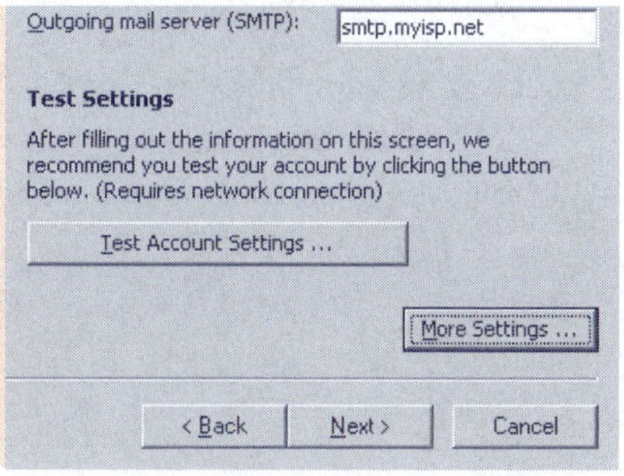

Tip

The graphic above, and the steps provided for this page of the wizard, apply only if you are using a POP3 account. If you are using a Microsoft Exchange Server account, you will see a different page, with different options.

This solution is continued on the next page.

I can't send and receive e-mail messages

(continued from page 83)

5. If there are no errors you'll see a check mark next to each test. If errors are reported, click the Tasks tab to see exactly which tests failed. ▶

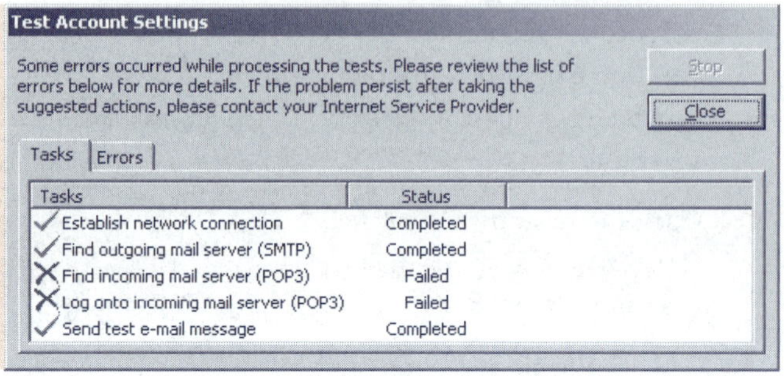

6. Click Close to close the Test Account Settings dialog box.

7. If all connection tests passed and you have other accounts, click Back in the E-mail Accounts Wizard, and repeat the previous four steps for each account to verify the connection.

8. If an Internet connection test fails, click the More Settings button, and when the Internet E-mail Settings dialog box appears, click the Connection tab. If you have an Internet e-mail account that you dial into with a modem, make sure the Connect Using My Phone Line option is selected, and then click OK to close the dialog box. ▶

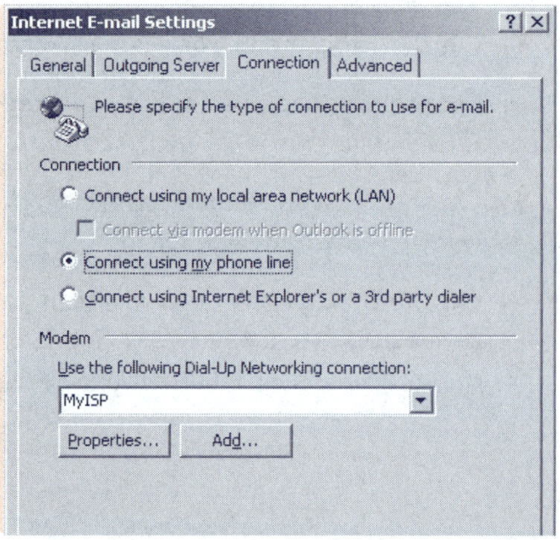

9. Click Finish in the E-mail Accounts Wizard when you're done checking all connections.

10. Look in your Inbox to see if a message titled "Microsoft Outlook Test Message" was received for each account test you performed.

After I send or receive e-mail, I get disconnected

Source of the problem

If you are using a dial-up connection and you need to limit your ISP connection time, it's very helpful to have Microsoft Outlook disconnect itself when it's finished performing its online tasks. But if connection time is not a problem (for example, if your computer has a dedicated phone line and your e-mail account provides unlimited connection time), automatic disconnection can be very annoying—you spend too much time dialing up and reconnecting every time you need to send and receive e-mail or visit a Web site. By changing a single setting, you can control when you disconnect from your ISP.

How to fix it

1. On the Tools menu, click Options.
2. In the Options dialog box, click the Mail Setup tab.
3. In the Dial-Up area, clear the Hang Up When Finished With A Manual Send/Receive check box.
4. Click OK to close the dialog box.

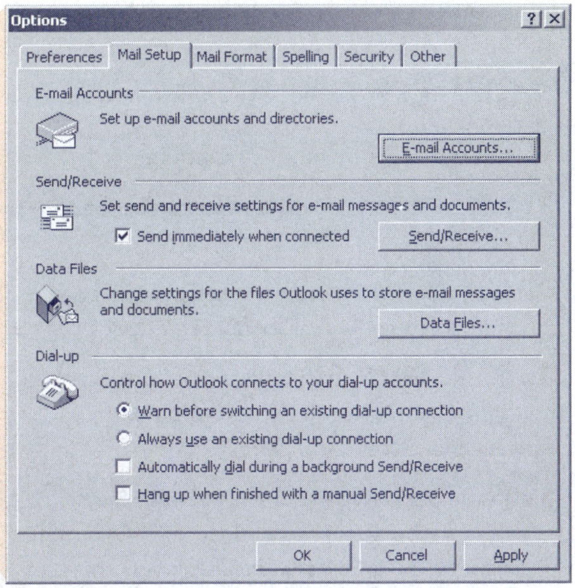

I don't know how to schedule a regular time for Outlook to automatically dial in and retrieve messages

Source of the problem

You connect to your Internet e-mail server over a dial-up connection, but you want to connect only periodically to receive e-mail, keeping the phone line open for other uses or maybe keeping the long-distance connection fees to a minimum. So how do you go about setting this up?

By default, Outlook should be automatically connecting, downloading e-mail, and disconnecting if you've set up a dial-up connection. If this is not working, you'll need to make sure all the settings are correct to make this happen correctly. If you want to set a different interval for automatic background connections, you can do that as well.

How to fix it

1. On the Tools menu, click Options.
2. In the Options dialog box, click the Mail Setup tab.
3. In the Send/Receive area, select the Send Immediately When Connected check box.
4. In the Dial-Up area, select the Automatically Dial During A Background Send/Receive check box. ▶
5. In the Send/Receive area, click the Send/Receive button. The Send/Receive Groups dialog box appears with All Accounts selected by default.

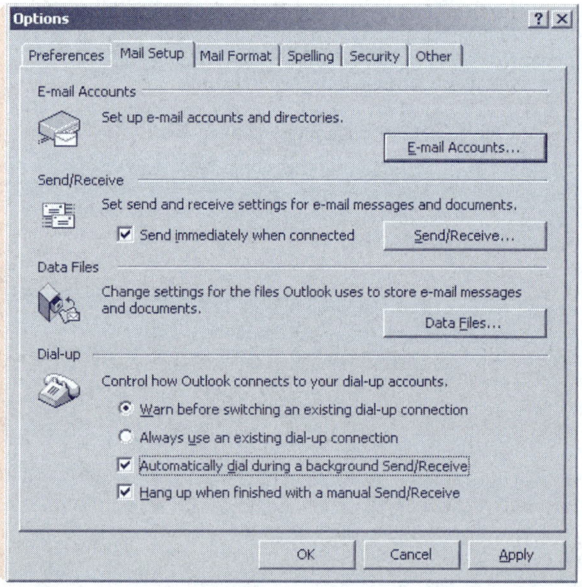

6. In the Settings For Group "All Accounts" area in the lower half of the dialog box, select the Schedule An Automatic Send/Receive Every check box, and set the interval you want. ▶

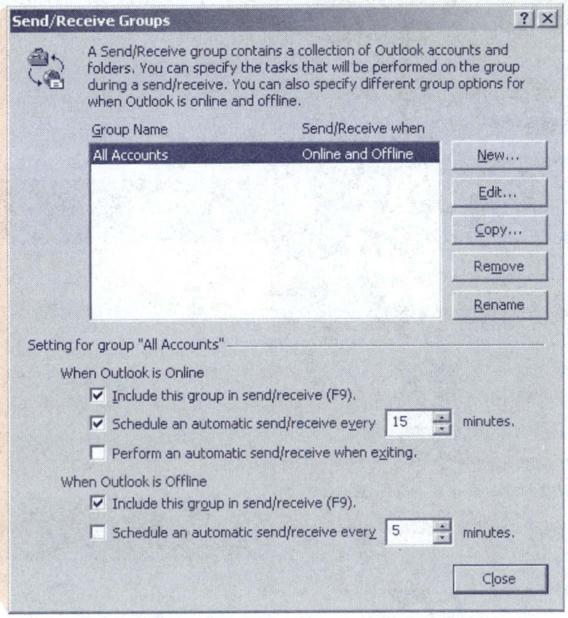

7. Click Close to close the Send/Receive Groups dialog box.

8. Click OK to close the Options dialog box.

Suppressing the logon prompt

The first time you log on, make sure you save your password with the Windows Dial-up Network connection so that future connections do not require you to type in a password. Also, to avoid having to click Logon each time you connect (you might not be at your computer when this prompt appears), right-click the dial-up connection in the Network And Dial-Up Connections folder, click Properties on the shortcut menu, and in the Dial-Up Connection Properties dialog box, click the Options tab, and then clear the Prompt For Name and Password, Certificate, Etc. check box.

Does your typing replace existing characters instead of adding new characters?

yes

no

Do you want to change your default message format?

yes

Do your message lines wrap and break in the wrong places?

yes

no

no

Do you want to change your message encoding format?

yes

Go to...

I don't know how to change my message encoding format, page 94.

Go to...

I don't know how to change my default message format, page 95.

no

Are you trying to place a picture in Outlook's Signature Picker?

yes

no

Do you want to change the message format of a single message?

yes

Go to...

I don't know how to change the format of a single message, page 90.

E-mail, creating

Quick fix

When I edit e-mail my typing overwrites what's there

If your typing replaces existing characters instead of adding new characters, you're typing in Overtype mode. It's easy to switch to Overtype mode by inadvertently hitting the Insert key on your keyboard while you type. To switch back to Insert mode, press the Insert key again.

Go to...
My message lines wrap and break in the wrong places, page 96.

Go to...
The Signature Picker won't accept a picture, page 92.

If your solution isn't here, see the general troubleshooting tips on page xvii.

I don't know how to change the format of a single message

Source of the problem

You generally send e-mail in the very businesslike Plain Text message format, but your grandmother (who recently discovered the joy of using e-mail) likes to exchange e-mail in HTML format with fancy stationery. You don't want to change your default Plain Text format, but you want to send messages to your grandmother in the HTML format. How you change the format of a single message depends on whether or not you are using Microsoft Word as your Microsoft Outlook editor.

How to fix it

If you are not using Word as your Outlook editor

- On the Message form's Format menu, click the message format you want—Plain Text, Rich Text, or HTML.

  If your open message is already formatted as HTML, you can't choose Rich Text; and if your open message is already formatted as Rich Text, you can't choose HTML.

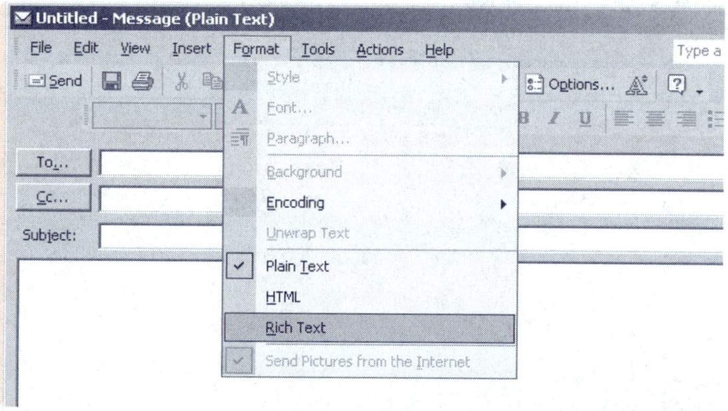

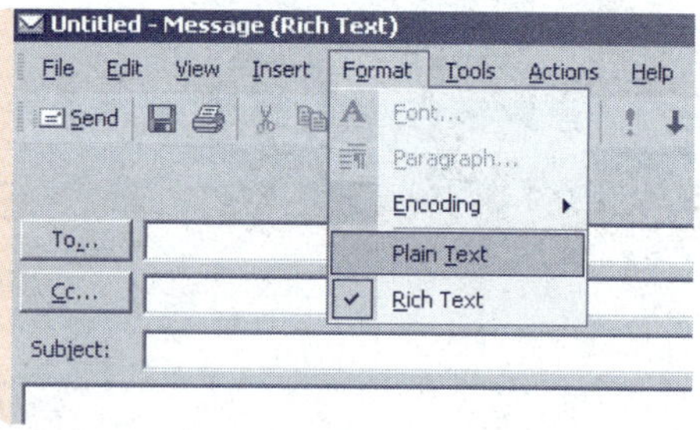

Here's a trick you might find useful: If you click Plain Text and then open the Format menu again, you can click the message format you want. However, keep in mind that you will lose any existing formatting in your open message when you click Plain Text!

Tip

These procedures change only the format of the individual message you are creating. See "I don't know how to change my default message format" on page 95 to change the format for all future messages you create.

If you are using Word as your Outlook editor

- In the Message form, click the down arrow to the right of the Message format list box on the toolbar, and click the message format you want—Plain Text, Rich Text, or HTML.

  Unlike Outlook's built-in e-mail editor, Word enables you to switch directly back and forth between HTML and Rich Text formatting without losing the formatting in your e-mail message. However, you will lose formatting if you switch between either Rich Text or HTML and Plain Text.

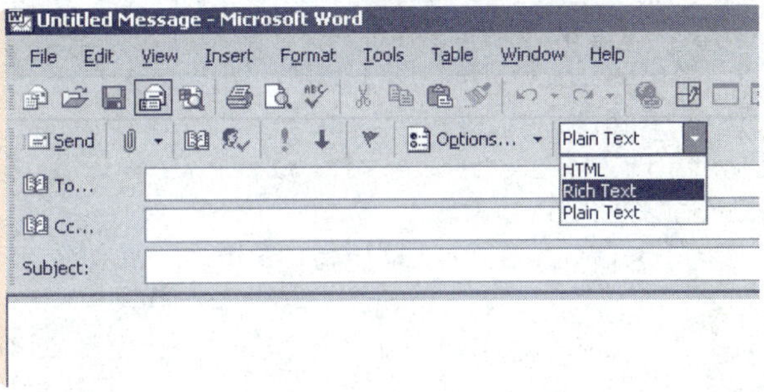

The Signature Picker won't accept a picture

Source of the problem

You've decided it would be nice to include a personal picture or a company logo with your signature. You're using HTML formatting, but you're not using Word as your editor. You create the signature, click Advanced Edit in the Edit Signature dialog box, and insert your picture. But although it looks fine in the Signature Preview window, the picture doesn't show up in new messages. Or maybe you created a signature when you were using Word as your editor, but after turning off Word, you notice that your signature is missing its picture.

If you're creating a signature with a picture, you have two choices: Use Word as your editor, or set your default HTML editor to another program, such as Microsoft FrontPage (or Notepad if you know HTML coding). If you're not comfortable using another HTML editor, stick with Word as your Outlook editor.

The problem here is that Outlook cannot use pictures you've inserted into an HTML signature using Word unless you've also used Word as the editor in Outlook. Also, if you need to change an HTML originally created in Word, you'll need to use Word to edit it.

How to fix it

Set your default HTML editor to the one you prefer using, and then insert your picture.

1. Start Microsoft Internet Explorer.
2. On the Tools menu, click Internet Options.
3. In the Internet Options dialog box, click the Programs tab.
4. Click the down arrow to the right of the HTML editor box, click your preferred HTML editor in the drop-down list, and click OK. ►

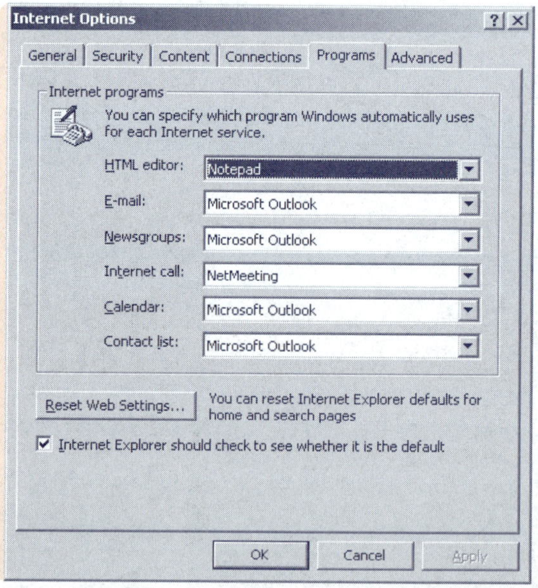

5. On Outlook's Tools menu, click Options, and in the Options dialog box, click the Mail Format tab, and then click Signatures.

6. In the Create Signature dialog box, select the signature you want to insert a picture in, and click Edit.

7. In the Edit Signature dialog box, click Advanced Edit. When you are informed that this will launch an editor that is not part of Outlook, click Yes.

   Your HTML editor should appear at this point. (If Word appears, you probably created this entire signature when Word was your Outlook editor.)

8. Insert your picture using the techniques appropriate to your default HTML editor.

More about inserting pictures in HTML

Because the amount of HTML needed to insert a picture is not overwhelming, you can get by using Notepad or any other text editor as your default editor. This example shows Notepad as the editor and the one line of HTML code that adds a picture in a file located at c:\mars30.gif. (Any basic HTML book will provide the code you need to do this.) ▶

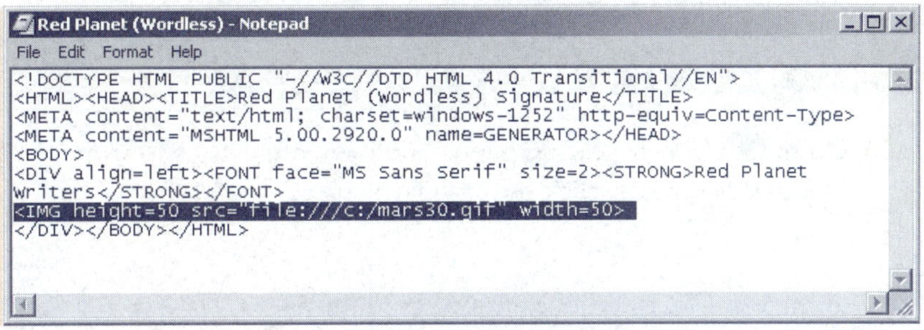

As you can see in the Create Signature dialog box, this inserts the picture after the text signature. ▶

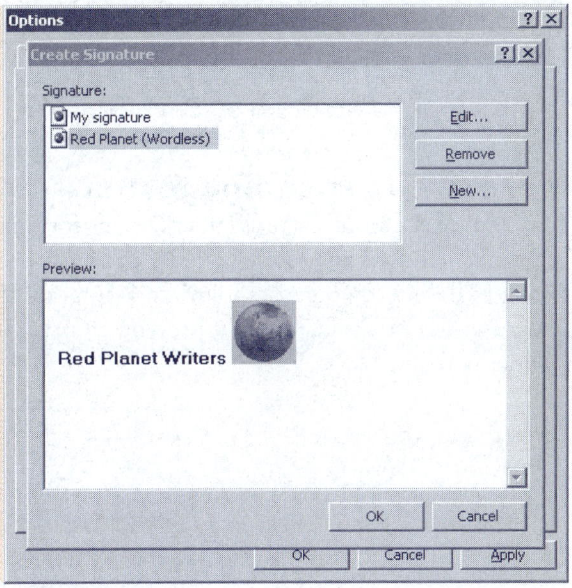

Tip

If you're using Word as your e-mail editor and want to change the default signature that's already been placed in a new message, a quick way is to right-click the signature, and then click the name of the replacement signature you want on the shortcut menu.

I don't know how to change my message encoding format

Source of the problem

An associate at a company you do business with has asked you to send a file to her in UUENCODE format, and you don't know how to switch your message encoding format in Outlook. It's easy enough to do—just follow these few steps before you add the encoded file to your e-mail message, and make sure you're sending the message as Plain Text. Don't forget to turn the UUENCODE format off after you send the file so that you'll be using the encoding format used by most servers (MIME).

How to fix it

1. On the Tools menu, click Options, and then in the Options dialog box, click the Mail Format tab.
2. Click Internet Format.
3. In the Plain Text Options area of the Internet Format dialog box, select the Encode Attachments In UUENCODE Format When Sending A Plain Text Message check box. ▶
4. Click OK to close each of the dialog boxes.

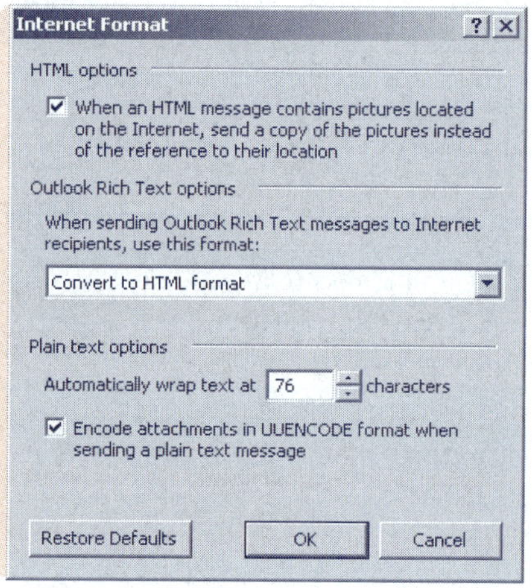

More about encoding formats

The two most common message encoding formats are MIME and UUENCODE. UUENCODE is the old standard and is readable by most mail servers (such as some UNIX-based operating systems); MIME is the new standard and supports the transfer of a wider range of file types. Outlook 2002 uses MIME as its default, but you can still send a UUENCODE format attachment when recipients request it.

I don't know how to change my default message format

Source of the problem

You generally send e-mail in the very striking HTML message format, but recently several business associates have asked you to send e-mail in Plain Text format. (They think it's more businesslike, and there's less threat of a script-borne virus arriving in their incoming mail.) You want to comply with the requests, but you don't remember how to change your default message format. Or, perhaps you've always sent messages in Plain Text format, but your new employer likes to see colorful, highly formatted e-mail. Whatever the reason, you can quickly set the default format that will be used for all new e-mail compositions.

How to fix it

1. On the Tools menu, click Options, and in the Options dialog box, click the Mail Format tab.
2. In the Compose In This Message Format box, click a default message format—Plain Text, Rich Text, or HTML.
3. Click OK.

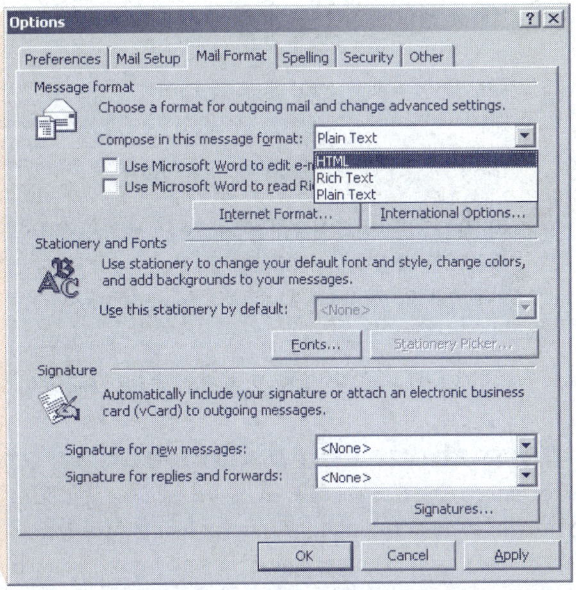

My message lines wrap and break in the wrong places

Source of the problem

You sent an e-mail message and received a reply that said your messages are hard to read because of too many line breaks. Or perhaps you posted a message to a newsgroup or a list server, and when you received the digest of posted messages the next day, you saw to your dismay that the last word or two of every line in your message was missing. The problem is the wrap length of lines in the messages you're sending out.

Fortunately, you can change the wrap length of the text in your outgoing messages. Shorter lines are more likely to remain intact when others reply to or forward your message, but shorter lines also break up the lines in messages that you reply to or forward. If the default wrap length of 76 characters doesn't work for you, experiment until you find a length that works better.

How to fix it

1. On the Tools menu, click Options.
2. In the Options dialog box, click the Mail Format tab, and then click the Internet Format button.
3. In the Plain Text Options area of the Internet Format dialog box, in the Automatically Wrap Text At box, type the number of characters at which you want your message lines to wrap. ▶
4. Click OK to close each of the dialog boxes.

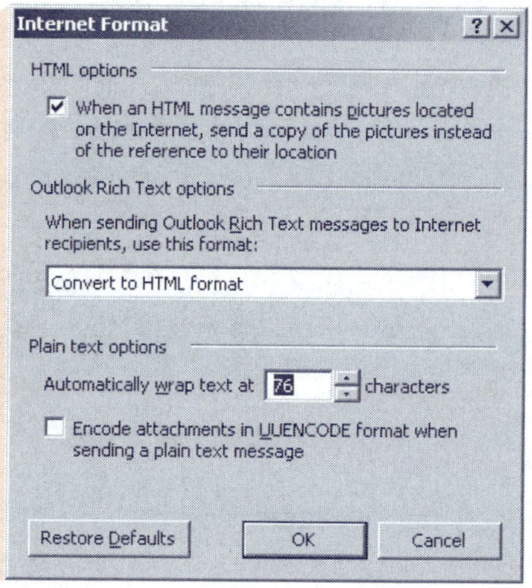

More about line breaks and wrapping

Not sure whether you really need to worry about setting your line length? How can you can tell if your messages' line lengths are causing problems?

You can often see the effects of wrap length in responses you get back that have your original messages embedded in them. For instance, if your original message is broken into short lines, it's because the sender's mail program wrapped your original lines into shorter pieces for sending. This often happens when a message has been forwarded several times.

Or you might see a message that has been truncated at the end of every line. This usually indicates that you sent the message with a long wrap length, and the receiving mail program cut the lines short rather than wrapping them. (Some older e-mail programs do that.)

Outlook 2002 automatically unwraps broken lines on incoming e-mail, so you might not notice the problem in other people's messages, or even in your own messages embedded in replies. But you should control the wrap length of the messages you send out because not everyone uses Outlook. If you want to see how your messages actually look to a recipient, e-mail a message to yourself and when you receive it, click the Information bar on "Extra line breaks in this message were removed. To restore, click here."

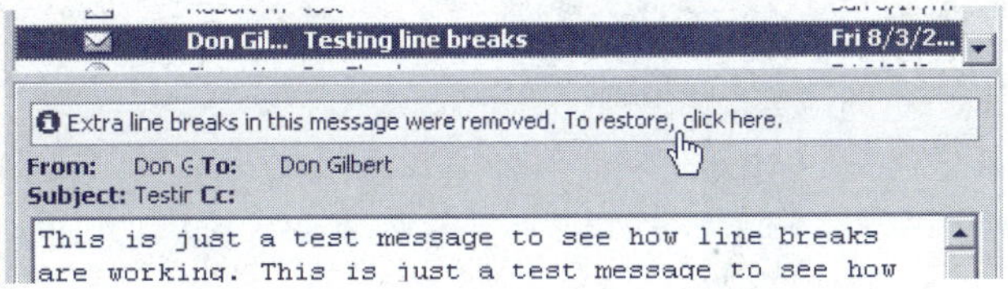

E-mail, im

Do you have all your e-mail addresses in a program that's not listed in Outlook's Import Wizard?

yes

no

Do you need to import your contacts list into a new computer?

yes

no

Are your e-mail addresses all stored in Netscape Messenger?

yes

Go to...
I don't know how to import my e-mail addresses from Netscape Messenger, page 100.

no

Do you have contact data in WordPerfect that you need to use in Outlook?

yes

Go to...
I can't import my WordPerfect mail-merge list into Outlook, page 101.

no

Are you trying to import a text file into Outlook?

yes

Quick fix

I need to import addresses, but the Import Wizard doesn't include my e-mail program Follow the procedure in the solution to "I can't import my Comma Separated Values text file into Outlook" on page 102. Export a Comma Separated Values text file (a *.csv* file) from your existing program as the intermediary file type, and then import the data into Outlook.

Quick fix

I don't know how to move my contacts to a new computer See the solutions "I don't know how to back up my data" on page 4 and "I don't know how to move my data to a different computer" on page 8.

Go to...

I can't import my Comma Separated Values text file into Outlook, page 102.

If your solution isn't here, see the general troubleshooting tips on page xvii.

I don't know how to import my e-mail addresses from Netscape Messenger

Source of the problem

You've been using Netscape Messenger, and that's where all your contacts and e-mail addresses are stored. Now that you're using Microsoft Outlook, you don't want to re-enter all that data—there must be an easier way to get your contacts and e-mail addresses into Outlook!

You're in luck—at least if you're importing from Netscape Messenger 4.0x or earlier—Microsoft anticipated your problem and made it easy to import Netscape Messenger contacts into Outlook.

How to fix it

1. On the File menu, click Import And Export.
2. On the first page of the Import And Export Wizard, click Import Internet Mail And Addresses, and then click Next.
3. Click the appropriate version of Netscape. ▶
4. Select the Import Address Book check box to import your e-mail addresses and contact information. You can also import existing e-mail from Netscape by selecting the Import Mail check box.
5. Click Next, and follow the rest of the steps in the wizard to finish importing your addresses.

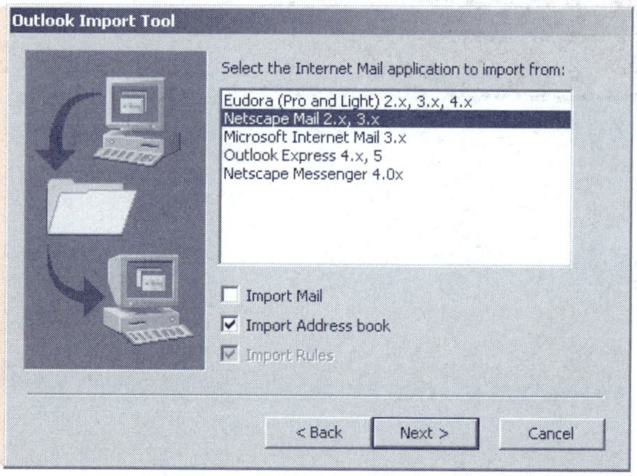

I can't import my WordPerfect mail-merge list into Outlook

Source of the problem

You have a sizable list of contacts built up in WordPerfect, and you want to import that information into Outlook. But in Outlook's Import And Export Wizard, there's no provision for importing addresses directly from WordPerfect.

The solution is to use a text file as an intermediary file type between WordPerfect and Outlook. First consult your WordPerfect documentation to find out how to save or export your address book as a text file with Comma Separated Values (*.csv*), and then follow the steps in this solution to import the new text file into Outlook.

How to fix it

1. On the File menu, click Import And Export.
2. On the first page of the Import And Export Wizard, click Import From Another Program Or File, and click Next.
3. Click the text file type you used to save or export your WordPerfect addresses, and follow the wizard steps to import the addresses into Outlook. ▶

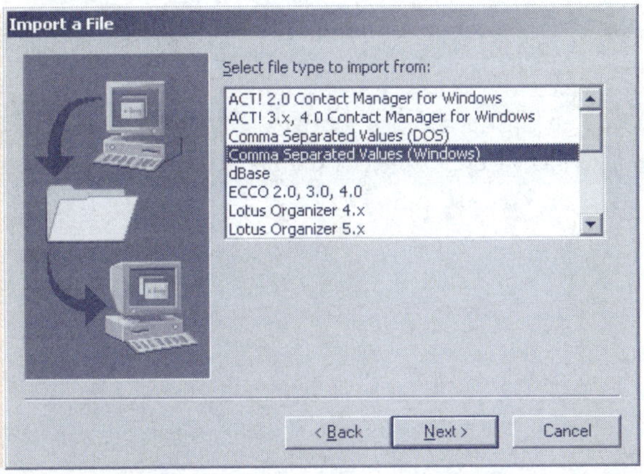

I can't import my Comma Separated Values text file into Outlook

Source of the problem

You exported or saved your contacts from another program as a Comma Separated Values (*.csv*) text file, but when you import the file into Outlook, you can't see the individual fields listed in the Map Custom Fields dialog box. Instead, all the imported fields are in a single row, separated by small box characters. Even with a text file, formatting might not be readable by the importing program, but that's a problem you can fix. If you open the text file in Microsoft Excel, the Text Import Wizard reformats the file so that Excel can read it. You can then save the file in Excel in either Comma Separated Values or Tab Separated Values format, and then import that file into Outlook.

How to fix it

1. On Excel's File menu, click Open.
2. In the Open dialog box, navigate to the text file, and click Open. ▶

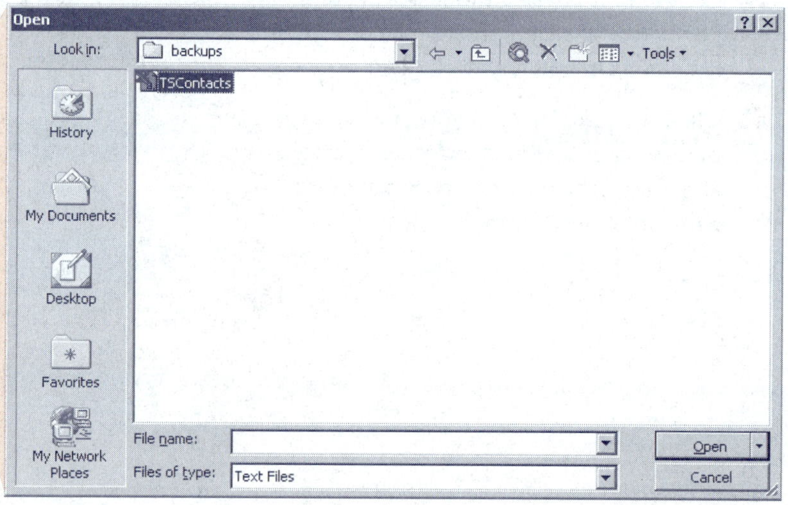

3. If the Text Import Wizard opens, click Finish.
4. On Excel's File menu, click Save As to display the Save As dialog box.
5. In the Save As Type box, click Text (Tab Delimited), and then click Save. ▶

6. If you're prompted to keep this format, click Yes.
7. Close the text file, and quit Excel.

Now you can import the resaved text file into Outlook.

Tip

You will see this option displayed as "Text (Tab Delimited) (*.txt*)" if the Hide File Extensions For Known File Types check box hasn't been selected in the Windows Folder Options dialog box.

Are you receiving all the messages people send you?

yes → Is the text in your Inbox and preview pane too small to read comfortably?

- yes → **Go to...** The text in my Inbox and preview pane is too small, page 108.
- no → Do all your messages open in the preview pane?
  - yes → Does Outlook download messages that flash through and disappear?
    - yes →
    - no → Do you want to control what gets downloaded when using a dial-up connection?
      - yes →
      - no → Do you want to sort your Inbox by category?
        - yes →
  - no → **Quick fix**

    I can't display some messages in the preview pane

    If a message is encrypted, you can't read it in the preview pane. Double-click the message to open it instead of reading it in the preview pane.

no → **Go to...** I'm not receiving some of the messages people send me, page 106.

E-mail, receiving

Quick fix

I see e-mail messages appearing briefly in my Inbox and then disappearing In Outlook, you can create a rule that permanently deletes an incoming message rather than sending it to the Deleted Items folder (where you can find it before you delete it permanently). Any incoming message that meets the criteria of that rule won't stop in your Inbox long enough for you to see it—it flashes through and gets permanently deleted. If you created this rule, and a message you're expecting inadvertently meets your "permanently delete this message" criteria, you'll never see the message.

If you have this problem with messages from specific contacts, add those contacts to your rule as "exceptions" so that the rule will ignore messages from them.

Go to...
It takes too long to download my e-mail messages, page 112.

Go to...
I don't know how to sort my Inbox by category, page 110.

If your solution isn't here, check these related chapters:

- E-mail, sending, page 120
- Upgrading, page 284

Or see the general troubleshooting tips on page xvii.

I'm not receiving some of the messages people send me

Source of the problem

You know people are sending you e-mail, but some of the messages people have sent you don't appear in your Inbox.

There are a few reasons why you might not see messages that you receive: a filter in your Inbox, a junk mail filter, or mail rules that are sending your mail to a subfolder.

How to fix it

Remove the filter

If you see the words Filter Applied in the lower-left corner of your Microsoft Outlook window or on the right side of the Folder banner, there's a filter applied to your Inbox. The filter might be hiding the new messages you can't find.

1. In your Inbox, right-click the column headings row, and click Customize Current View on the shortcut menu.
2. In the View Summary dialog box, click the Filter button.
3. In the Filter dialog box, click the Clear All button.
4. Click OK to close each open dialog box.

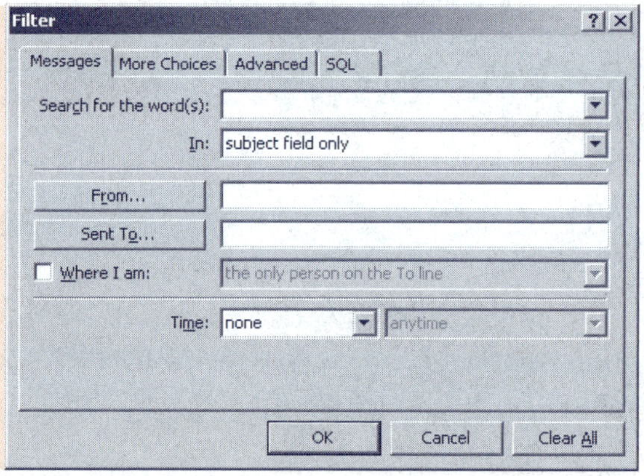

Turn off the junk mail filter

If you have the junk mail filter turned on, any messages that appear to be junk mail are swept directly to your Deleted Items folder. The built-in junk mail filter looks for specific words and phrases in incoming messages that are likely to be found in junk mail, such as "advertisement," "money back," "over 18," and "100% satisfied." Unfortunately, some legitimate messages can contain junk mail filter criteria, and they, too, get swept into the Deleted Items folder. To avoid this problem, you need to turn off the filter.

1. In the Inbox, on the Tools menu, click Organize.

2. In the Ways To Organize Inbox pane, on the left side, click Junk E-Mail.

   A Turn Off button in either the Junk or the Adult Content option means the filter is turned on.

3. In the Junk option, click the Turn Off button.
4. Click the Close button in the upper-right corner of the Ways To Organize Inbox pane to close it.

Check your mail rules

If you created a mail rule that delivers incoming mail to a mail subfolder, the messages you're expecting might be in that subfolder. It's easy to forget that you created the rule or that the subfolder exists, but you can check the rules that are currently at work in Outlook.

1. On the Tools menu, click Rules Wizard.
2. In the Rules Wizard dialog box, scan the list of rules in the Apply Rules In The Following Order box. If you want to know what a specific rule does, click the rule, and read its description in the Rule Description box.
3. If you want to turn a rule off, clear its check box. If you want to delete the rule, click the rule in the list, click the Delete button, and then click Yes to confirm the deletion.
4. Click OK to close the dialog box.

Tip

To see the list of criteria that the junk mail filter uses, open the file *filters.txt* (in the folder where Outlook is installed, most likely C:/Program Files /Microsoft Office/Office10 /1033/). You can add or delete words and phrases to change the filter.

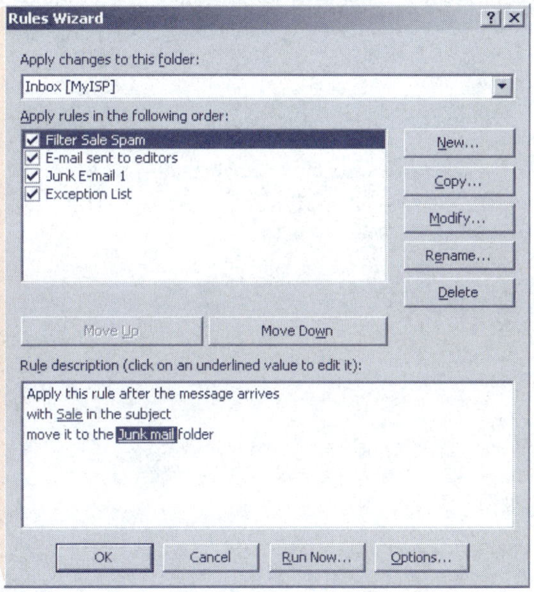

The text in my Inbox and preview pane is too small

Source of the problem

You sit in front of that darn computer too many hours a day, and when your eyes are tired, the text in your messages seems to get uncomfortably small. Wouldn't it be great if you could make the text bigger and easier to read? Well, you can.

Tip

This procedure changes the text that you see, but your Plain Text messages still go out without formatting, so your recipients read your messages in whatever font they've chosen in their mail program.

How to fix it

Change the font size in plain text messages

1. On the Tools menu, click Options.
2. On the Mail Format tab of the Options dialog box, in the Stationery And Fonts area, click the Fonts button.
3. In the Fonts dialog box, click the Choose Font button next to the When Composing And Reading Plain Text box.
4. In the Font dialog box, click a font and font size.
5. Click OK to close each dialog box.

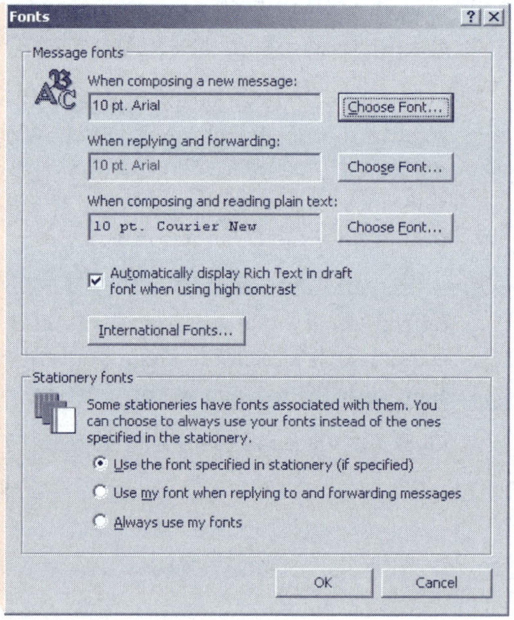

Change the font in the message headers

1. On the View menu, point to Current View, and then click Customize Current View.
2. In the View Summary dialog box, click the Other Settings button.
3. In the Other Settings dialog box, in the Rows area, click the Font button. ▶
4. Make your font changes in the Font dialog box.
5. Click OK to close each dialog box.

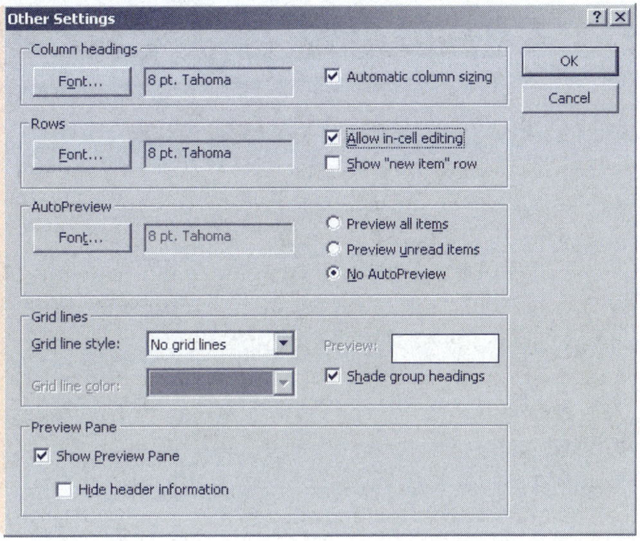

Tip

In the Other Settings dialog box, you can also change the font for AutoPreview lines and column headings.

I don't know how to sort my Inbox by category

Source of the problem

You've discovered the convenience of assigning categories to messages as you read them, and now you want to view your Inbox sorted by category. But when you display the Sort dialog box, the Categories field doesn't show up.

The problem is that you cannot sort by category: Outlook won't do it. This is because one item can fit into more than one category, which would make it impossible to sort. However, you can group e-mail by category so that each message appears in each category to which it's been assigned (that is, a message with two categories will appear in both groups). The categories themselves are sorted alphabetically, and you can further sort the messages within each group.

There are a couple of ways to group a folder by category: You can use the Group By button in the View Summary dialog box, or you can use the Group By Box button on the Advanced toolbar.

Tip

The procedure for grouping by category can be done in any folder where contents are listed in table format. You can apply categories to e-mail messages, tasks, contacts, or notes, but you'll need to select a table view first if you don't see a headings row.

How to fix it

You can sort by category even if you don't have Categories showing as a column in your Inbox.

1. In the Inbox, right-click the column headings row, and click Customize Current View on the shortcut menu.
2. In the View Summary dialog box, click Group By.
3. In the Group By dialog box, click the down arrow to the right of the Group Items By box, and click Categories in the drop-down list. ▶

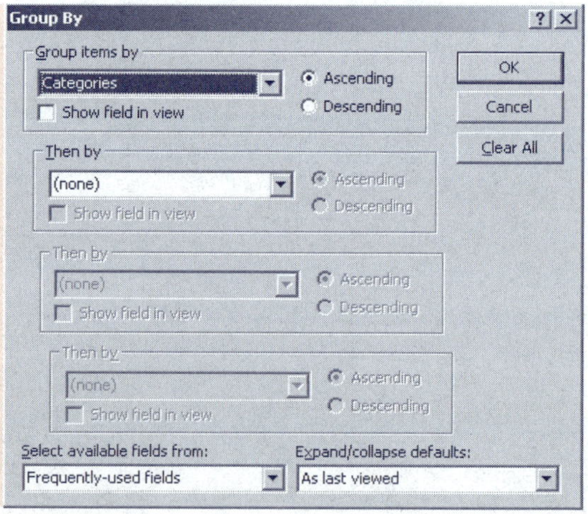

4. Click OK to close each open dialog box.

If you have a Categories column in your Inbox, you can sort by category very quickly.

1. Right-click the Categories column heading.
2. On the shortcut menu, click Group By This Field.

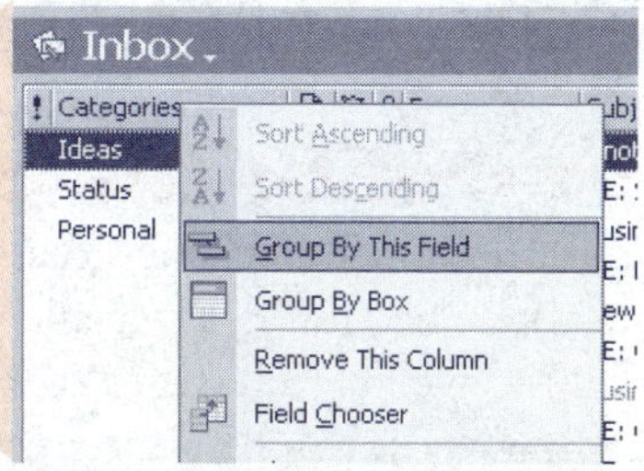

How do I remove this grouping?

1. Right-click the column headings row, and click Customize Current View on the shortcut menu.
2. In the View Summary dialog box, click Group By.
3. In the Group By dialog box, click Clear All.
4. Close each open dialog box by clicking OK.

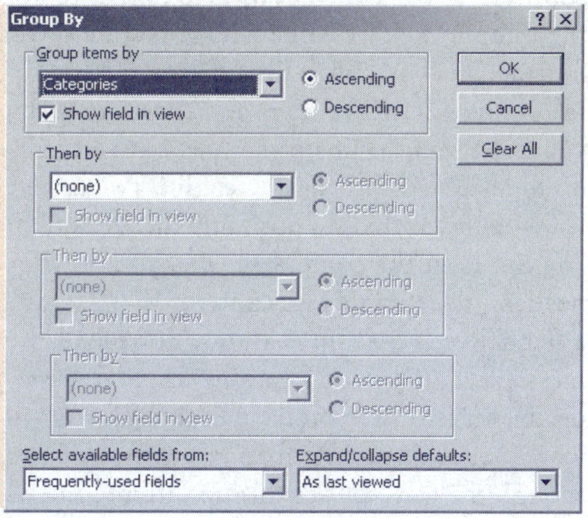

Tip

To assign a category to an e-mail message, right-click the message, click Categories on the shortcut menu, select a category (or more than one), and click OK.

It takes too long to download my e-mail messages

Source of the problem

You occasionally need to access your e-mail when a fast (or local) connection is not available, and invariably that's when you receive long messages that you really don't need to see right away. It can be quite frustrating to make a long-distance connection to pick up a business e-mail reply and then watch the minutes tick by while a huge picture of your cousin's dog is downloaded with his e-mail message! Or maybe you share the telephone line with others and there are certain times when you don't want to tie up the line, but you still would like to log on to check at least the subject lines of any e-mail sent to you.

If any of this sounds familiar, Outlook has an answer—you can limit the content of what you download to only the headers (the subject line content). For example, you can set up a Send/Receive group that only downloads the headers of any messages that exceed a certain size and leaves those messages on the server until you have time to download them. This works for both internet mail accounts and those connected to Microsoft Exchange Server, although the way you set this up differs somewhat. To learn more about working with Microsoft Exchange Server offline, see chapter 36, "Synchronizing data."

Before you start

When you work with headers, never click the Send/Receive button unless you want everything downloaded. Instead, either download headers directly or create a Send/Receive group that downloads headers. After you have the headers in your Inbox, you can mark and download only the messages you want.

How to fix it

Download just the headers

- If you have only one e-mail account, on the Tools menu, point to Send/Receive, point to Work With Headers, and click Download Headers.

Tip

You won't see Work With Headers on the Send/Receive menu unless you're in the Inbox.

- If you have multiple accounts, on the Tools menu, point to Send/Receive, point to Work With Headers, point to Download Headers From, and then click the account from which you want to download headers.

Process the headers to download only what you want

After you've downloaded headers, you need to determine which messages you want to download, if any, and then download them.

1. Look at the headers and decide which ones you don't want to download. You can delete these messages, which will also delete them from your mail server.
2. Right-click a message header you want to download, and click either Mark To Download Message(s) or Mark To Download Message Copy on the shortcut menu.

   The latter command leaves a copy on the server—a good idea if you want to retrieve that e-mail later from a different computer.
3. On the Tools menu, point to Send/Receive, point to Work With Headers, and click Process Marked Headers. (If you have multiple accounts, point to Process Marked Headers From, and click the account you want to download messages from).

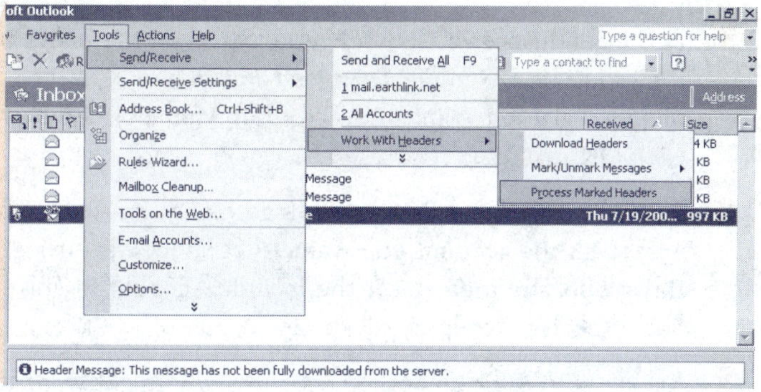

If this solution didn't solve your problem, go to the next page.

It takes too long to download my e-mail messages

(continued from page 113)

Use a Send/Receive group to selectively download headers

A Send/Receive group enables you to set parameters for exactly what you want to download from any account. The options in a Send/Receive group are different depending on the account type. For Internet accounts, as described here, you can specify whether to download just headers, entire messages with attachments, or headers only for messages over a certain size. It's easy to create a group and set its parameters.

1. On the Tools menu, point to Send/Receive Settings, and click Define Send/Receive Groups.
2. In the Send/Receive Groups dialog box, click New.
3. In the Send/Receive Group Name box, type the name of the group (for example, *Download limited size* if you're setting up a group to limit the size of downloads), and then click OK.

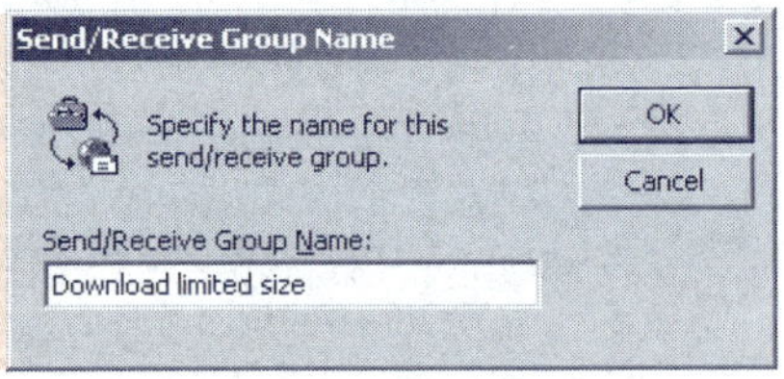

4. In the Send/Receive Settings dialog box, in the Accounts area, click the account you want to connect with using this group, and then select the Include Account In This Send/Receive Group check box.
5. Repeat step 4 for any other accounts you might want to include in this group.
6. In the Check Folders To Include In Send/Receive box, select the check boxes of all the folders you want included in the Send/Receive group.

   The folders that you can include here depend on the type of account you are using. For example, if you are using an Internet account or a Remote Mail account, you'll only be able to select the Inbox; if you are connecting to a Microsoft Exchange Server mailbox or using a Hotmail account you'll see more folders.
7. If you want to limit the download to just subject lines and no message text or attachments, click the Download Item Description Only option.

8. If you want to download messages but limit the size, click the Download Complete Item Including Attachments option and then select the Download Only Item Descriptions for Items Larger Than check box. Then enter the size to which you want to limit downloaded messages.

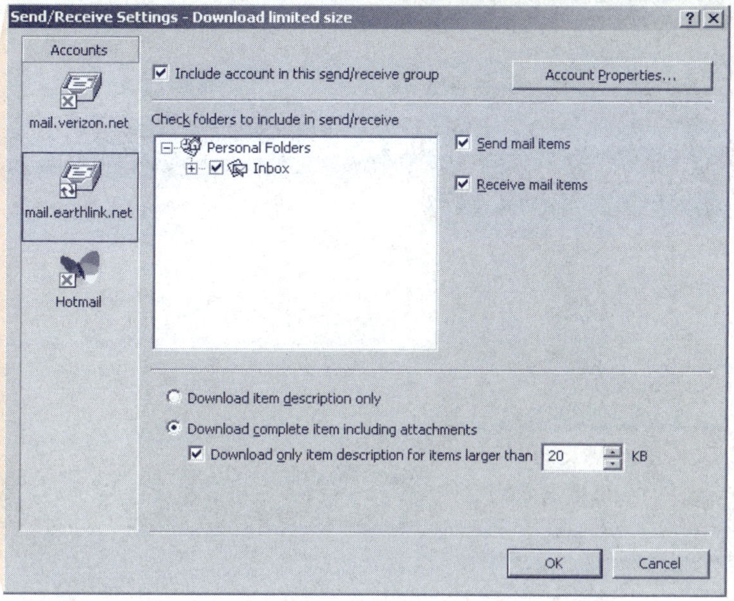

9. Click OK to close the Send/Receive Settings dialog box.

10. Click Close to close the Send/Receive Groups dialog box.

Use a Send/Receive group to retrieve messages

To use a Send/Receive group, on the Tools menu, point to Send/Receive, and click the group name.

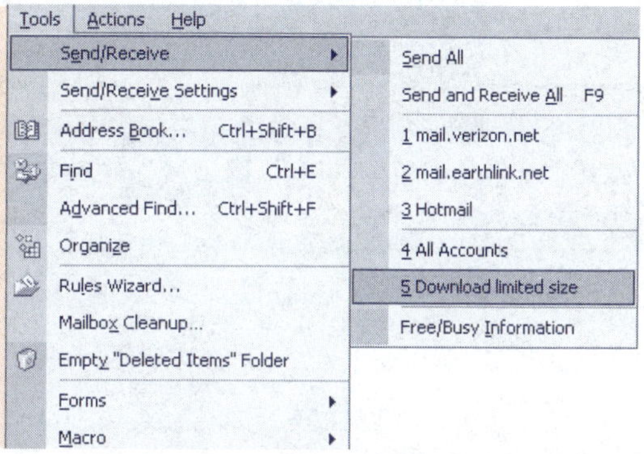

If only headers are downloaded, you can select which messages you want to download. See "Process the headers to download only what you want" earlier in this solution to learn how to work with downloaded headers.

Did you send a message that was never received?

yes

no

Did your recipient get your message with a *winmail.dat* attachment?

yes

Go to...

My recipient got my message with a *winmail.dat* attachment, page 118.

no

Did your recipient get your message without all the features you sent?

yes

Can your recipient see the voting buttons in the message you sent?

yes

no

Quick fix

Voting buttons work only when sending messages to others who run Outlook on Microsoft Exchange Server If you send voting buttons to a recipient who is not on your network, include a line in your message that says "Please respond by using the voting buttons—if you don't see voting buttons in this message, send a reply specifying your choice."

E-mail, recipients

Quick fix

The e-mail message I sent was never received
Send the message again. Sometimes a mail server goes down, and messages can be lost permanently.

Go to...

My recipient doesn't receive the message features I send, page 119.

If your solution isn't here, **check these related chapters:**

- E-mail, sending, page 120
- E-mail, receiving, page 104
- E-mail, creating, page 88
- Hidden names, page 176

Or see the general troubleshooting tips on page xvii.

My recipient got my message with a *winmail.dat* attachment

Source of the problem

You sent a message from Microsoft Outlook to an associate. The message was in Rich Text format, with indented, bulleted lines of text and a variety of colors that emphasized the important parts. But the message your recipient got had a mysterious attachment named *winmail.dat* (which the recipient couldn't open) and none of your colorful formatting.

The problem lies in your recipient's e-mail program or in an e-mail server through which the message must pass to reach your recipient. The program or server either can't or won't read your message. All the accessory coding for colors and bullets and extra features, such as voting buttons, that can't be read by the recipient's e-mail server or e-mail program are contained in the attached file *winmail.dat*. The attachment is useless, but it serves to keep the message clean so that your recipient can read the plain text of your message.

Tip

Your recipient might get an attachment with a name that starts with *ATT0000*. It's the same as the *winmail.dat* attachment, but your recipient's e-mail program doesn't recognize the *winmail.dat* attachment name.

How to fix it

Always send e-mail to that recipient in Plain Text format so that he or she doesn't get the extra attachments. You can either change all your messages to plain text or change individual messages.

- To make plain text your default message format so that everyone gets plain text messages, on the Outlook Tools menu, click Options. In the Options dialog box, click the Mail Format tab, and in the Compose In This Message Format box, click Plain Text.
- To create a Plain Text message for that recipient, on the Message form's Format menu, click Plain Text.

  If Word is your editor, select Plain Text from the toolbar list box.

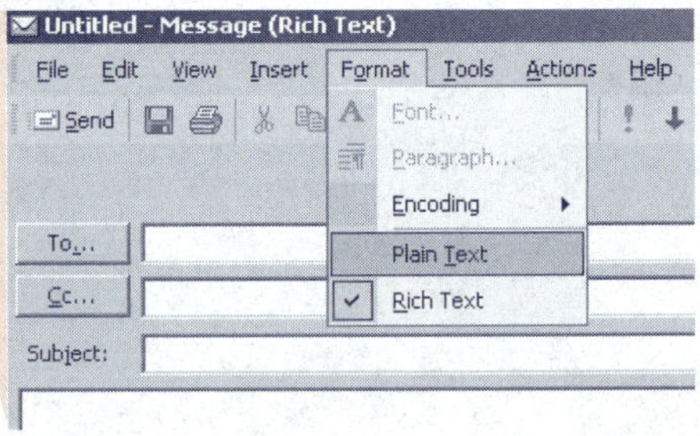

My recipient doesn't receive the message features I send

Source of the problem

You sent a message to an associate that was in Rich Text format with indented, bulleted lines of text and a variety of colors that emphasized the important parts of your message. But when your recipient opened the message, it was in Plain Text format, with no colors or indents. So what happened to all your detailed formatting?

Your recipient is probably using an e-mail program that doesn't recognize Rich Text formatting. Also, some e-mail servers (such as Microsoft Exchange Server) provide the option of removing the extra coding from Rich Text messages, so those recipients who choose that option always receive plain text messages. The only way you can transmit formatted messages to these recipients is to use HTML format. Or you can limit yourself to plain text messages so that you know exactly what your recipient will see.

By default, Outlook converts Rich Text formatting to HTML formatting for Internet e-mail, but if this setting has been altered in your profile, you can get it back.

How to fix it

1. On the Tools menu, click Options.
2. In the Options dialog box, click the Mail Format tab.
3. In the Message Format area, click Internet Format.
4. In the list box under Outlook Rich Text Options, click Convert To HTML Format.
5. Click OK to close each open dialog box.

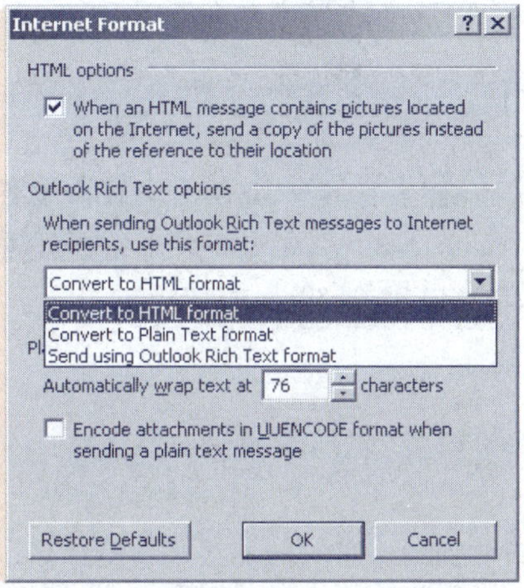

Are messages stuck in your Outbox?

yes

Go to...
Messages are stuck in my Outbox, page 122.

no

Did you get an "undeliverable" message returned to your Inbox?

yes

no

Was your recipient's e-mail server down when your message was supposed to be delivered?

yes

E-mail, sending

Quick fix

I received an "undeliverable" message This can happen if your recipient's e-mail address is incorrect, or if your ISP is busy or out of service. You should first check the recipient's address and make sure it's entered correctly. If it is, resend the message when the ISP is available (either at a different time of day, or after any problems at the ISP have been fixed).

Quick fix

I don't know how to resend a message When your recipient tells you the e-mail server is up again, resend the original message from the Sent Items folder.

1. In the Sent Items folder, open the message.
2. On the message's Actions menu, click Resend This Message.
3. When the original message appears, click the Send button on the message's toolbar.

If your solution isn't here, check these related chapters:

- E-mail, accounts, page 56
- Error messages, page 130

Or see the general troubleshooting tips on page xvii.

Messages are stuck in my Outbox

Source of the problem

You're trying to send e-mail, but the messages don't leave your Outbox. There are several possible reasons (and solutions) for messages stuck in the Outbox.

The most common reason why messages don't leave your Outbox is that you opened and then closed the message while it was in your Outbox. That changes the status of the message, so it doesn't get sent. A visual clue that this is the problem is in the message title—the title of a message that's ready to be sent is formatted in italics, so a message that doesn't have an italicized title isn't going to be sent.

Assuming that your e-mail account is set up correctly, there are other reasons why a message might be stuck in the Outbox: you're working offline, the message is corrupt, you're sending e-mail from an account that doesn't match the e-mail message account, or your Personal Folders file is damaged.

Try the following short solutions first. If the message is still stuck, try repairing the Personal Folders file.

How to fix it

Return the message to Send status

If you open and then close a message while it's in the Outbox, you need to return the message to Send status.

1. Open the message.
2. Click the Send button on the message toolbar.

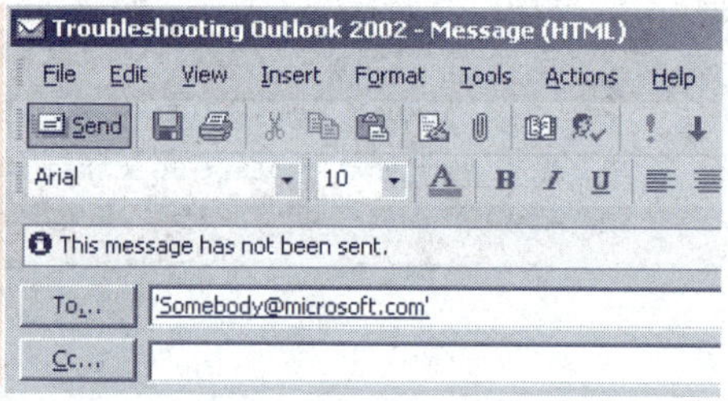

The message closes, and the message title is italicized. The next time you send outgoing mail, Microsoft Outlook sends the message.

Make sure you're working online

If you're using an Internet e-mail account and have the option of going offline, make sure you're working online.

- On the File menu, click Work Offline if it has a check mark beside it.

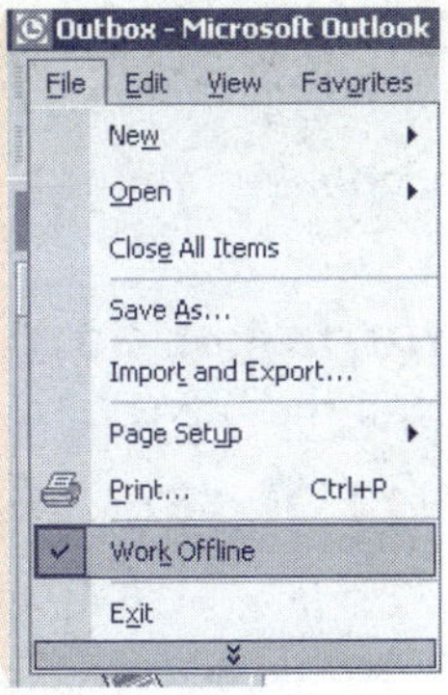

Make sure you're using the right account

If you have multiple accounts in the same profile, make sure you are sending your e-mail message using the right account. If you specifically select an account from which to send an e-mail message (by clicking the Accounts button in the message), and then click a different account on the Send/Receive submenu, the message will not be sent.

Even if you don't specify an account in the e-mail message, you might be clicking the wrong account on the Send/Receive submenu. If you have multiple accounts but want to send a message from only one of them, click the specific account on the Send/Receive submenu that matches the account you selected in the message.

To summarize, if you select an account from which to send an e-mail message, when you point to Send/Receive on the Tools menu, make sure you either:

- Click Send All, Send/Receive All, or All Accounts.
- Click the account that matches the specific account you chose in the message.

Check if the message is corrupted

To find out whether a message is corrupted, move the message out of the Outbox, and try to send a different message.

1. Move the message in question into your Deleted Items folder.
2. Create a short new message addressed to yourself or to a colleague who doesn't mind helping you.
3. Send the new message.

If the new message is sent successfully, the first message is somehow corrupted—you should delete it and re-create it. If the new message isn't sent successfully, move the first message back into your Outbox, and try the following solution.

If this solution didn't solve your problem, go to the next page.

Messages are stuck in my Outbox

(continued from page 123)

Repair a damaged Personal Folders file

Run the Inbox Repair Tool to repair your Personal Folders file.

1. On the File menu, click Data File Management.
2. In the Outlook Data Files dialog box, double-click the Personal Folders entry in the list.
3. In the Personal Folders dialog box, make a note of the path to your personal storage file (*.pst*), which appears in the Filename box. Click Cancel, and then click Close to close each dialog box.
4. On the File menu, click Exit to quit Outlook.
5. On the Start menu, point to Programs, point to Accessories, point to System Tools, and then click Inbox Repair Tool.
6. If you don't see Inbox Repair Tool on your System Tools menu, on the Start menu, point to Search, click For Files Or Folders, and search for the file *scanpst.exe*. In the Search Results dialog box, double-click the file *scanpst.exe* to run the Inbox Repair Tool.

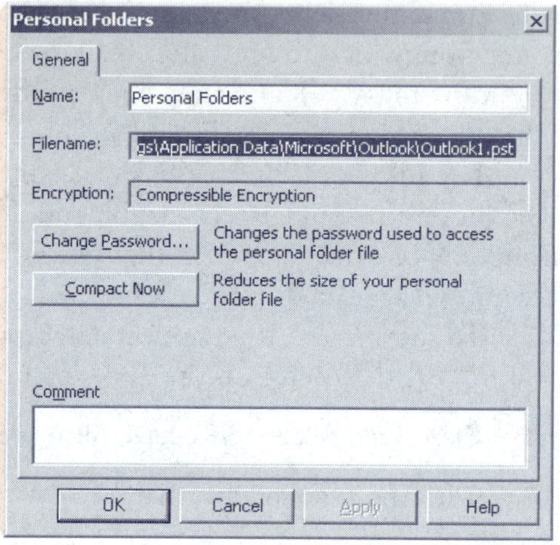

Tip

In step 3, you can select the entire path in the Filename box, and press Ctrl+C to copy it. Then you can paste it into the Inbox Repair Tool in step 7.

7. In the Inbox Repair Tool dialog box, click Browse, navigate to the personal storage file (*.pst*) you wrote down in step 3, click the file name, and then click Open.

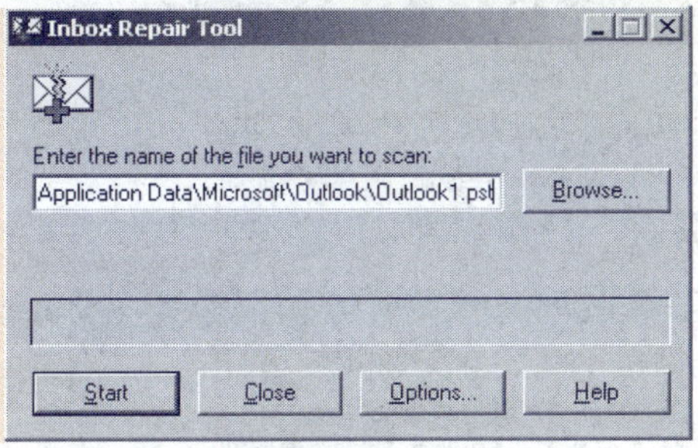

8. In the Inbox Repair Tool dialog box, click Start. Follow the instructions to repair the *.pst* file if errors are found.
9. When the Inbox Repair Tool is finished, click OK to close the Inbox Repair Tool dialog box.
10. Restart Outlook.
11. Open the message that you're having trouble sending, and copy the contents of the message.
12. Create a new message, and paste the contents you just copied into the new message.
13. Delete the original message, and try sending the new message.

Do you have a current anti-virus protection program running on your computer?

yes → Do you always open the attachments you receive in e-mail messages?

yes

no → Do you always open every message you receive, even if you don't recognize the sender?

yes

no → Do you want to know how to protect yourself from e-mail viruses?

yes →

Go to...

I don't know how to protect my computer from e-mail viruses, page 128.

no →

Quick fix

I don't use an anti-virus program on my computer

A good anti-virus program is your first line of defense against any computer virus, regardless of its source, and it's well worth whatever it costs. Norton and McAfee are two prominent companies which develop reliable anti-virus programs. But remember that you need to update your anti-virus program often with new virus definitions so that you can stay one step ahead of any new viruses.

Quick fix

I don't see what's wrong with opening attachments sent to me through e-mail Even though Outlook blocks the attachments that are most likely to be infected with a virus, you still run a risk of infecting your computer with a virus if you open attachments. You can get viruses even from presumably safe files sent to you by friends or colleagues if they don't know the files are infected. It's also possible that a virus on their system sent you the file without them even knowing about it. You can reduce your risk of infection by not opening any attached file if you aren't expecting it.

Quick fix

I don't know whether it's safe to open messages from strangers Opening messages from strangers is risky these days. HTML-formatted messages can carry viruses that infect your computer. In Outlook 2002, scripts in an HTML message cannot run when the message is opened in the preview pane, so view the message in the preview pane first to see if it has HTML formatting before deciding whether you want to open it.

If your solution isn't here, see the general troubleshooting tips on page xvii.

I don't know how to protect my computer from e-mail viruses

Source of the problem

As of the publication of this book, e-mail viruses are the latest and most damaging craze in malicious computer programs. Microsoft Outlook is an especially promising target for creators of computer viruses because it's widely used and easy to program, and all your contacts, as well as the rest of your hard disk, are within easy reach of any virus-borne programming.

Not so long ago it was easy to avoid e-mail viruses because they always arrived in attached files, and you had to open the attached file for the virus to run. But now some viruses are being sent as scripts hidden in the coding of HTML-formatted messages, and the viruses are released when the HTML message is opened and the scripts it contains are run. In the not-so-distant future, virus creators are likely to find even more insidious ways to use Outlook (and other e-mail programs) to carry and propagate viruses.

How to fix it

Visit Slipstick Systems, at *www.slipstick.com*—it's a great source of current Outlook information. While you're there, look up anything related to viruses—you'll find links for downloading lots of security updates and instructions for more ways to protect your computer by making changes in Microsoft Windows and Microsoft Internet Explorer.

You can increase your protection from HTML viruses by turning off ActiveX controls and scripting within Outlook.

1. On the Tools menu, click Options, and in the Options dialog box, click the Security tab.
2. Click Zone Settings, and then click OK in the warning message.
3. Click one of the four zones across the top of the Security dialog box (a description of the selected zone appears beneath the four zones). For example, to disable ActiveX Controls on Internet sites, click the Internet zone. ▶

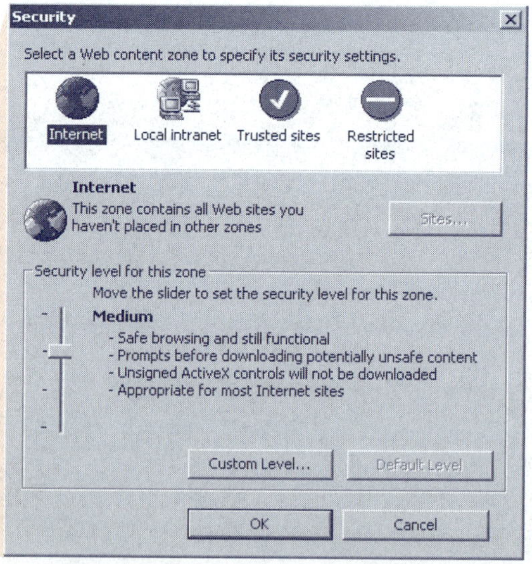

4. Click Custom Level.

5. In the Security Settings dialog box, select the Disable option for all the settings under ActiveX Controls And Plug-Ins.

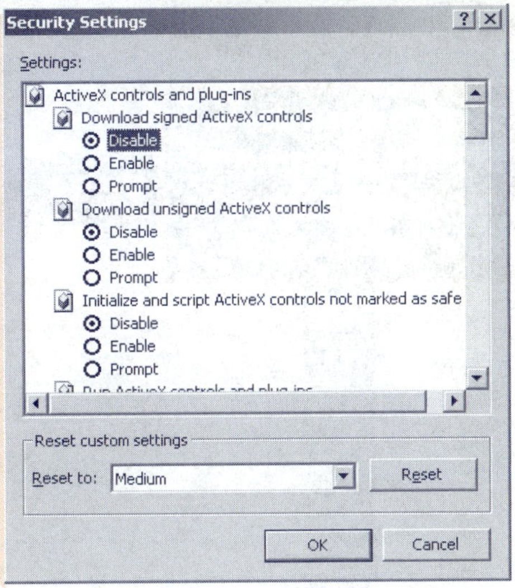

6. Still in the Security Settings dialog box, scroll down and select the Disable option for all the settings under Scripting.

7. Click OK to close each dialog box, and click Yes in any warning messages.

> **Tip**
> When you turn off ActiveX controls and scripting, Web pages that depend on these features won't work. It's a trade-off—more security for less Web page functionality.

If you want to know more about protecting your computer from e-mail viruses

If you are up to programming in Microsoft Visual Basic for Applications (VBA), you can find sample code that converts incoming HTML messages to Plain Text format (which removes scripting and active content but also, of course, removes formatting). Check out this Web page for more information—*www.slipstick.com/dev/code/zaphtml.htm*—and read the accompanying information carefully before you undertake any reprogramming of Outlook.

Another source of protection against HTML-type viruses can be found at *www.slipstick.com/outlook/htmlmail.htm*. Read the accompanying information carefully to be sure any patch you download is right for your system.

No doubt the future holds more new e-mail viruses with new techniques for infecting your system. The best ways to protect yourself from viruses, both old and new, are to run an updated anti-virus program regularly and to stay up-to-date with Outlook security patches as they're released by Microsoft.

Do you understand the error messages you are getting?

yes

Have you updated your anti-virus program recently?

yes

no

Quick fix

I don't know if a virus is causing an error message to occur The only way to be sure that your error is not being caused by a virus is to install a good anti-virus program, update your virus lists at least every two weeks, and run the anti-virus program often. (Norton and McAfee are two developers of popular and reliable anti-virus programs.)

no

Are you getting an error message when you access e-mail from your second computer?

yes

Go to...

A message with the words "Rules conflict" appears when I access my e-mail from my second computer, page 138.

no

Are you trying to look up your error message in Microsoft's Knowledge Base?

yes

Go to...

I don't know how to get help from the Microsoft Knowledge Base, page 134.

Error messages

Do you keep getting an error message that tells you that a program is trying to access your e-mail or send messages?

yes → **Go to...** A message says that a program is trying to access e-mail addresses or send e-mail on my behalf, page 136.

no ↓

Have you tried running Outlook's Detect And Repair?

yes → **Go to...** I don't know how to repair Office XP, page 133.

no ↓

Go to... I don't know how to repair Outlook, page 132.

If your solution isn't here, check this related chapter:

- E-mail, viruses, page 126

Or see the general troubleshooting tips on page xvii.

I don't know how to repair Outlook

Source of the problem

There are lots of different error messages. Some you might see often, and others you'll never see at all. There are also many different causes for them, such as outdated or mismatched versions of program files, outdated or damaged driver files, and corrupted files. (In other words, it's probably not your fault.)

There are very few error messages that actually tell you anything worthwhile—most are quite cryptic, which makes them enormously frustrating. Fortunately, there are easy procedures you can do that might banish the error message that's currently pestering you. One of those procedures is to run Microsoft Outlook's Detect And Repair, which instructs Outlook to find and fix its own mismatched or corrupted files.

Tip

A single error message that doesn't reappear might be just an "electron cramp"—ignore it, save your current work, and continue working.

How to fix it

First, quit and restart Outlook. Sometimes closing and restarting the program (or even closing all your open programs and then shutting down and restarting Windows) straightens out whatever's wrong. If that doesn't solve the problem, it's time to repair Outlook.

1. On Outlook's Help menu, click Detect And Repair.
2. In the Detect And Repair dialog box, make sure the Restore My Shortcuts While Repairing check box is selected. You can also select the Discard My Customized Settings And Restore Default Settings check box if you suspect your custom settings are causing the problem.
3. Click Start.

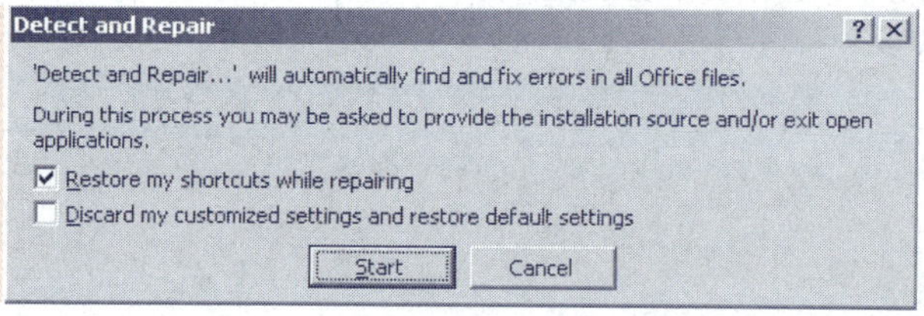

4. Wait several minutes while the program checks your files and makes any needed repairs. You'll be asked to restart Windows if repairs were made.

After you restart Windows, your problem might well be solved. If it isn't, try repairing Microsoft Office XP. (See "I don't know how to repair Office XP" on the facing page.)

I don't know how to repair Office XP

Source of the problem

Error messages are pretty mysterious, and the same error message can be generated by any number of different, totally unrelated problems. Sometimes the quickest approach to fixing an error message is to repair the whole program, and then probably whatever was wrong will be fixed.

If you've already run Outlook's Detect And Repair (see the previous solution, "I don't know how to repair Outlook") and you still get the error message, try repairing Office. This solution shows you how to make sure all its program files are current and appropriate for your installation by reinstalling Office XP.

Tip

To complete these steps you need the Office XP CD or access to the network location from which it was installed, and you should be logged on with administrative privileges.

How to fix it

1. On the Start menu, point to Settings, and then click Control Panel.
2. In Control Panel, double-click the Add/Remove Programs icon.
3. In the Add/Remove Programs dialog box, select Microsoft Office XP, and click Change.

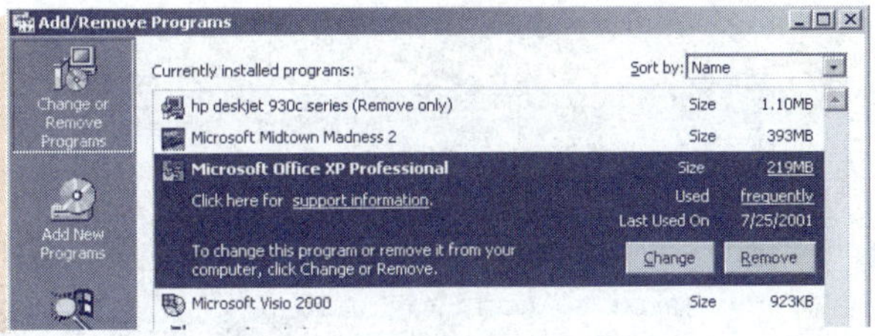

4. In the Maintenance Mode Options page of the Microsoft Office XP Setup Wizard, select the Repair Office option, and then click Next.
5. In the wizard's Reinstall Or Repair Office Installation page, select the Reinstall Office option, and click Install.

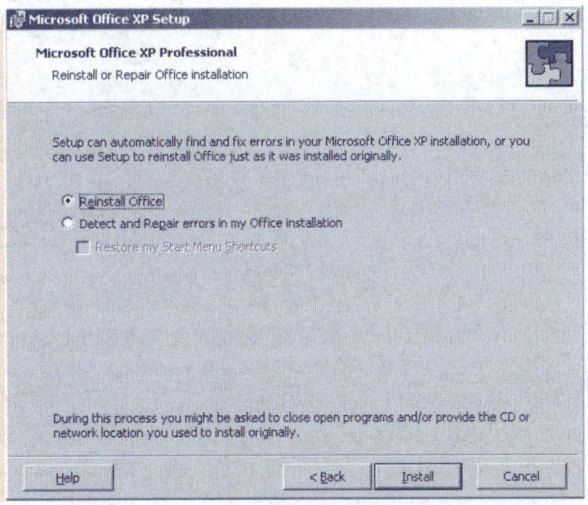

Tip

Depending on the particular files that need to be fixed or replaced, you might receive error messages during the reinstallation process. Click the Ignore button in each error message to continue the reinstallation.

I don't know how to get help from the Microsoft Knowledge Base

Source of the problem

If running Outlook's Detect And Repair doesn't help, and reinstalling Office XP doesn't solve the problem of recurring error messages, you might need more in-depth help. You can find lots of detailed help and fix-it procedures online, in the Microsoft Knowledge Base. The Microsoft Knowledge Base is a storehouse of articles that address specific problems, and there's a search engine to help you locate information about your specific problem.

How to fix it

1. Write down the complete wording of your error message, including any file names it mentions. You need this information to focus your Knowledge Base search.
2. Launch your Web browser, and go to the site *http://search.support.microsoft.com/kb.* ▶

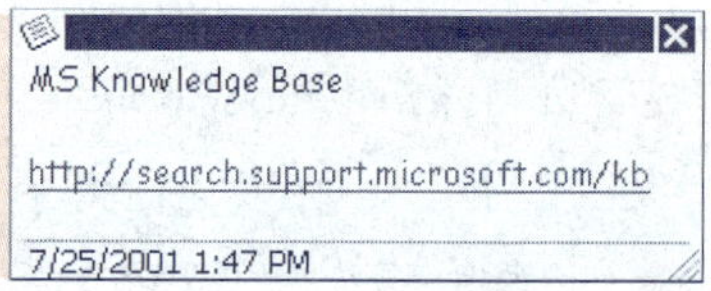

3. On the Microsoft Knowledge Base page, set up your search by clicking the down arrow to the right of the My Search Is About box and selecting Outlook 2002 in the drop-down list. ▶

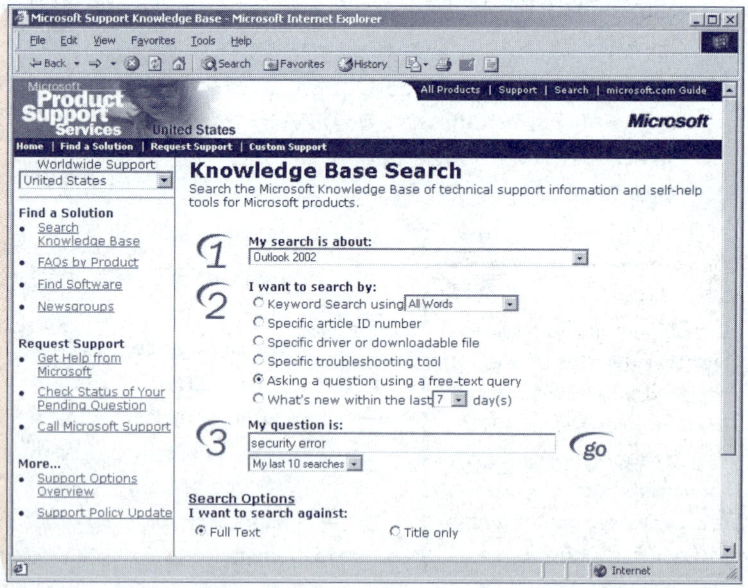

Tip

Store the Web address for the Microsoft Knowledge Base as a Note in Outlook, or you can add it to your Favorites list.

4. If you know the specific article ID number you want, select the Specific Article ID Number option, and type the article ID number (beginning with a *Q*), in the My Question Is box.
5. If you want to look for articles containing specific words, select the Keyword Search Using option, click the down arrow to the right of the Keyword Search Using box, click All Words or Any Words in the drop-down list, and type the words in the My Question Is box.
6. If you don't know a specific article ID number or words to search for, click the Asking A Question Using A Free-Text Query option, and type a question in your own words in the My Question Is box.
7. Click Go, and then click a prospective article's title to open it.
8. When you find a potentially helpful article, print it so that you can refer to it while you carry out whatever procedures it prescribes.

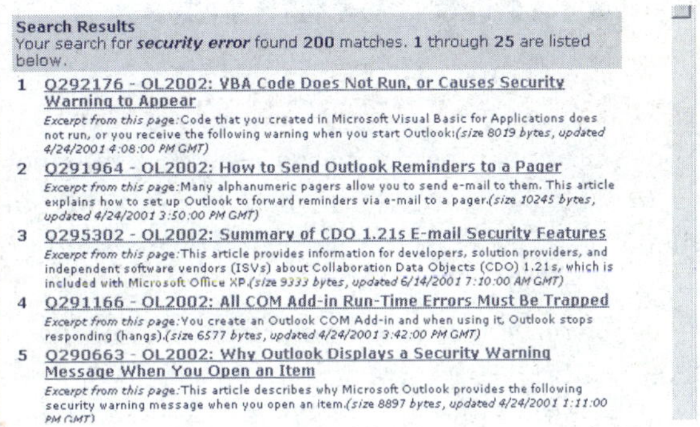

A message says that a program is trying to access e-mail addresses or send e-mail on my behalf

Source of the problem

You're being bombarded with messages telling you that a program is trying to access e-mail addresses stored in Outlook, or that a program is trying to automatically send e-mail messages on your behalf.

If you've recently installed an add-in, that's the most likely culprit—try turning it off to see if your problem goes away. Another possibility is that another program has automatically installed a Component Object Model (COM) add-in. Your best option is to turn it off or remove it.

If you installed the add-in, you probably know that you can turn it off by using the Add-In Manager in the Advanced Options dialog box. If a COM add-in has been installed without your knowledge, you need to turn it off a different way.

Tip

A common cause of this problem is ICQ 2000—a popular messaging program that installs an ICQ Express COM add-in, which monitors selections you make in Outlook. Although this add-in is automatically disabled in Outlook, it might have been re-enabled from the Disabled Items dialog box, accessed from About Outlook on the Help menu.

How to fix it

1. On the Tools menu, click Options.
2. In the Options dialog box, click the Other tab, and in the General area, click Advanced Options.
3. In the Advanced Options dialog box, click COM Add-Ins. ▶

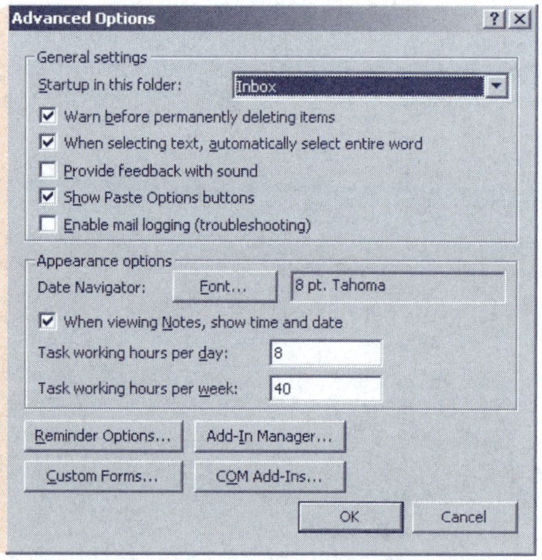

4. In the Add-Ins Available list in the COM Add-Ins dialog box, clear the check boxes for all add-ins.

5. Click OK to close each open dialog box.

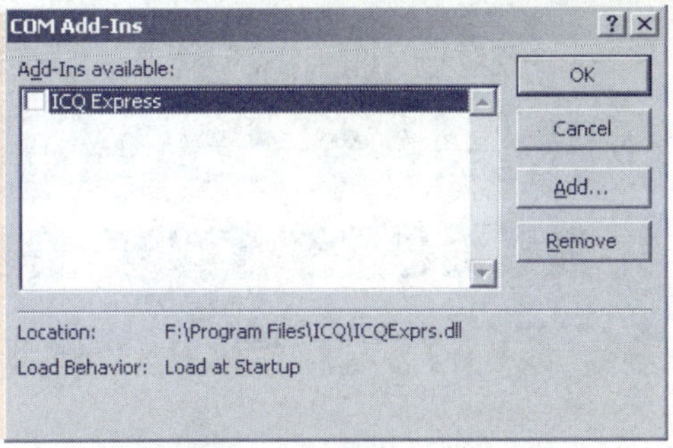

Make add-ins trusted so that you can use them

If you're on a network with Microsoft Exchange Server and have specific add-ins that you need to use—to send out bulk e-mail when you're not at your computer, for instance—ask your administrator to give these programs full access to your e-mail and address book. The resources to accomplish this are available as part of the Microsoft Office XP Resource Kit (ORK), located on the Web at *www.microsoft.com/office/ork/xp*.

A message with the words "Rules conflict" appears when I access my e-mail from my second computer

Source of the problem

You want to use a Microsoft Exchange Server account from two different computers. On the first computer, you've created some rules and set e-mail to go to a personal storage file (*.pst*), but as soon as you connect from the second computer, you get an error message that says "The rules on this machine do not match the rules on your Exchange server. Only one set of rules can be kept. You will usually want to keep the rules on the server. Which rules do you want to keep?"

The problem is that you need to keep your rules where they can be accessed from both computers—on the Exchange server instead of in a local *.pst* file. (After Exchange fails to find the rules on the second computer, even your Outlook account on the first computer will generate an error message, making a fix even more imperative!)

To fix this problem, you need to set up both your computers so that e-mail is delivered to the Exchange server instead of to a local *.pst* file. (This makes sense—because you want to access your stored e-mail from both computers.)

How to fix it

1. On the Tools menu, click E-mail Accounts.
2. On the first page of the E-mail Accounts Wizard, make sure the View Or Change Existing E-mail Accounts option is selected, and then click Next.

3. Click the down arrow to the right of the Deliver New E-mail To The Following Location box, and click your Exchange mailbox in the drop-down list.
4. Click Finish.
5. Click OK to close the Account Manager message that appears.

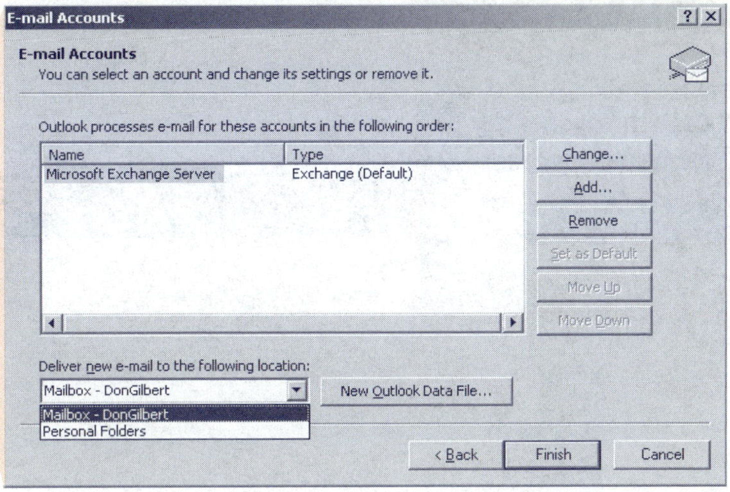

When you exit Outlook, are you prompted to empty your Deleted Items folder?

yes

no

When you exit Outlook, does it continue to run?

yes

Go to...
After I exit Outlook, it continues to run, page 142.

Exiting

Quick fix

Every time I close Outlook, I'm prompted to empty the Deleted Items folder If you find this bothersome, you can put a stop to it with a quick change. Your deleted items will then remain in your Deleted Items folder until you delete them.

1. On the Tools menu, click Options to display the Options dialog box.
2. On the Other tab, clear the Empty The Deleted Items Folder Upon Exiting check box.
3. Click OK. .

If your solution isn't here, check this related chapter:

- Error messages, page 130

Or see the general troubleshooting tips on page xvii.

After I exit Outlook, it continues to run

Source of the problem

You've got several programs open and your computer is running low on available memory, so you decide to close a few programs, including Microsoft Outlook. But Outlook doesn't close; it continues to run and use a portion of that currently scarce available memory.

Outlook can continue to run under these circumstances if a Microsoft Visual Basic for Applications (VBA) or a Microsoft Visual Basic (VB) program is using Outlook data or if you're running a Microsoft Office program that's attempting to record an entry in the Outlook Journal.

How to fix it

Close Outlook, check whether Outlook or any programs that might be using Outlook are still running, and then close them.

1. On the File menu, click Exit to quit Outlook.
2. Press Ctrl+Alt+Del to open the Windows Security dialog box in Windows 2000, and then click Task Manager.
3. In the Windows Task Manager dialog box, click the Applications tab and check the list of programs for any reference to Outlook. In the list, you'll also see what other programs are still running that might be using Outlook and keeping it open.

Warning

Don't click the Shut Down button—you'll quit Windows while programs are still running, and that creates a mess for Windows.

Tip

In some versions of Windows, such as Windows 98, you won't see the Windows Security dialog box when you press Ctrl+Alt+Del. Instead you'll see a Close Window dialog box that you can use to close any programs that are keeping Outlook open.

4. Click the name of the program you think might be keeping Outlook open, and click the End Task button. If Outlook disappears from the list in the Windows Task Manager, you chose correctly. Otherwise, continue to close programs until Outlook closes.

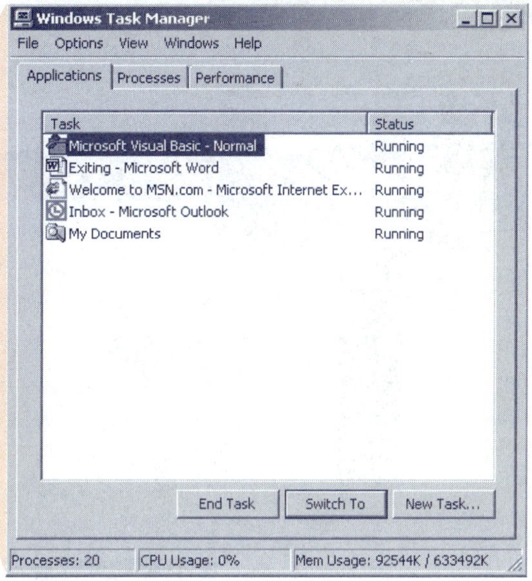

5. On the File menu, click Exit Task Manager.

Tip

When you close a program, be sure to look carefully to see if you are prompted to save data before closing. Because the Windows Task Manager dialog box stays on top of all other windows, it might obscure any prompts that appear. You can minimize the Windows Task Manager dialog box to get better access to any dialog box that appears as you close the program. Then you can restore the minimized dialog box to close another program or to close the Windows Task Manager.

Are you able to send and receive faxes from Outlook?

yes

Are you unable to find your contacts in the Windows 2000 Fax Wizard?

yes

no

Are you unsure which fax programs work with Outlook 2002?

yes

no

Are you unsure how to send faxes?

yes

Go to...
I don't know how to send faxes from Outlook, page 146.

no

Are you unsure how to set up Outlook to receive faxes?

yes

Go to...
I don't know how to set up Outlook to receive faxes, page 148.

Faxing

Go to...

My Contacts list doesn't appear in the Windows 2000 Fax Wizard, page 152.

Quick fix

I don't know which fax programs work with Outlook 2002 Outlook 2002 supports only the Windows 2000 Fax Service, which is installed by default with Windows 2000 if you have a supported fax/modem in your computer.

If your solution isn't here, see the general troubleshooting tips on page xvii.

I don't know how to send faxes from Outlook

Source of the problem

You're using Microsoft Windows 2000 and Microsoft Outlook 2002 but you've never sent a fax from Outlook—perhaps you've never sent a fax from Windows 2000 either, and aren't even sure if its Fax Service is set up.

If you've never sent a fax from Windows 2000, you need to check the Windows 2000 Fax Service to make sure it's online and set up a fax printer if you don't have one. Then you should be able to send a fax from Outlook.

How to fix it

Verify your fax device and printer

The Windows 2000 Fax Service is automatically set up for outgoing faxes as soon as Windows 2000 detects a fax device, so if you have a fax/modem in your computer, the Fax Service should be ready to go.

1. Log on to your computer as Administrator or as a user who has Administrator privileges.
2. On the Start menu, point to Programs, point to Accessories, point to Communications, point to Fax, and then click Fax Service Management.
3. In the Fax Service Management window, on the Tree tab, click Devices. If you see a device listed, it should have Yes in the Send list. If a device isn't listed, you need to install a fax/modem on your computer or troubleshoot to see why it isn't recognized.

4. Click the Close button in the upper-right corner to close the Fax Service Management window.

Tip

If Fax Service is installed but doesn't appear to be working, make sure the problem isn't operator error. Open Windows 2000 Help and, on the Search tab, type *Fax*, and click List Topics. Then select *Common tasks: Fax* to find procedures for most operations involving faxes.

You also need to make sure there's a Fax printer installed.

1. On the Start menu, point to Settings, and click Printers. If you see a Fax printer listed in the Printer window, you're ready to send a fax from Outlook.
2. If you don't see a Fax printer listed, on the Start menu, point to Settings, and click Control Panel.
3. In Control Panel, double-click the Fax icon.
4. In the Fax Properties dialog box, click the Advanced Options tab, and then click Add A Fax Printer. ▶
5. When the Add A Fax Printer dialog box appears, click OK.

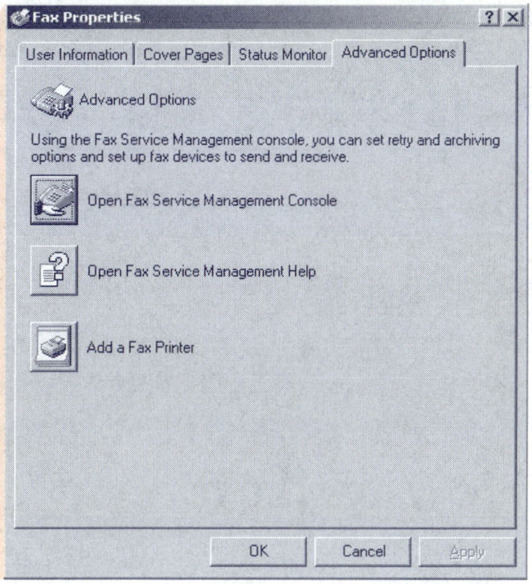

Send a fax

Now that you know your fax is ready, try sending a fax from Outlook. You'll need a fax number you can test this out with—perhaps a friend with a fax who can verify that the fax was received.

1. In Outlook, open a folder or item you want to fax—perhaps your Contacts folder or an e-mail message in your Inbox.
2. On the File menu, click Print.
3. In the Select Printer area of the Print dialog box, click Fax, and then click Print. ▶
4. Follow the Send Fax Wizard's steps to send the fax.

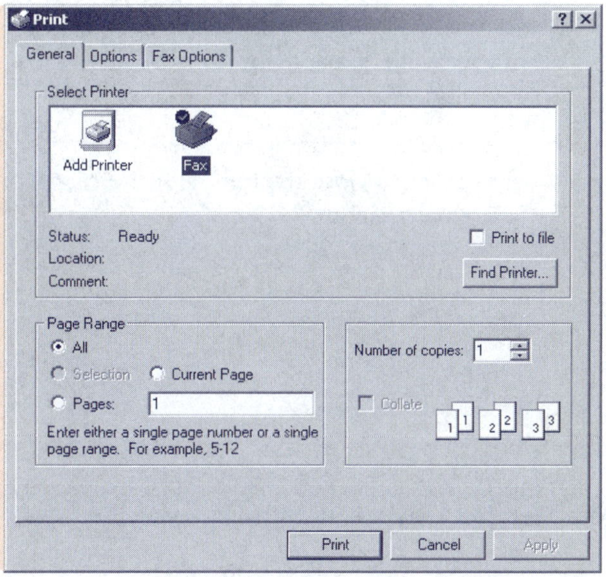

Tip

If you have a dial-up connection and a single fax/modem, you might need to disconnect from your Internet connection to use the fax device.

I don't know how to set up Outlook to receive faxes

Source of the problem

You're running Outlook 2002 and Windows 2000, and you've been able to send faxes. Now you'd like to receive faxes and have them delivered electronically to your Inbox.

Although this takes several steps to set up, it's worth the effort to see your faxes waiting for you in your Inbox.

Tip

If you've never sent a fax from Windows 2000 and aren't sure if your fax device is enabled, see "I don't know how to send faxes from Outlook," earlier in this chapter.

How to fix it

Enable your computer to receive faxes

1. Log on to your computer as Administrator or as a user who has Administrator privileges.
2. On the Start menu, point to Programs, point to Accessories, point to Communications, point to Fax, and click Fax Service Management.
3. In the Fax Service Management window, on the Trees tab, click Devices.
4. On the right side of the window, right-click the fax device, and if Receive does not have a check mark next to it on the shortcut menu, click Receive.

5. Click the Close button in the upper-right corner to close the Fax Service Management window.

Set up a fax service account

1. On the Start menu, point to Settings, and click Control Panel.
2. In Control Panel, double-click the Internet Options icon.
3. In the Internet Properties dialog box, click the Programs tab, make sure Microsoft Outlook is selected in the E-mail box, and click OK.
4. Open Outlook, and on the Tools menu, click E-mail Accounts.
5. On the first page of the E-mail Accounts Wizard, select the Add A New E-mail Account option, and click Next.
6. On the wizard's second page, select the Additional Server Types option, and click Next.
7. On the wizard's third page, select the Fax Mail Transport option, and click Next.
8. On the wizard's fourth page, click OK in the message that informs you that the e-mail account won't be started until you exit and restart Outlook.
9. On the File menu, click Exit.

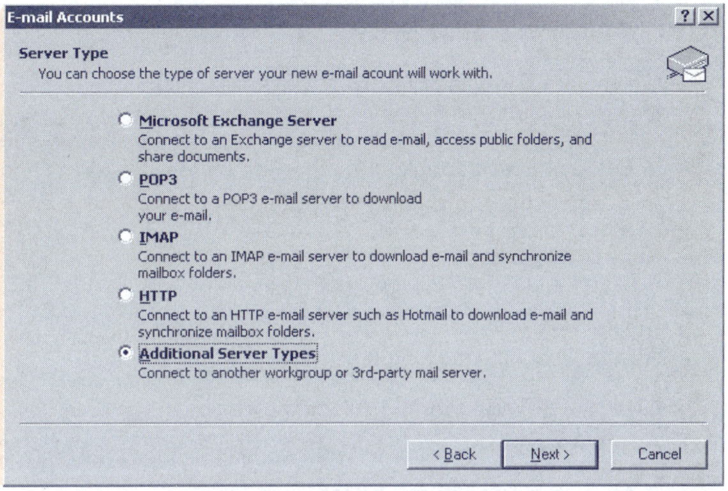

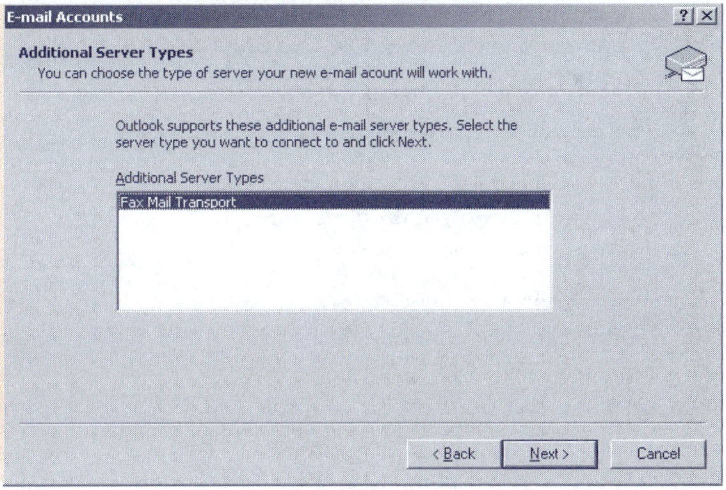

If this solution didn't solve your problem, go to the next page.

I don't know how to set up Outlook to receive faxes

(continued from page 149)

Enable the fax service to log on to your account and send faxes to your profile

1. On the Start menu, point to Settings, and click Control Panel.
2. In Control Panel, double-click the Administrative Tools icon, and then double-click Services in the Name list.
3. In the Services window, double-click Fax Service in the Name list to open the Fax Service Properties dialog box.
4. Click the Log On tab, and select the This Account option.
5. Click Browse, and in the Select User dialog box, click the account that you want this service to use, and then click OK.
6. In the Password and Confirm Password boxes, type the account's password.

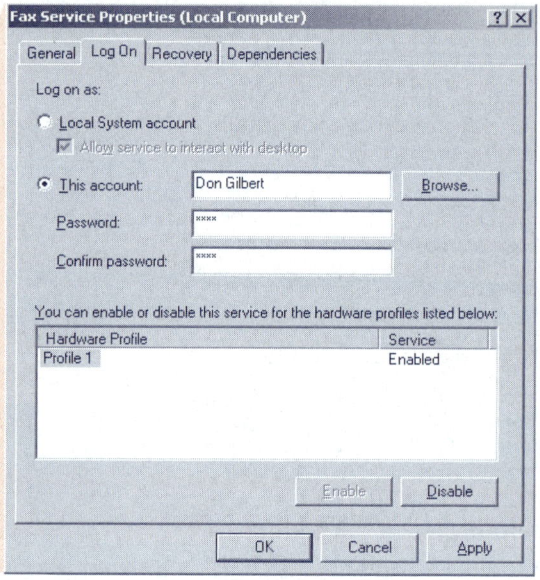

7. Click OK three times to close the dialog box, answer Yes to the prompts, and return to the Services window.
8. In the Services window, right-click Fax Service, and click Stop on the shortcut menu. Then right-click Fax Service again, and click Start on the shortcut menu.

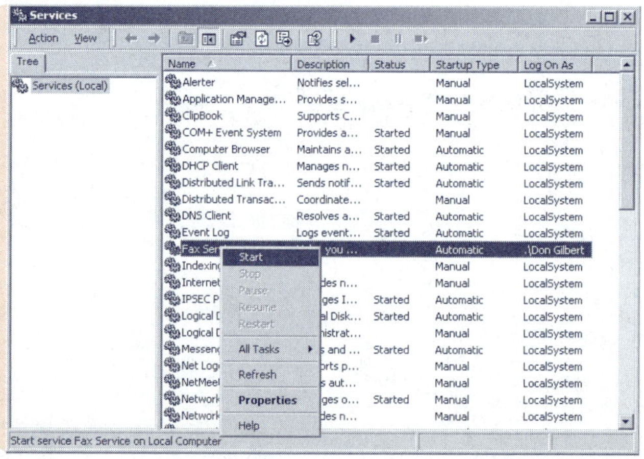

9. On the Start menu, point to Programs, point to Accessories, point to Communications, point to Fax, and click Fax Service Management.

10. In the Fax Service Management window, click Devices on the Tree tab, and double-click the fax/modem device listed on the right side of the window.

11. On the Received Faxes tab of the Fax Modem Properties dialog box, select the Send To Local E-mail Inbox check box. Then click the down arrow to the right of the Profile Name box, and in the drop-down list, click the name of the account that you added the Fax service to earlier. ▶

12. Click OK.

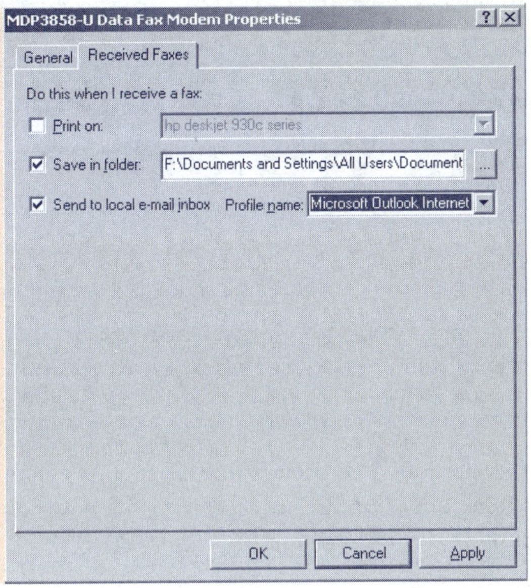

My Contacts list doesn't appear in the Windows 2000 Fax Wizard

Source of the problem

You store all your contact information, including fax numbers, in your Contacts folder. But when you send a fax, your Contacts list doesn't appear in the Windows 2000 Fax Wizard. Unfortunately, the Windows 2000 Fax Wizard uses the Windows Address Book (WAB), and Outlook 2002 doesn't share its Contacts folder with the Windows Address Book.

There is a workaround, however, so you're not out of luck—you'll just need to do a little extra preparation. The trick is to export all your contacts to the WAB so that the Fax Wizard can display them. Then, when you want to add a new contact with a fax number, add it to the WAB and import it into Outlook.

How to fix it

Export your contacts to Windows Address Book

1. On the File menu, click Import And Export.
2. On the first page of the Import And Export Wizard, click Export To A File in the Choose An Action To Perform List, and then click Next.
3. On the wizard's second page, click Comma Separated Values (Windows) in the Create A File Of Type list, and then click Next.
4. On the wizard's third page, click the Contacts folder in the Select Folder To Export From list, and click Next. ▶
5. On the wizard's fourth page, click the Browse button, locate a folder in which to store the file, type a name for the exported file (for example, *mycontacts*) in the File Name box, click OK, and then click Next.

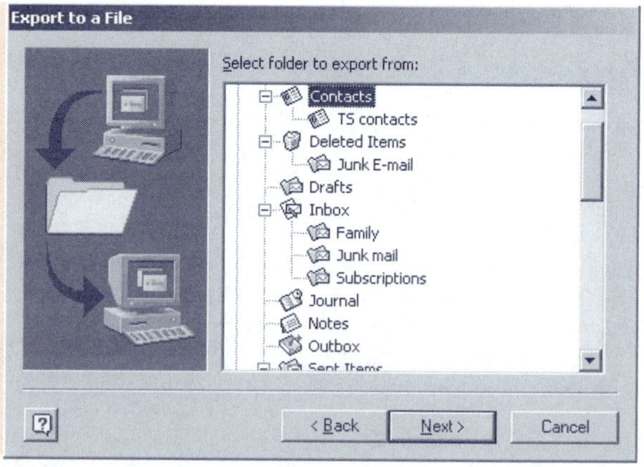

6. On the wizard's final page, click Finish.
7. On the File menu, click Exit to close Outlook.
8. On the Start menu, point to Programs, point to Accessories, and click Address Book. (If a message appears asking if you want the Windows Address Book to be your default vCard viewer, click No.)
9. On the File menu, point to Import, and click Other Address Book.
10. In the Address Book Import Tool dialog box, click Text File (Comma Separated Values), and click Import.

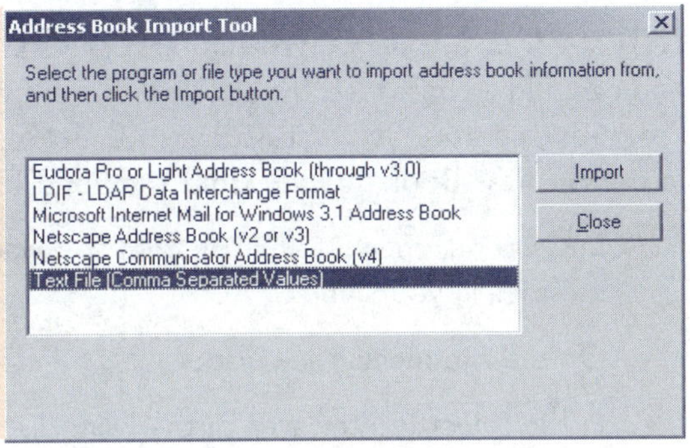

11. In the CSV Import Wizard, click Browse, locate the file that you saved in step 5, click its name, click Open, and then in the CSV Import Wizard, click Next.
12. Select the check boxes next to the fields you want to import. (For example, you might want to import only names and fax numbers.) Click Finish.
13. Click OK in the message that appears when the process is finished, and then click the Close button in the Address Book Import Tool.

All your contacts should now show up in the Send Fax Wizard. All phone numbers stored in the Fax fields of your contact forms will be available in Windows 2000 Fax Wizard. (You'll be asked to choose the correct number if there is more than one fax number for any contact.)

Tip

If you already have some of the same contacts in the Windows Address Book, you'll be asked if you want to replace them. It's probably safe to do so—you'll want your Outlook contacts to be the central repository of your addresses.

If this solution didn't solve your problem, go to the next page.

My Contacts list doesn't appear in the Windows 2000 Fax Wizard

(continued from page 153)

Import a new contact into Outlook's Contacts folder

You can add a contact to the Address Book from within Outlook or by clicking Start, pointing to Programs, pointing to Accessories and clicking Address Book. You can also add the new contact to the Address Book directly from the Send Fax Wizard.

1. In Outlook, open a folder or item you want to fax—perhaps your Contacts folder or an e-mail message in your Inbox.
2. On the File menu, click Print.
3. In the Select Printer area of the Print dialog box, click Fax, and then click Print.
4. On the first page of the Send Fax Wizard, click Next.
5. On the wizard's second page, select the Keep The Current User Information option, and then click OK.
6. On the Recipient And Dialing Information page of the Send Fax Wizard, click Address Book.
7. In the Address Book dialog box, select either Main Identity's Contacts or Contacts (whichever appears) in the drop-down list, and then click New Contact.
8. In the Properties dialog box, enter all the necessary information for the new contact, and then click OK.
9. Double-click the new contact's name in the Name list of the Address Book dialog box, and then click OK to close the dialog box and return to the Recipient And Dialing Information page of the Send Fax Wizard.
10. On the Recipient And Dialing Information page of the Send Fax Wizard, click Next, and then follow the rest of the wizard's instructions to complete the procedure.

Add a new contact with a fax number

If you want to add a new contact with a fax number, add it to the Windows Address Book, and then import it into Outlook.

1. In Outlook, on the File menu, click Import And Export.
2. On the first page of the Import And Export Wizard, click Import Internet Mail And Addresses in the Choose An Action To Perform list, and then click Next.
3. On the wizard's second page, click Outlook Express 4.x, 5 in the Select The Internet Mail Application To Import From list.
4. Clear the Import Mail and Import Rules check boxes, select the Import Address Book check box, and then click Next.

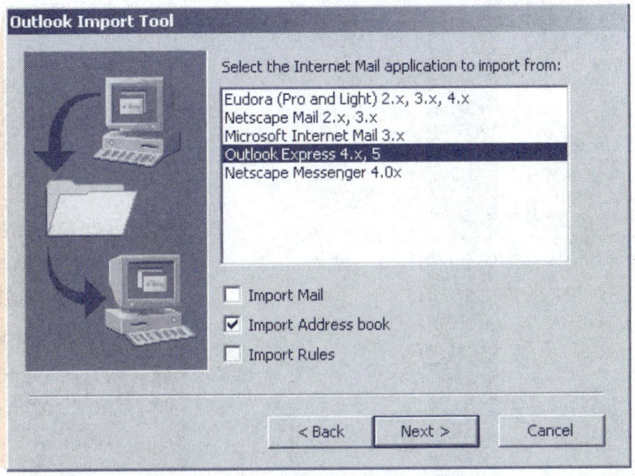

5. On the wizard's third page, select the Outlook Contacts Folder option as the destination (or another Contacts folder if you prefer). In the Options area, select the Do Not Import Duplicate Items option, and then click Finish.

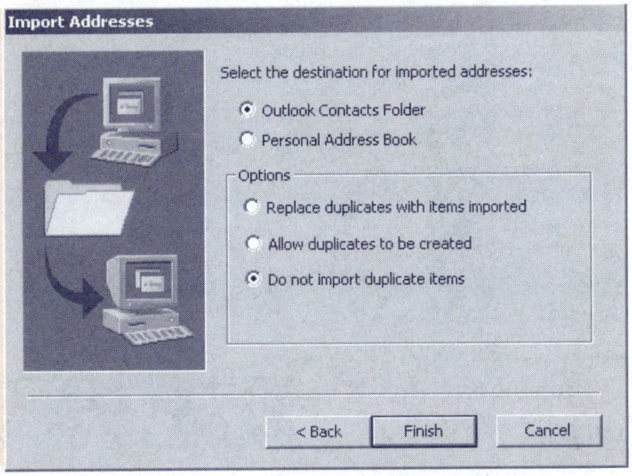

6. Click OK in the message that appears when the process is complete, or click Save In Inbox if you want to maintain a record of what was imported.

Is it impossible to open a file you received?

yes → Do you have the correct program and version on your computer?

yes →

no ↓

Quick fix

An attached file does not have an icon associated with it To open any file on your computer, you need the correct program and version for the file. Ask your correspondent to save the file in a format that you can open and then send it to you again. (Many files can be saved for use with an earlier version of the program.) If the file is compressed or zipped, you'll need a copy of a program that can uncompress or extract it.

no ↓

Is your message full of unreadable characters?

yes →

no ↓

Do you want to be given the option of saving or opening attachments when you double-click the attachment?

yes →

Go to...

Attached files are always opened automatically, page 160.

Files, receiving

Is the file being blocked because of security reasons?

yes → Do you want to override the security and receive blocked files?

yes → **Go to...**

I don't know how to receive files that Outlook is blocking, page 158.

no (security override) →

Quick fix

An attached file that I need is blocked by Outlook Outlook blocks some files, such as programs, to help prevent the spread of viruses. Ask your correspondent to use a program such as WinZip to compress the blocked attachment file. Then save the zipped attachment to your hard drive, and extract the file.

no (security) →

Quick fix

An attached file isn't blocked but won't open
Ask your correspondent to resend the file. Sometimes a file is corrupted before or while it's being sent.

Go to...

My message is full of gibberish, page 162.

If your solution isn't here, check these related chapters:

- Files, sending, page 164
- E-mail, receiving, page 104

Or see the general troubleshooting tips on page xvii.

I don't know how to receive files that Outlook is blocking

Source of the problem

Since installing Microsoft Outlook 2002, you can't receive some file types—primarily programs—that come as e-mail attachments. Although the security restrictions enforced by Outlook 2002 on attached files are an effective way of blocking viruses, you'd rather bear the responsibility of deciding which files to open yourself. Fortunately, you can work around the blocking with a simple registry edit.

Before you start

It is important to understand that editing the registry can create serious computer problems if you make a mistake. If the thought of editing the registry makes you cringe (and it probably should if you've never done it before), read "More about receiving blocked files" at the end of this solution for other alternatives. If you decide to edit the registry, the first few steps here create a backup of the current registry information, in case you want to return it to its previous state. You should also update your Emergency Repair Disk, just to be on the safe side.

How to fix it

1. On the Start menu, click Run.
2. In the Run dialog box, type *Regedit*, and click OK.
3. In the Registry Editor window, on the Registry menu, click Export Registry File.
4. In the Export Range area at the bottom of the Export Registry File dialog box, select the All option.
5. Type a name in the File Name box (such as *backup*), and click Save to save a backup copy of your current registry information.

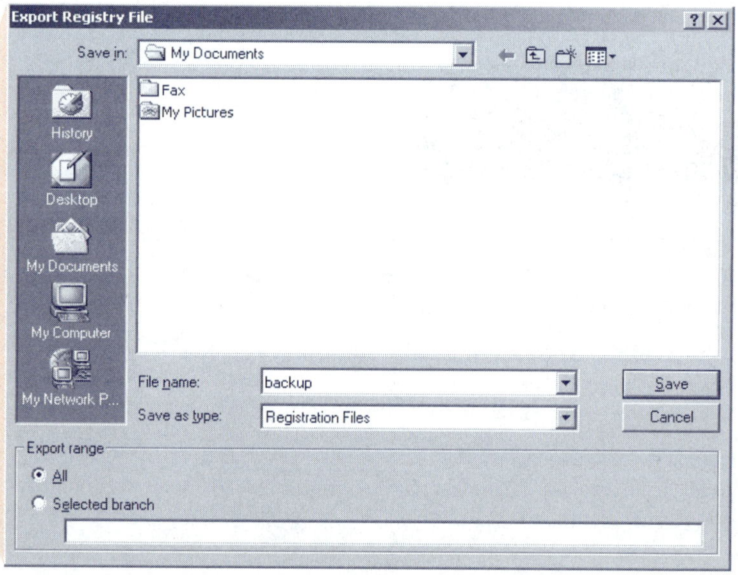

6. In the Registry Editor window, navigate to HKEY_CURRENT_USER\Software\Microsoft\Office\10.0\Outlook\Security.
7. On the Edit menu, point to New, and click String Value.

8. Type *Level1Remove* to replace the highlighted text, and then press Enter.

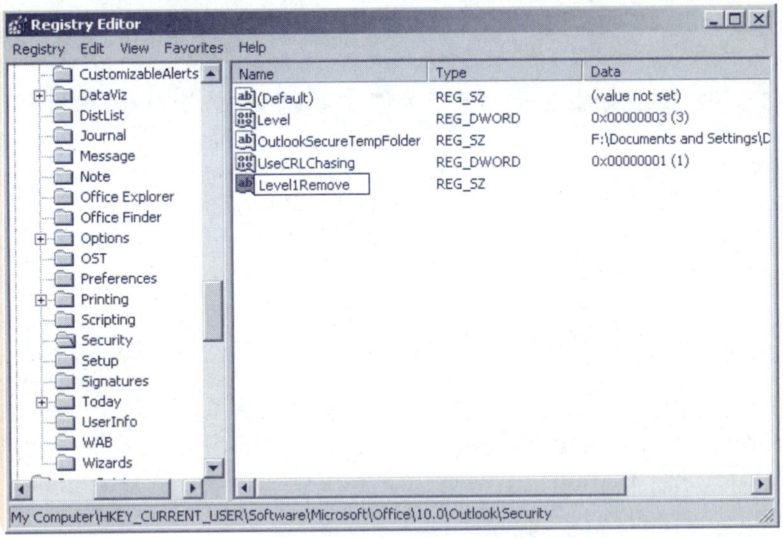

9. Right-click Level1Remove, and click Modify on the shortcut menu.

10. In the Edit String dialog box, in the Value Data box, type the extensions of the blocked file types you want to allow. If you want to allow more than one type, type a semi-colon after each one to separate them. For example, to unblock programs with the extension *.exe* and *.com*, type *.exe;.com*.

11. Click OK.

12. On the Registry menu, click Exit.

If Outlook is currently open, you'll need to close it and open it again for the changes to take effect. To verify that the changes have been made, on the Help menu, click About Microsoft Outlook. In the middle of the About Microsoft Outlook dialog box, you should see "Security Mode: User Controlled."

More about receiving blocked files

The safest way to receive the file types that Outlook blocks is not to receive them as e-mail attachments. It's no mystery why Microsoft chose to block certain file types as e-mail attachments—these file types are extremely accessible as virus hosts and too many computer users still open attachments with little or no thought. If you regularly transfer files with particular correspondents via e-mail and are now hampered because of Outlook's security feature, consider setting up an account with an online storage Web site where you can upload and download files with correspondents you trust.

Alternatively, ask your correspondents to use a compression program such as WinZip (*www.winzip.com*). You can send WinZip files as attachments in Outlook 2002 and extract them using the same program.

Finally, if you're convinced you really do want to un-block certain file types but you don't want to edit the registry, visit *www.slipstick.com/outlook/esecup/getexe.htm,* where you'll find both a free plug-in and a free stand-alone program that accomplishes the same thing that using the registry approach described here does.

Attached files are always opened automatically

Source of the problem

When you open an e-mail that contains an attachment with a certain file type, the attached file opens automatically instead of opening a dialog box that asks you whether you want to open it or save it.

This is probably happening because, at some point after double-clicking an attachment, you cleared the Always Ask Before Opening This Type Of File check box in the Opening Mail Attachment dialog box. With the increasing threat that a virus is in an attached file, you need to have better control of what files you open, so it's a good idea to make sure you're prompted for every file type. As it turns out, this is a Microsoft Windows setting, not an Outlook setting (even though you might have made the change in Outlook), so you just need to visit the Folder Options dialog box in Windows to set things right again.

Tip

If you don't find Folder Options in the Control Panel, on the Start menu, point to Settings, and click Folder Options (depending on your operating system).

How to fix it

1. On the Start menu, point to Settings, and click Control Panel.
2. In the Control Panel, double-click the Folder Options icon.
3. In the Folder Options dialog box, click the File Types tab.
4. In the Registered File Types box, scroll down, and click the file type that is opening automatically.

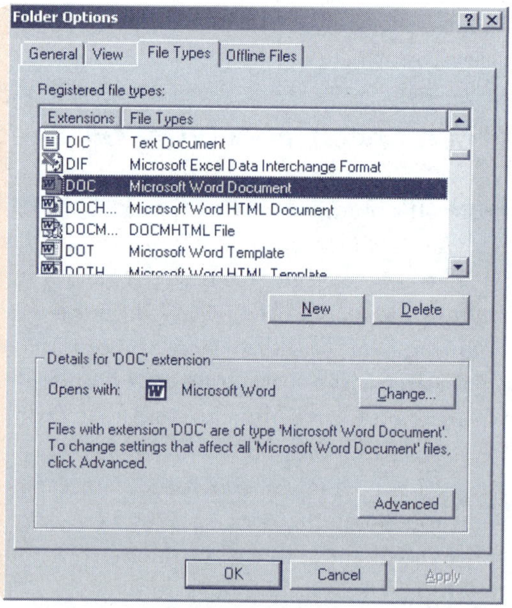

Tip

To group all file type extensions together by application, click the File Types header.

5. In the Folder Options dialog box, click Advanced.
6. In the Edit File Type dialog box, select the Confirm Open After Download check box.
7. Click OK, and then click Close.

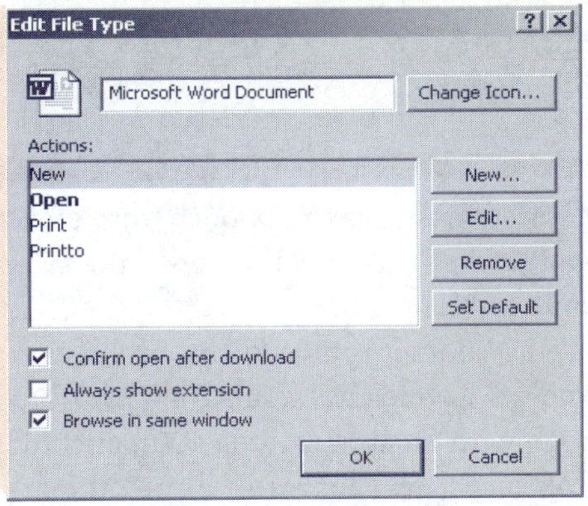

Tip

If the Confirm Open After Download check box is already selected, you've selected the wrong file type to edit—many programs recognize several extensions. Just click Cancel to close the Edit File Type dialog box, and select another extension of the same file type to see if that's the one that's opening automatically.

My message is full of gibberish

Source of the problem

E-mail messages can bounce from server to server around the world before they arrive at your Inbox. Sometimes an e-mail server in the system fails to pass along your bouncing message completely and correctly.

Another source of this problem is that there are several e-mail encoding formats in use around the world, and they don't always work well with every e-mail system. If someone sends you a message with an attached file in an encoding format that your e-mail server can't read, or that some Internet gateway can't interpret, the attached file might be converted into pages and pages of garbage characters.

How to fix it

There are three possible solutions.

- Ask your correspondent to resend the message in MIME format.
- Ask your correspondent to use a compression program, such as WinZip, to compress the file and then send it to you. Sometimes compressed attached files are carried through Internet gateways more easily.
- If the file is fairly short and doesn't need formatting, ask your correspondent to send it as text in the body of the message rather than sending it as an attachment.

More about e-mail encoding formats

When a binary file is attached to an e-mail message, the file is encoded so that it travels to its destination rapidly and intact. When the file arrives, most e-mail programs can decode the file, regardless of the encoding format.

The most common file encoding type is MIME. Another older file type that is still in use is UUENCODE. MIME stands for Multipurpose Internet Mail Extensions, and UUENCODE stands for Unix to Unix Encode. UUENCODE was the standard for a long time and was originally designed primarily to support the transfer of text-based files. MIME is newer and supports the transfer of a wider range of file types, such as audio, video, graphics, and e-mail.

Files, receiving

Are you having problems sending attachments?

yes

When you send a message with an attached file, does your e-mail server try for a long time, and then not send the message?

yes

no

When you click Send, do you receive a warning that says your attachment is potentially unsafe?

yes

no

Do your recipients receive unreadable attachments?

yes

Are you sending the attached files to an AOL address?

yes

no

Quick fix

Recipients can't open or view my attachments If your non-AOL recipients don't have the correct program or version to open the file you sent, they won't be able to read your file. Save and resend the file in a format they can open and read.

Files, sending

Go to...
My message with attached files doesn't get sent, page 166.

Go to...
I receive a warning when I send some attachments, page 169.

Go to...
My AOL recipient can't read my message or attached files, page 168.

If your solution isn't here, check these related chapters:

- Files, receiving, page 156
- E-mail, recipients, page 116
- E-mail, sending, page 120

Or see the general troubleshooting tips on page xvii.

My message with attached files doesn't get sent

Source of the problem

If a message has a very large attached file (more than 2 MB, for example), many e-mail servers won't handle it—so you can't send it. But suppose you've got a huge, complex database to send to your client. How can you get it there electronically?

First, open your Outbox, and look at the size of the outgoing message. Then you can decide what to do.

How to fix it

Check the size of the outgoing message

If the Size field isn't displayed, you can easily display it.

1. In the Outbox, right-click the row of column headings, and click Field Chooser on the shortcut menu.
2. Drag the Size field from the Field Chooser to the headings row. It is positioned correctly when you see two red arrows. ▶
3. Close the Field Chooser by clicking its Close button.

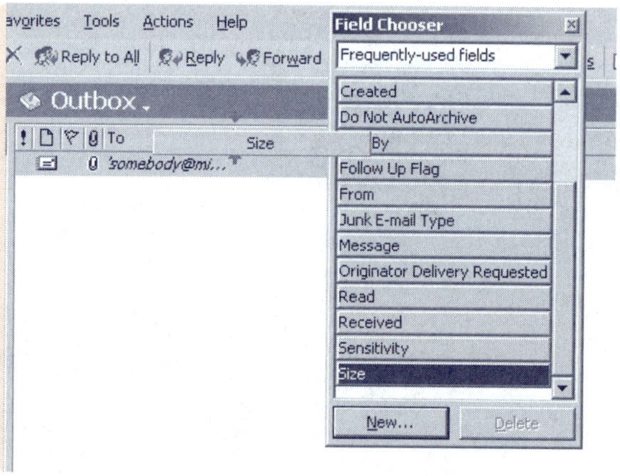

Decide what to do

- If your message is larger than 2 MB (2000 KB), use WinZip, which you can find at *www.winzip.com,* or another file compression program to reduce the size of the attached file. (The compressed file is commonly called a "zipped" file.)
- If the message is large because it contains multiple attached files, either send the files in separate messages, or zip the multiple files together, and attach the single zipped file to your message.
- If your message is still too large, consider uploading the file to a Web storage site and giving your recipient a link to the site and permission to retrieve it.

My AOL recipient can't read my message or attached files

Source of the problem

When you use Microsoft Outlook to send single messages that contain multiple attached files to America Online (AOL) addresses, your recipients might not be able to read either the message or the attached files. AOL's e-mail server combines the message and all its attachments into a single file, making it difficult to view.

How to fix it

There are a couple of ways to work around the problem of getting multiple files to colleagues who use AOL.

- Send multiple separate messages to your recipient and attach a single file to each message.
- Combine all the attached files into a single compressed file (using a compression program such as WinZip), and attach the zipped (compressed) file to your message.

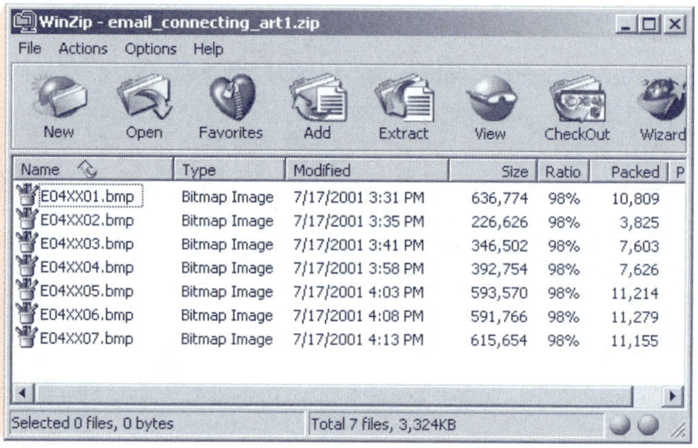

If you use the second method, you need to tell your recipients that they can open the compressed file using their own copy of WinZip. If recipients use WinZip 7.0 or earlier to access the AOL combined files, they'll need to use WinZip in Classic mode instead of using the WinZip Wizard, which won't open the combined file type in these earlier versions. WinZip 8.0 can extract compressed files from the AOL combined file type and is the preferred version when dealing with AOL files.

Tip

WinZip is a popular and widely used file compression program created by Nico Mac Computing, Inc. It can be downloaded from *www.winzip.com.*

I receive a warning when I send some attachments

Source of the problem

You want to send a file to someone as an e-mail attachment but when you click Send, a message appears telling you that the attachment is "potentially unsafe" and that recipients who use Outlook might not be able to open it.

How you handle this depends on whether your recipients are using Outlook 2002 or Outlook 2000 with the Microsoft Office 2000 SR-1 update. (Both of these versions of Outlook block the same file attachment types.) If your recipients tell you that your attachment is blocked, it's likely they are using one of these versions of Outlook, and in that case it's best to find another means of sending the file.

Tip

To learn more about the Office 2000 SR-1 update and other Office updates, visit *http://office.microsoft.com/downloads/default.aspx*

How to fix it

- Use WinZip to compress the file, and then send the zipped version as an attachment. (WinZip files are not blocked.) Go to *www.winzip.com* for more information.
- Post your file on a Web storage site and give your recipients permission to download it. Then send your recipients the file name and a link or URL to the Web storage site. This works especially well for large files, or when your recipients do not have access to (or don't want to install) a compression program to extract your file. It is also an efficient method of distributing a file to several recipients at once—you have to upload it only once, rather than sending out several copies. Some examples of Web storage sites are *www.freedrive.com*, *www.xdrive.com*, and *www.driveway.com*.

Tip

If you want to tell the recipient how to turn off the blocking on certain file types, see "I don't know how to receive files that Outlook is blocking," earlier in this book.

Do you need more than one Calendar (or other folder)?

yes → **Go to...** I need more than one Calendar, page 172.

no

Do you need to see the contents of two Outlook folders (such as Inbox and Calendar) simultaneously?

yes

no

Do you need to hide private Outlook items in a shared folder?

yes → **Go to...** Other people can see my private Outlook items, page 173.

no

Are you having trouble opening a co-worker's shared folder?

yes → **Go to...** I can't open my co-worker's folder, page 174.

no

Are you having trouble entering items in a co-worker's shared folder?

yes

Quick fix

I need to view two folders at the same time If you want to see the contents of two folders simultaneously (for example, your Inbox and Calendar, or your Inbox and Web page), you can open a separate Outlook window for a second (or even a third) folder.

1. On the View menu, click Folder List.
2. In the Folder List, right-click the folder you want to see in a second window, and then click Open In New Window on the shortcut menu.

Go to...

I can't enter items in my co-worker's folder, page 175.

If your solution isn't here, check these related chapters:

- Calendar, scheduling meetings, page 32
- Multiple users, page 204
- Outlook Bar, page 222

Or see the general trouble-shooting tips on page xvii.

I need more than one Calendar

Source of the problem

If you have a full load of work appointments and personal appointments, or you have busy schedules going for multiple work projects, your Calendar can be both full and confusing.

You can solve the confusion by creating separate Calendar folders.

How to fix it

1. If the Folder List is not visible, on the View menu, click Folder List.
2. In the Folder List, right-click the Calendar folder, and then click New Folder on the shortcut menu.
3. In the Create New Folder dialog box, in the Name box, type a name for your new Calendar.
4. Be sure the Folder Contains box reads Calendar Items. ▶
5. In the Select Where To Place The Folder list, click either the top-level folder (named Personal Folders, Outlook Today, or Mailbox) or Calendar. If you click the top-level folder, the new calendar will be on the same level as the main Calendar folder. If you click Calendar, the new calendar will be a subfolder of the main Calendar folder.
6. Click OK.

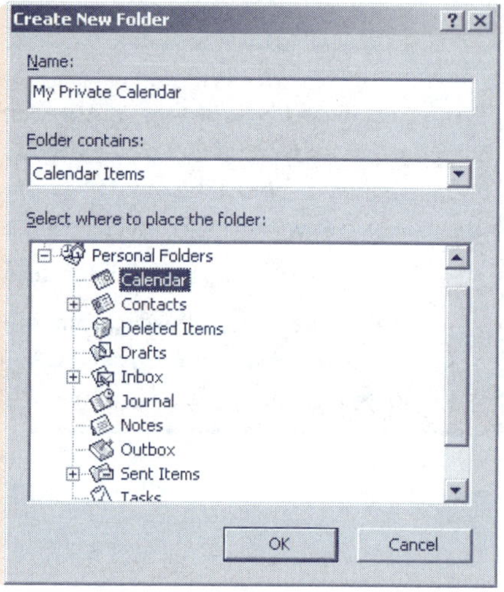

Tip

A message might appear asking if you want to add a shortcut to this folder to the Outlook Bar. (In fact, it will appear unless you've previously selected the Don't Prompt Me About This Again check box.) If you have disabled the prompt, you can always create an Outlook Bar shortcut for any existing folder by right-clicking the folder in the Folder List, and then clicking Add To Outlook Bar on the shortcut menu.

Other people can see my private Outlook items

Source of the problem

Shared Calendar and Contacts folders are very efficient in a work environment, but there are items (perhaps appointments or contacts) that you don't need to share with your co-workers.

There are two ways to keep items private: keep them in a private folder that's not shared, or mark individual items as private so that they don't appear for anyone else who opens the shared folder.

How to fix it

- Keep all your private items in a folder hidden from others, and don't make the folder a public folder. (That one was easy.)
- To keep specific items private, even if they're in a public folder, select the Private check box in the lower-right corner of the open item. Every item in the Contacts, Calendar, Tasks, and Journal folders can be marked private.

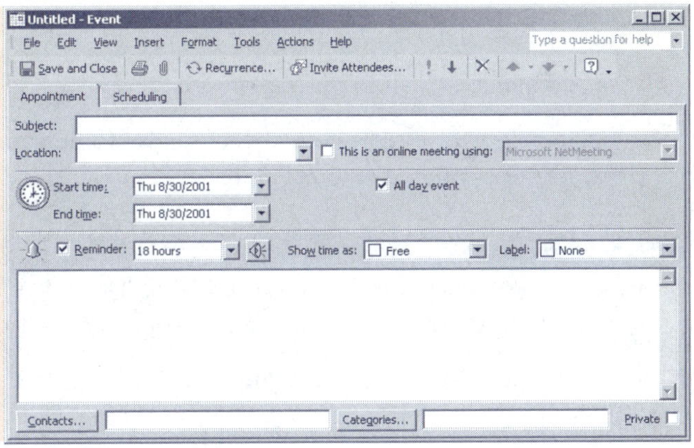

If you don't see the Private check box, drag the lower-right corner of the open item to make the item larger (until you can see the check box).

I can't open my co-worker's folder

Source of the problem

If you're using Microsoft Outlook on a network that uses Microsoft Exchange Server, you and your co-workers have the capability of sharing Outlook folders, such as the Calendar folder. Now you need to get into your co-worker's shared calendar to find some scheduling details, but you can't open it.

You need to have a chat with your co-worker. Because it's her Calendar folder, she has to give you permission to open it—and you can tell her how to do that.

Tip

This procedure must be carried out on the computer where the shared folder is stored—it can't be done from another computer. If the shared folder is on a server, ask your system administrator to change permissions for you.

How to fix it

1. If the Folder List is not visible, on the View menu, click Folder List.
2. In the Folder List, right-click the Calendar folder, and click Properties on the shortcut menu.
3. In the Properties dialog box, click the Permissions tab.
4. Be sure your name is listed in the Name list—if it's not there, click the Add button, and add your name to the list.
5. In the Name list, click your name.
6. Click the down arrow next to the Permission Level box, and then click a permission level that grants you permission to at least read items and view folders in your co-worker's Calendar folder. (Look at the options below the box as you select each role, to see which permissions apply to the role.)
7. Below the Permission Level box is a set of options and check boxes for specific activities for which you can be granted or denied permission. Be sure that (at least) the Read Items and Folder Visible check boxes are selected.
8. Click OK.

Tip

Any role *except* Contributor and None gives you permission to open the folder and read the items.

I can't enter items in my co-worker's folder

Source of the problem

You're using Outlook on a network that uses Microsoft Exchange Server, and you share your supervisor's Calendar folder so that you can schedule appointments for him. Now you need to add some appointments to your supervisor's shared calendar, but Outlook won't let you create new items. Your supervisor forgot to give you the appropriate permissions.

If your supervisor is too busy to schedule his own appointments, he's probably too busy to make the permission change. As usual, you have to do it yourself, but it's not difficult.

Tip

This procedure must be carried out on your supervisor's computer, where the shared folder is stored. If the shared folder is on a server, ask your system administrator to change permissions for you.

How to fix it

1. If the Folder List is not visible, on the View menu, click Folder List.
2. In the Folder List, right-click the Calendar folder, and click Properties on the shortcut menu.
3. In the Properties dialog box, click the Permissions tab.
4. In the Name list, click your name.
5. In the Permission Level box, click a permission level that grants you permission to at least read items and files in your supervisor's Calendar folder. (Look at the options below the box as you select each role, to see which permissions apply to the role.)
6. Below the Permission Level box is a set of options and check boxes for specific activities for which you can be granted or denied permission. Be sure that (at least) the Create Items and Folder Visible check boxes are selected.
7. Click OK.

Tip

Any role *except* Reviewer and None gives you permission to open the folder and create new items.

Can you find the Bcc field in your message?

yes

When you send a message to several people, do you want recipients to see only their own names?

yes

no

When you send a message to a group, do you want recipients to see only the group name?

yes

no

Quick fix

I don't see a Bcc field in my new message If the Bcc field isn't displayed in the message below the Cc field, on the View menu, click Bcc Field. If you are using Word as the editor for Outlook, turn off Word as editor, display the Bcc field in a new message, then turn on Word as the editor again.

Hidden names

Go to...
Some of my recipients want their identities hidden, page 178.

Go to...
I don't know how to send a message to a group name, page 179.

If your solution isn't here, check this related chapter:

- E-mail, addressing messages, page 72

Or see the general troubleshooting tips on page xvii.

Some of my recipients want their identities hidden

Source of the problem

When you send a message to a large group of people (or a distribution list), each recipient sees a long list of all the recipient names in the To or Cc field. The long list of names is often annoying to a recipient, and some of those recipients might not want their names and e-mail addresses broadcast to the whole list. So how can you send a message to the whole group while keeping the list of addressees confidential?

Tip

Bcc means *blind courtesy* (or *carbon*) *copy*. Addresses in the Bcc field are hidden from everyone in the To and Cc fields who receives the message, so the To and Cc recipients are *blind* to the Bcc recipients.

How to fix it

To hide names and addresses of message recipients, use the Bcc field. Any recipient names in the Bcc field are hidden from all recipients.

1. Open a new message.
2. If you don't see the Bcc field below the Cc field, on the View menu, click Bcc Field.
3. In the Bcc field, enter all the names and distribution lists that you don't want to display. You don't need to enter any name in the To field—if you leave the To field empty, some recipients will see *your* name there and some will see *their* name there, depending on their mail system.
4. Compose and send your message.

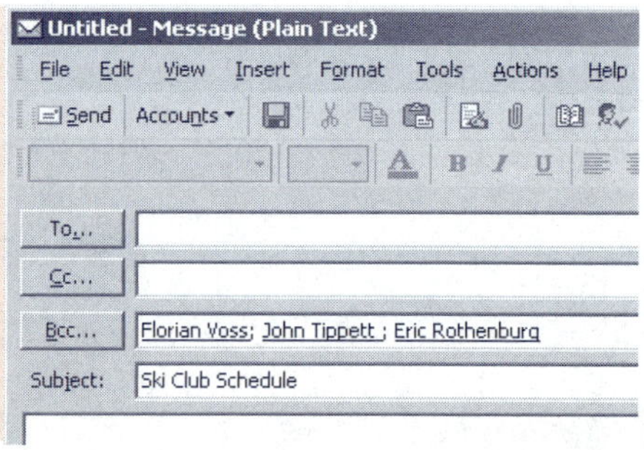

Tip

The Bcc field option appears only if you are not using Word as your editor. To disable Word as the editor, on the Tools menu, click Options. In the Options dialog box, click the Mail Format tab, clear the Use Microsoft Word To Edit E-mail Messages check box, and click OK. Then enable the Bcc field, and enable Word as editor again.

Tip

Any names in the To and Cc fields are visible to all recipients.

I don't know how to send a message to a group name

Source of the problem

You need to send a message to all the members of your ski club (The Mogul Maniacs), and you want each recipient to know that this is a message to the entire Mogul Maniacs club. But if you send blind copies to the members, the e-mail message appears to be addressed to each individual instead of the whole club. How can you send a message that's addressed to The Mogul Maniacs?

How to fix it

Send the message to a group name (that has your own e-mail address), and put all the recipient names in the Bcc field. Everyone will receive the message addressed from you to the group name.

1. Create a new contact.
2. Put the group name in the Company field and your e-mail address in the E-mail field. Don't put any other information in the new contact. ▶

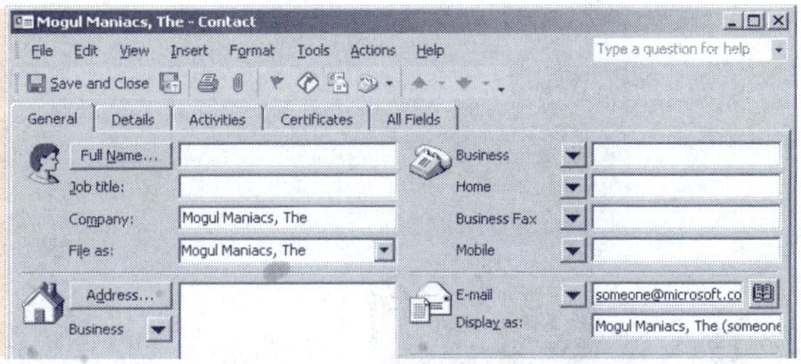

3. Click the Save And Close button to save and close the new contact.
4. Create a new message, and address it to the new contact (the name from the Company field) in the To field.
5. Place all the recipient and/or distribution list names in the Bcc field, separated by semicolons. ▶
6. Compose and send the message.

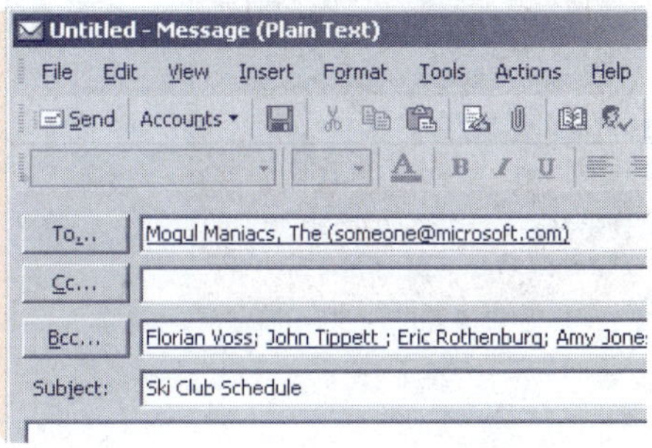

Hype

Is your hyperlink blue and underlined?

yes

no

Did you punctuate the hyperlink correctly?

yes

Are you using Word as your Outlook e-mail editor?

yes

Does your hyperlink start with *www*?

no

no

no

Quick fix

I don't know if I punctuated my hyperlink correctly Hyperlinks are punctuated with periods and forward slashes (/). Be sure you haven't inadvertently typed a comma or a backslash in the hyperlink.

Go to...

My Outlook automatic hyperlinks don't work, page 183.

Go to...

My hyperlink doesn't start with *www*, page 182.

Did your recipient receive your hyperlink as an active link?

yes

Does clicking the hyperlink launch your recipient's browser?

yes

Quick fix

The hyperlink I sent is not working If your recipient has active scripts disabled on his or her computer as a security measure, Web pages that depend on active scripting to function will open mostly or entirely blank.

See the "E-mail, viruses" chapter to learn more about disabling and enabling active scripting (and tell your recipient about it, too).

no (Does clicking the hyperlink launch your recipient's browser?)

Quick fix

My hyperlink doesn't launch a browser when clicked Your recipient's browser might not support the hyperlink protocol. Recipients of your message must have an Internet browser that supports the hyperlink protocol (such as Microsoft Internet Explorer) installed on their computer.

no (Did your recipient receive your hyperlink as an active link?)

Quick fix

My recipient received a hyperlink that is inactive Your recipient's e-mail program might not support hyperlinks. If it doesn't, he or she can still copy and paste the inactive link into the browser's address box.

If your solution isn't here, **check these related chapters:**

- E-mail, creating, page 88
- E-mail, recipients, page 116

Or see the general troubleshooting tips on page xvii.

My hyperlink doesn't start with *www*

Source of the problem

If you type a URL (universal resource locator, or Web site address) that begins with *www* in an Outlook message, the URL is formatted as a live hyperlink. More and more Web sites have URLs that don't begin with *www*, however, and lots of Internet addresses are not Web sites, which means they don't have *www* prefixes, either. So how do you get Outlook's e-mail editor to turn the URL into a live hyperlink?

How to fix it

First, try typing the entire Internet address in the message, especially if there's no *www* at the start of the address. Outlook adds a hidden *http://* prefix when you type the *www* part of a URL, but if there's no *www* prefix, you need to type the URL beginning with *http://* so that Outlook recognizes and formats it as a link.

Also, if the URL is not a Web site (for example, if it is a gopher, news, or ftp site), you need to include the *gopher://*, *news:*, or *ftp://* prefix and punctuation when typing the URL.

Tip

After you finish typing the hyperlink, you can switch the message format back to Plain Text or Rich Text without losing the hyperlink formatting.

If you're creating a message in HTML format, you can insert a hyperlink. The method for doing this depends on whether you are using Word as your e-mail editor. If you're not, you can insert a hyperlink by choosing from a list of prefixes:

1. Make sure the message is in HTML format, and click the body of the message where you want to place the URL.
2. On the Message form's Insert menu, click Hyperlink.
3. In the Hyperlink dialog box, click the down arrow next to the Type box, and click a prefix for the URL in the drop-down list. ▶
4. Click in the URL box, on the right side of the prefix, and type the remainder of the URL.
5. In the Hyperlink dialog box, click OK to insert the hyperlink in the message.

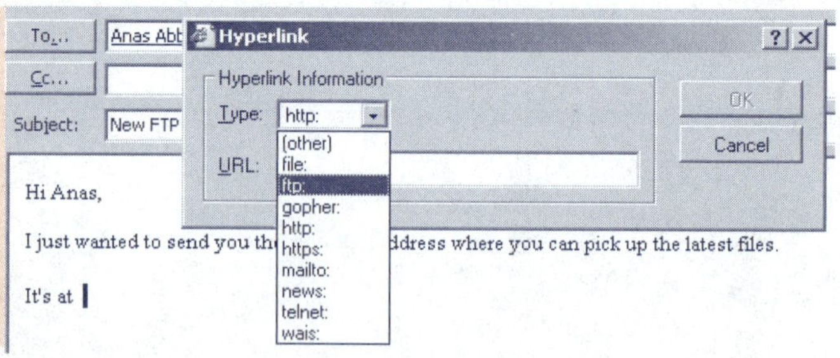

My Outlook automatic hyperlinks don't work

Source of the problem

If you're using Outlook with Word as your e-mail editor (so that your messages can be formatted with bullets and other Word formatting) and your automatic hyperlink formatting isn't working, it's probably been turned off. When you use Word as your Outlook e-mail editor, you can turn the automatic hyperlink formatting on or off; but if you don't use Word as your e-mail editor, hyperlinks are always formatted as live links (blue and underlined).

How to fix it

One way to solve the problem is to turn off Word as your Outlook e-mail editor. (On the Tools menu, click Options. In the Options dialog box, click the Mail Format tab, clear the Use Microsoft Word To Edit E-mail Messages check box, and then click OK.)

If you want to continue using the Word e-mail editor, you can turn the automatic hyperlink formatting back on.

1. Open a new e-mail message.
2. Click in the body of the message to place the insertion point there.
3. On the Message form's Tools menu, click AutoCorrect Options.
4. In the AutoCorrect In Email dialog box, click the AutoFormat As You Type tab, and then select the Internet And Network Paths With Hyperlinks check box.
5. Click OK.

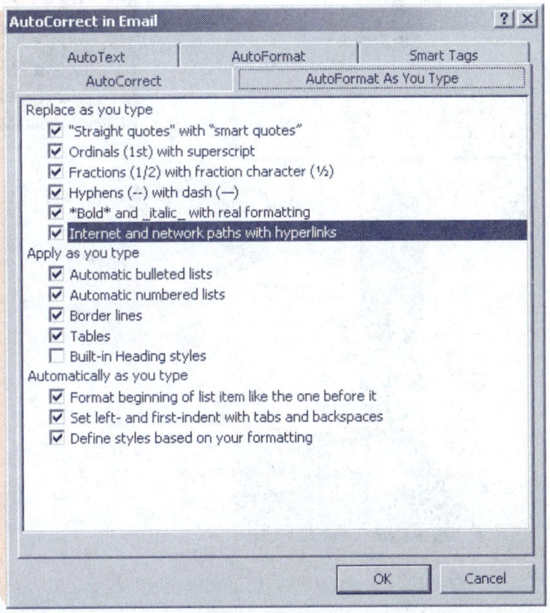

Tip

When using the Word e-mail editor with the option to automatically format hyperlinks selected, you can easily unformat an address you've just typed by clicking Undo AutoFormat on the message form's Edit menu.

Impor

Are you having a problem exporting data out of Outlook?

yes

no

Is the data you imported into Outlook missing some fields?

yes

no

Is your imported data correct?

no

Go to...
My imported data is wrong, page 188.

Quick fix

The data I imported from another program is missing fields If you imported data from another program and some of the fields didn't get imported, you need to "map" your imported fields to match Outlook's field names:

1. In the last page of the Import Wizard, click the Map Custom Fields button. In the Map Custom Fields dialog box, the existing field names are in the list on the left, and the Outlook field names are listed on the right.
2. Click the small plus symbols in the list on the right to expand the Name group, the Home Address group, and so forth.
3. Drag each existing field name from the left to the corresponding Outlook field name on the right.

Are you trying to export custom fields in Outlook to Access or Excel?

yes

Go to...
I can't export custom fields to an Access database, page 186.

If your solution isn't here, check these related chapters:

- E-mail, importing addresses, page 98
- Contacts, general, page 48
- Contacts, custom data, page 38

Or see the general trouble-shooting tips on page xvii.

I can't export custom fields to an Access database

Source of the problem

You've created custom fields in the Tasks folder (or any Microsoft Outlook folder), and you want to export all the fields in that folder, including the custom fields, to a Microsoft Access database. But when you export Outlook items, the Export Wizard exports only Outlook's built-in fields.

How to fix it

The trick is to use Microsoft Excel as an intermediate translator between Outlook and Access. Export your custom fields from Outlook to Excel without using the Export Wizard, and all your fields, including the custom fields, will be exported.

1. Switch the Outlook folder (in this example, a subfolder of the Contacts folder) to a table view, and display all the fields you want to send to the Access database (including your custom fields—in this example, Employee ID).
2. Start Excel, and resize both the Excel and Outlook windows so that they are side-by-side or overlapping a little. ▶

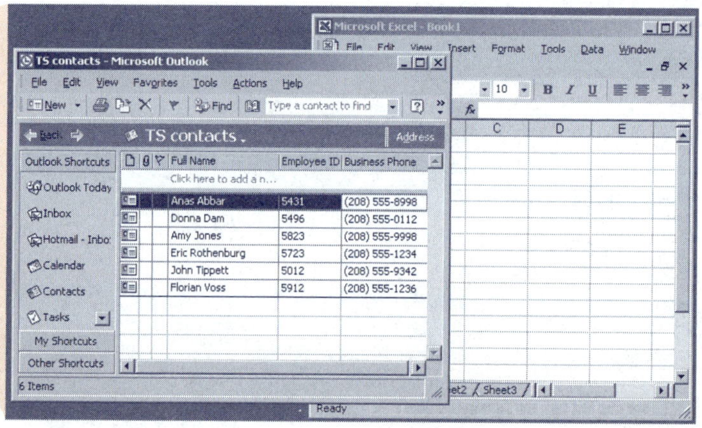

3. In Outlook, select all the records you want to send to Access. (Drag down the left side of the table to select them all, or use the Ctrl or Shift key and click to select specific records.)

4. In Outlook, point to the border of the selected records, and drag the selection into the Excel window. (You'll see a "move" mouse pointer icon when the mouse moves into the Excel window.) ▶

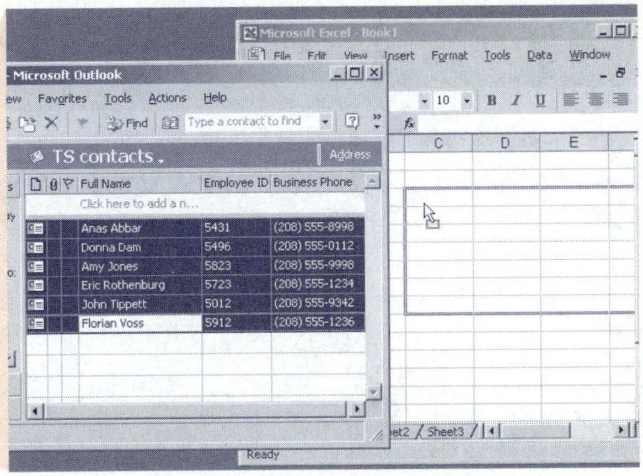

5. Before you drop the selected records in Excel, hold down the Ctrl key while you release the mouse button. This drops a copy of the records. ▶

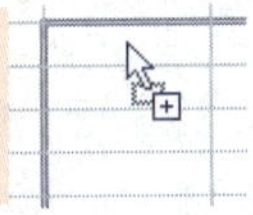

6. Now the records, including your custom fields, are in an Excel table. Use any Access import procedure to import the Excel table into Access. (You can drag the selected Excel table into the Table pane of an Access database to create a fast Access table.) ▶

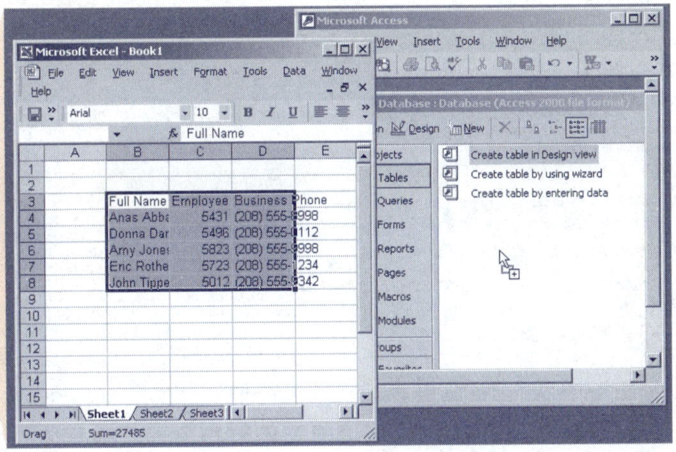

My imported data is wrong

Source of the problem

You imported a contacts list from Excel, and some of the phone numbers were imported incorrectly. (They appear in Outlook with extra characters in them.) It's a long list with lots of phone numbers, and you don't want to have to go through and correct them one by one. How can you import an Excel list into Outlook with all its data intact and correct?

How to fix it

The most important part of importing correct Excel data is setting up the Excel worksheet properly before you begin the import process. You need to format all the phone number and ZIP code columns as text.

1. In the Excel worksheet, click the column heading for any column that contains phone numbers or ZIP codes to select the entire column.
2. On the Format menu, click Cells.
3. In the Format Cells dialog box, on the Number tab, click Text in the Category list.
4. Click OK.
5. Save and close the Excel Workbook.
6. In Outlook, import the Excel file.

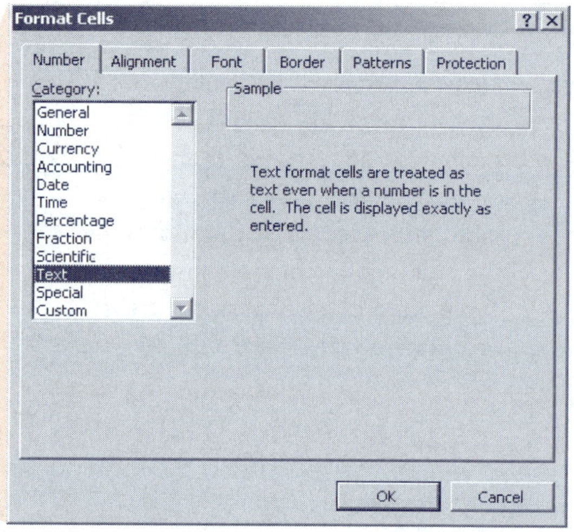

More about pre-import formatting in Excel

The correct formatting for Excel data that's not going to be used in calculations (for example, ZIP codes and phone numbers) is text. Excel has special formats to make data entry in worksheets more efficient, but those special formats might not translate properly when you export the Excel data to another program. Before you export Excel data to any other program (including Outlook), it's a good idea to go through the worksheet and reformat the columns as either text or numbers so that the data is exported with the simplest possible formatting.

Although this solution describes Excel in particular, proper pre-import formatting is important in any program from which you import data into Outlook.

ting and exporting

Can you find the Mail Merge command on the Tools menu?

yes

Can you do a mail merge for a selected group of contacts?

yes

no

Go to...

When I do a mail merge, all my contacts are included, page 192.

no

Quick fix

The Mail Merge command is missing You won't see the Mail Merge command on the Tools menu unless you have Contacts or a Contacts subfolder displayed in Outlook.

Also, if your menus are set to hide seldom-used commands, the Mail Merge command might be hidden until you display the full menu. If there's a down-pointing chevron at the bottom of your menu, click the chevron to display all the commands on the menu.

Mail merge

Do you need to use Outlook contacts for a mail-merge operation in Microsoft Access?

yes

Go to...

I don't know how to do an Access mail merge using my Outlook contacts, page 194.

no

Do you need to use Outlook contacts for a mail-merge operation in a program other than Microsoft Word?

yes

Go to...

I don't know how to mail merge my Outlook contacts in a non-Word program, page 193.

If your solution isn't here, check this related chapter:

- Importing and exporting, page 184

Or see the general troubleshooting tips on page xvii.

When I do a mail merge, all my contacts are included

Source of the problem

You need to send a form letter to a select group of your contacts, but when you do a mail merge, all your contacts are included. You need to tell Microsoft Outlook which contacts you want to include in the merge.

How to fix it

If there's a common criterion among your select group of contacts, you can do a mail merge to the group by filtering the contacts list before you run the merge. You can also select specific contacts manually. (Click the first contact, and then click the rest while you hold down the Ctrl key.)

1. Select the contacts, either by clicking or with a filter. ▶
   If you filter your Contacts view, only the contacts displayed in the filtered view are included in the mail merge. If you manually select the contacts you want, whether the view is filtered or not, only the selected contacts are included in the mail merge.

2. On the Tools menu, click Mail Merge.
3. If you used a filter to display the contacts you want, in the Mail Merge Contacts dialog box, select the All Contacts In Current View option.
4. If you manually selected the contacts you want, select the Only Selected Contacts option. ▶

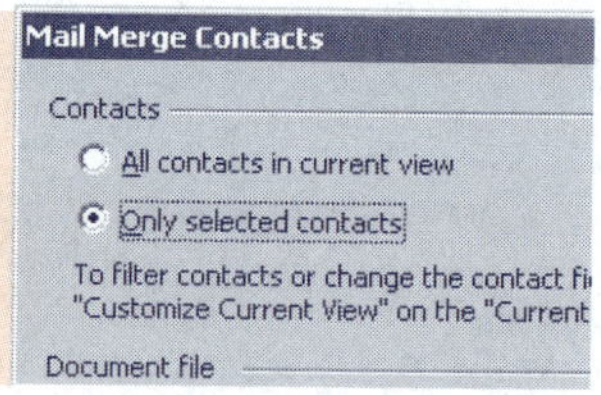

5. In the Document File area, specify the location of the document you want to merge, and then click OK to merge the document and the select list.

Tip

To learn what each option in the dialog box does, right-click the option label to see a brief explanation.

I don't know how to mail merge my Outlook contacts in a non-Word program

Source of the problem

You keep all your contact information in Outlook, but you don't have Microsoft Word installed on your computer. How can you do a mail merge in another word-processing program, using your Outlook contacts as the data source?

Tip

If you need only a select group of contacts for your mail merge operation, make the process easier by exporting only those contacts to the intermediary text file. Create a new Contacts subfolder, and copy the contacts you want to export into the subfolder. Then, export that subfolder to the text file.

How to fix it

You can use an intermediary data file that can be opened and used by both Outlook and your word-processing program.

1. Check your word-processing program to see which file types it can open or use as a data source. (Most programs can read a Comma Separated Values text file.)
2. Export your Outlook Contacts folder to a text file of that type. For example, if your word-processing program can use a Comma Separated Values text file, click Comma Separated Values (Windows) on the second page of the Export Wizard.

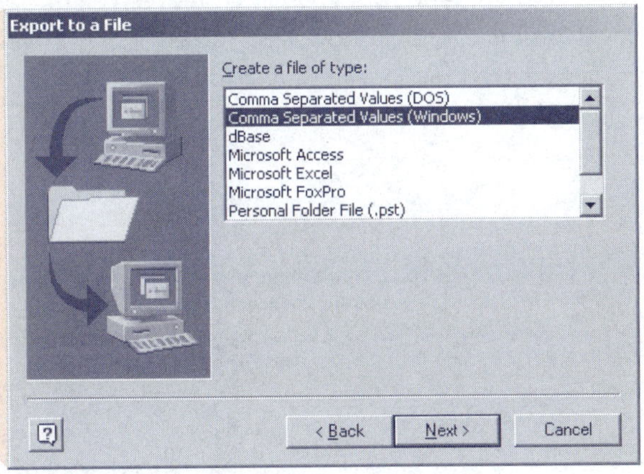

3. Run your mail merge procedure in the word-processing program, using the text file you exported from your Outlook Contacts folder as the data source.

I don't know how to do an Access mail merge using my Outlook contacts

Source of the problem

You use Microsoft Access to create mailing labels, and you need to create mailing labels from your Outlook contacts. But you don't know how to get Access to use contacts from Outlook as a data source for your mailing labels report. Not a problem—Access can use Outlook's current contact data if you set up the Contacts folder or subfolder as a table in the Access database.

How to fix it

1. In your Access database, with the Tables pane open, click the New button in the Database window.
2. In the New Table dialog box, double-click Link Table.
3. In the Link dialog box, click the down arrow to the right of the Files Of Type box, and click Outlook in the drop-down list to display the Link Exchange/Outlook Wizard.

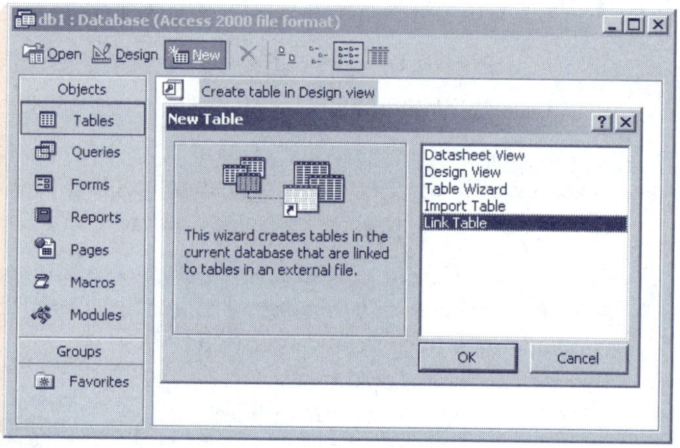

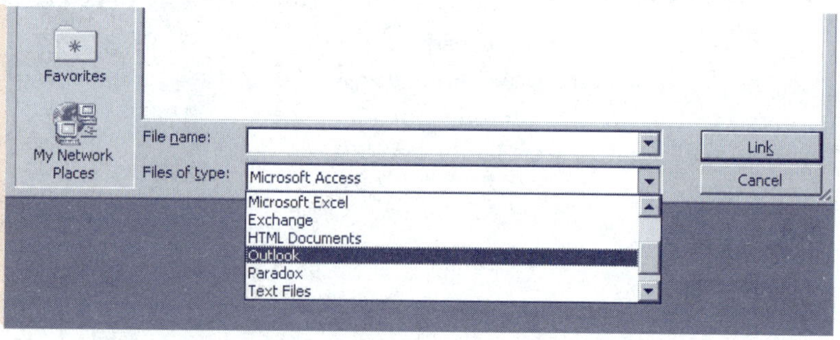

4. In the Link Exchange/Outlook Wizard, click the small plus symbol next to Personal Folders (or, if you're using Microsoft Exchange Server, click the plus symbol next to Mailbox – *username*, where *username* is your mailbox name). ▶

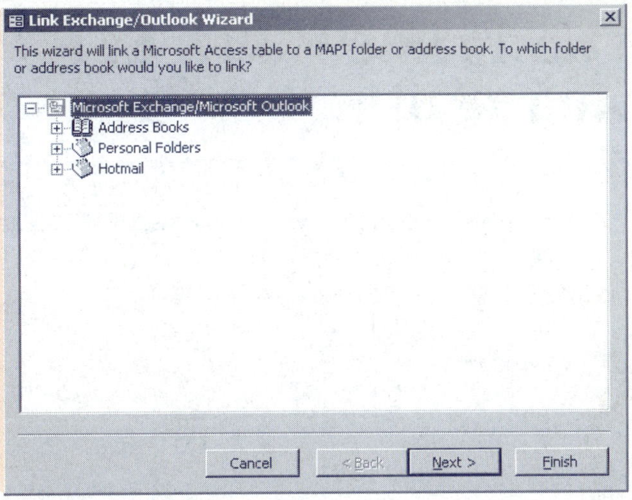

5. If there is a small plus symbol next to Contacts, click it to open a list of your Contacts subfolders.
6. Click the Contacts folder or subfolder you want to use for a linked Access table, and then click Next. ▶

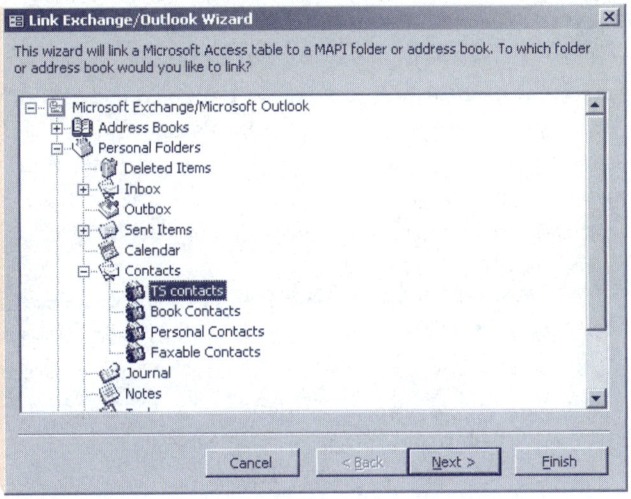

7. On the last page of the Link Exchange/Outlook Wizard, click Finish, and when the wizard tells you it's finished, click OK.

   A new linked table is created in your Access database.

8. In the Access Database window, click Reports, and then click the New button.

This solution is continued on the next page.

I don't know how to do an Access mail merge using my Outlook contacts

(continued from page 195)

9. In the New Report dialog box, click Label Wizard, click the down arrow next to the Choose The Table Or Query Where The Object's Data Comes From box, and then click the linked table name in the drop-down list. ▶

10. Click OK, and then follow the steps in the Label Wizard to create your Access mailing labels report.

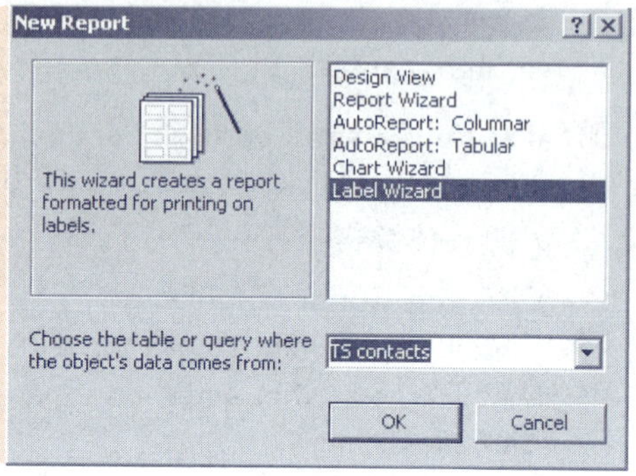

More about using Outlook data in an Access database

You can import or link to your Outlook Contacts folder to create a new Access table. Linking the Access table to the Outlook source is a good idea if the Outlook data is likely to change (as contacts often do), because then the data for your Access labels will always be current. The alternative—importing the Outlook data—creates a static table in Access that doesn't change when your Outlook contacts data changes. This means you must run a fresh import every time you want to print current mailing labels.

When you link to your Outlook data, not only does the linked Access table always have current data, but also your Access mailing labels are always ready to print. If you save the Mailing Labels report in your Access database, the finished report uses linked, current data. To print a current mailing labels report in Access—anytime—right-click the name of the report, and click Print on the shortcut menu.

Mail merge

Are some of your items (contacts, messages, and the like) missing?

yes

Do you know whether AutoArchiving is turned on?

yes

no

Quick fix

I'm not sure whether AutoArchiving is turned on If AutoArchiving is turned on, the item you're looking for might have been archived, in which case you should look for your items in the Archive Folders folder that appears in the Folder List, as described in "Some of my Outlook items are missing" (page 200). You can easily check whether AutoArchive is turned on.

1. On the Tools menu, click Options.
2. In the Options dialog box, on the Other tab, click the AutoArchive button.
3. In the AutoArchive dialog box, if the Run AutoArchive Every check box is selected, AutoArchive is turned on (the Days box tells you how often your items are AutoArchived).

You can also see whether AutoArchive is turned on in a specific folder.

1. Right-click that folder's icon in either the Outlook Bar or the Folder List.
2. Click Properties on the shortcut menu.
3. In that folder's Properties dialog box, on the AutoArchive tab, if the Do Not Archive Items In This Folder option is selected, AutoArchive is turned off in that folder.

Missing items

Are you unable to find an e-mail message you sent or received?

yes

Go to...
I can't find an e-mail message, page 203.

no

Go to...
Some of my Outlook items are missing, page 200.

If your solution isn't here, check this related chapter:

- Backing up and moving data, page 2

Or see the general troubleshooting tips on page xvii.

Some of my Outlook items are missing

Source of the problem

You've opened your Contacts folder to look up an associate's telephone number, and the contact you're looking for isn't there. Or perhaps you're looking for an e-mail message you received some months ago, and you can't find it. You're sure you didn't delete the item. There must be another reason why it's hidden—perhaps you're looking in the wrong folder, or you're searching in a view that has a filter applied, or you've archived the item.

How to fix it

First make sure you're looking in the correct folder. For example, you might have moved the item you need into a subfolder. Next make sure you're looking at a view that's not filtered. Then check the Archive folder. Finally, if you still haven't found the item, search everything using Find.

Check all your subfolders

1. On the View menu, click Folder List.
2. If any folders in the Folder List have small plus signs next to them, click the small plus signs to display subfolders.
3. Search each of the subfolders that contain the type of item you're looking for. (For example, if you're looking for a contact, search every subfolder of the Contacts folder.)

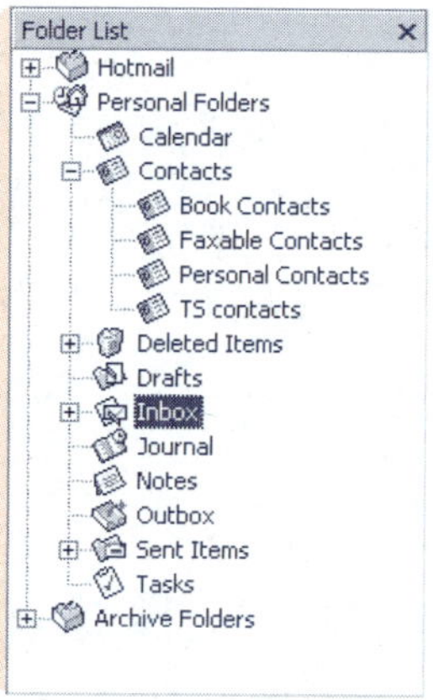

Check your view for filters

1. Look at the lower-left corner of the Outlook window. If you see the message "Filter applied," the filter applied to the current view might be hiding the item you're looking for.
2. To switch views, on the View menu, point to Current View, and click a different (unfiltered) view name.

3. To remove filters from the current view, on the View menu, point to Current View, and then click the Customize Current View option.
4. In the View Summary dialog box, look at the label next to the Filter button. The label tells you whether a filter is applied. ▶
5. If a filter is applied, click the Filter button.
6. In the lower-right corner of the Filter dialog box, click the Clear All button.
7. Click OK to close each dialog box.

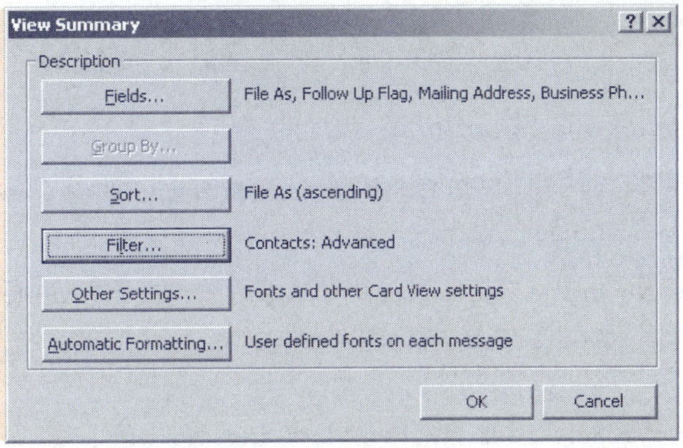

Tip

If you still can't find the item, search your backup files—even if you've deleted the item, you might have backed it up.

Check your archive files

If the Archive Folders folder appears in your Folder List and you haven't yet checked all the subfolders in Archive Folders, do that now by opening and examining each subfolder.

The Archive Folders folder automatically appears in your Folder List after you perform the first archive operation. If you know you have an Archive Folders folder but it doesn't currently appear there, you must have closed it. The fastest way to get it to reappear in the Folder List is to perform a manual archive. On the File menu, click Archive, select any folder (use an empty folder like Drafts if you don't really want to archive now), and click OK.

Search all folders using Find

1. Click a subfolder of Personal Folders, such as Inbox.
2. On the toolbar, click Find.
3. In the Look For box on the Find Bar, type some text that you know the item contains (for example, an e-mail address, part of a subject line, or a contact name).

Tip

If you're looking for an e-mail message, select an e-mail folder option, such as All Mail Folders, in the Search In drop-down list. See "I can't find an e-mail message" on page 203 for these steps.

This solution is continued on the next page.

Some of my Outlook items are missing

(continued from page 201)

4. On the Find Bar, click Search In, and click Choose Folders in the drop-down list.
5. In the Select Folder dialog box, select a top-level folder to search (such as Personal Folders or Archive Folders).
6. Select Search Subfolders, and click OK.
7. Click Find Now.
8. Repeat this procedure for every top-level folder in your Folder List. (You can select only one at a time.)

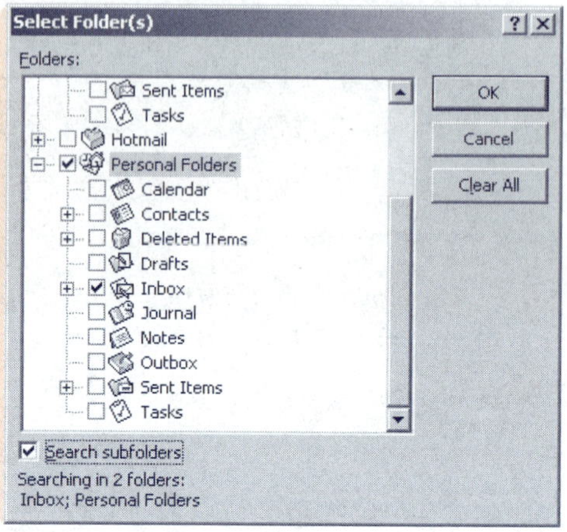

I can't find an e-mail message

Source of the problem

You've sent an e-mail message to, or received a message from, one of your contacts, and now you can't find it. One of the fastest ways to look for e-mail messages in Outlook is to use the Find tool, which looks for messages of the type displayed in the current folder.

How to fix it

1. In the Folder List, click Inbox (or whatever folder you want to search).
2. On the toolbar, click the Find button to display the Find Bar.
3. In the Look For box, type the name of the contact as it would appear in an e-mail message.
4. If you don't want to search only the current folder, click the down arrow to the right of the Search In box, and click the location you want to search in the drop down list. If you're not sure, click All Mail Folders.

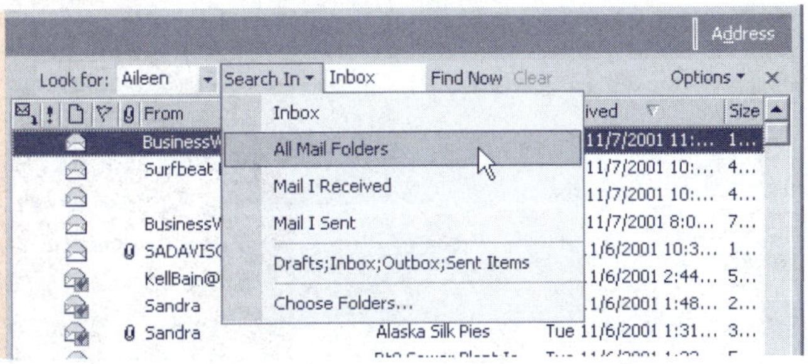

5. To search only the address and subject lines of messages, on the Find Bar, click Options, and clear the Search All Text In Each Message check box.
6. Click Find Now to perform the search. The search results will be displayed in the current folder.
7. To redisplay all the current folder contents, click Clear to clear the results of the search.

Tip

By default, you will search only the current folder and not any of its subfolders.

More about finding e-mail

A fast way to find all the e-mail messages associated with a contact is to open that contact's form, click the Activities tab, click the down arrow to the right of the Show box, and click E-mail in the drop-down list. Outlook then displays all the e-mail in every folder associated with that contact. To sort these messages by folder, click the In Folder heading.

Do you need to set up a second e-mail address in Outlook?

yes

Are the people sharing the existing Internet account also sharing the same Windows account?

yes

no

Quick fix

I want to add a second e-mail address to an existing ISP account outside my Windows profile If you want to add a second e-mail address to your ISP account, but the person who will use the new e-mail address logs on to Windows as a separate user, have them set up Outlook as a new user with the second e-mail address. Because the two of you are not sharing a single Windows account, Outlook will present wizards to walk the the new user through the steps of setting up a new e-mail account.

Multiple users

Go to...
I don't know how to set up additional e-mail addresses in my Internet account, page 206.

If your solution isn't here, see the general trouble-shooting tips on page xvii.

I don't know how to set up additional e-mail addresses in my Internet account

Source of the problem

Your family members all use the same computer, and each person needs a separate, password-protected e-mail address. Your Internet service provider (ISP) allows a single Internet account to have multiple e-mail addresses, but how do you set that up?

Tip

If you're adding an additional e-mail address to an existing ISP account, it's a good idea to write down your account information before you start. To view your e-mail settings, on the Tools menu, click E-mail Accounts. On the first page of the E-mail Accounts Wizard, click Next, and then click Change. After you've written down the settings, click Cancel.

How to fix it

Each user can log on to a separate Windows account, start Outlook, and follow the wizard to set up his or her own e-mail account. See "Create a new windows 2000 user account" later in this solution if you're not sure how to create separate user accounts in Windows 2000, and then see "Set up a new e-mail account" for further detailed steps.

If you don't currently log on to Windows (if it just appears without a logon prompt) and several users share the same account on your computer, you can still create separate Outlook profiles so that each user has a separate Personal Folders file (*outlook.pst*) and accesses only his or her own e-mail. This technique, described here for Windows 2000, also works with other versions of Windows, and the steps are basically the same.

To set up a new Outlook profile

1. Close Outlook.
2. Click the Windows Start button, point to Settings, and click Control Panel.
3. In the Control Panel window, double-click the Mail icon.
4. In the Mail Setup dialog box for this account, click Show Profiles.
5. In the Mail dialog box, select the Prompt For A Profile To Be Used option.
6. Click Add. ▶

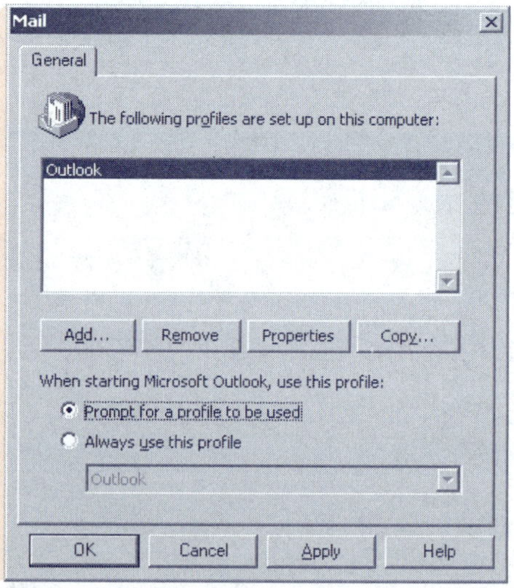

7. In the New Profile dialog box, type the profile name (for example, the name of the person using this profile), and click OK.

8. On the first page of the E-mail Accounts Wizard, the Add A New E-mail Account check box is selected by default, so click Next.

9. Select the server type for this account. If the additional users are using the same ISP as the original account, use the same server type as that account—POP3 or IMAP for Internet users. Click Next.

10. Type the user information (name and e-mail address), logon information (your ISP user name and password if you're sharing an ISP connection), and server information. If your ISP requires it (MSN does, for example), select the Log On Using Secure Password Authentication (SPA) check box.

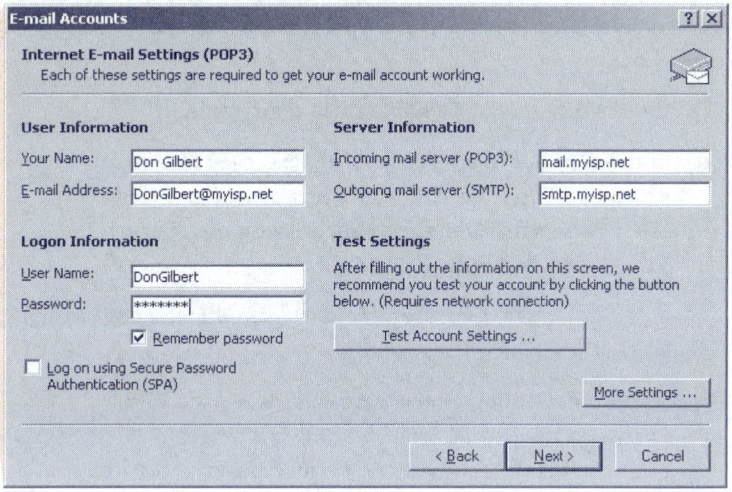

11. If you're setting up a POP3 account, click Test Account Settings to make sure the information you entered is correct. Otherwise skip to step 13. If there are no errors in the Test Settings dialog box, click Close.

12. If there are errors in the Test Settings dialog box, re-enter the information, and click Test Account Settings again; otherwise, click Next, and then click Finish.

13. Click OK to close the Mail dialog box.

Now, each person who opens Outlook will be prompted with a Choose Profile dialog box so that he or she can choose the individual profile you've set up and privately display the e-mail and other Outlook data associated with that profile.

This solution is continued on the next page.

I don't know how to set up additional e-mail addresses in my Internet account

(continued from page 207)

Add Personal Folders file security

All users should enable password-protection for their Personal Folders file. By protecting your Personal Folders file with a password, you protect your Outlook profile at the same time, because Outlook requires a password to open a profile that's associated with a password-protected Personal Folders file. This keeps other users of your computer from inadvertently opening your profile and viewing your e-mail.

1. On the File menu, click Data File Management.
2. In the Outlook Data Files dialog box, click Settings. If this data file is already password-protected, you'll see a Personal Folders password dialog box. Enter a password, and click OK to continue.
3. If you don't see a Personal Folders password dialog box, click Change Password.
4. If you are creating a new password, leave the Old Password box blank, type the new password in both the New Password and Verify Password boxes, and click OK.
5. Click OK, and then click Close to close each open dialog box.

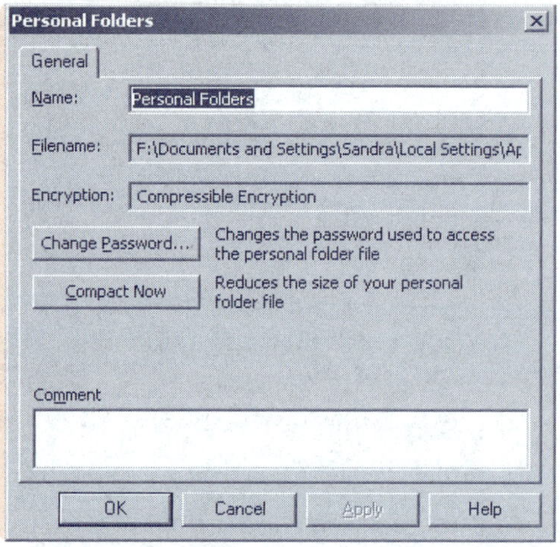

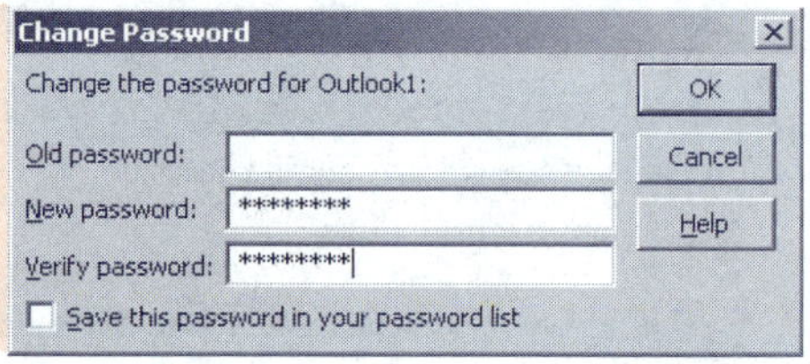

Tip

Do not select the Save This Password In Your Password List check box when you're setting this up, or when you're prompted for a password to open a profile. If you do, everyone using your account will have access to this profile without knowing the password.

Create a new Windows 2000 user account

If you're sharing a computer with other users, it's usually best to create a separate Windows account for each one, so each user's Outlook data—as well as everything else—is kept separate and private. If you originally installed Outlook while logged on to an account that has Administrator privileges (such as your default account), Outlook will be automatically available to other accounts and all users will be able to set up their own e-mail accounts the first time they run Outlook while logged on to their Windows 2000 account.

> **Note**
> If your computer is connected to a domain network, ask your administrator for help in creating new Windows accounts.

1. Log on to Windows 2000 as Administrator. If you don't log on to Windows now, you already have Administrator privileges.
2. Click the Windows Start button, point to Settings, and click Control Panel.
3. Double-click the Users And Passwords icon.
4. If you don't currently log on to Windows (if it just appears without a logon prompt), in the Users And Passwords dialog box, select the Users Must Enter A User Name And Password To Use This Computer check box. ▶

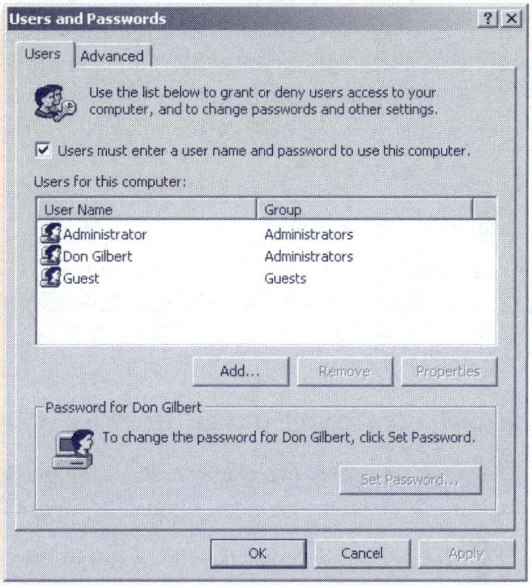

5. Click the Add Button.
6. In the Add New User Wizard, type the user name for the new account (the name that will be used to log on to Windows), the new user's full name (for administrative purposes only), and any description you care to provide, and then click Next. ▶

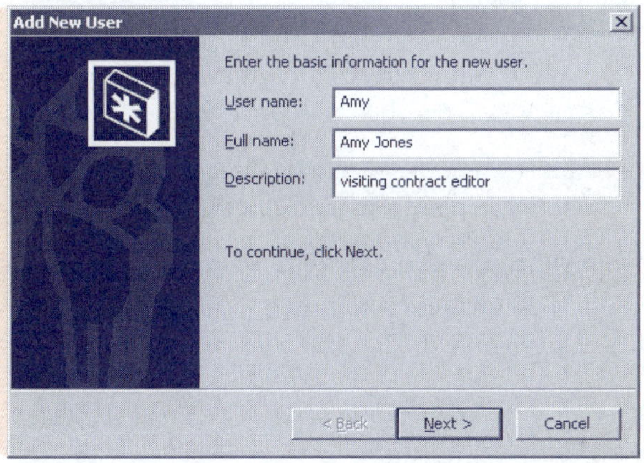

7. Type the password for this account in both the Password and Confirm boxes, and click Next.

This solution is continued on the next page.

I don't know how to set up additional e-mail addresses in my Internet account

(continued from page 209)

8. Select the user level appropriate for the new account. The Standard User option is sufficient for ensuring privacy of Outlook files. (The Restricted User option might not allow users to add Outlook or Office components that they need, and Administrator privileges are usually granted to only one user on the system.)

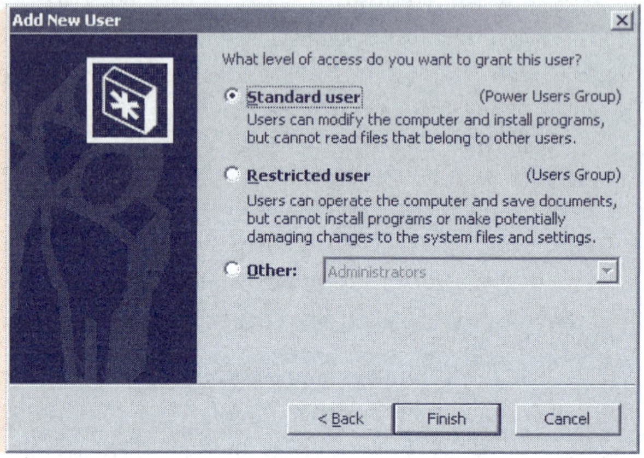

9. Click Finish.
10. Click Close to close the User Settings dialog box, and then close the Control Panel.

Set up a new e-mail account

1. Quit any open programs, and then log off Windows by clicking the Windows Start button, clicking Shut Down, selecting Log Off <username>, and clicking OK.
2. Start Windows again, and log on with the new user name. In the Enter Network Password dialog box, type the new user's name and password, and click OK.
3. In the Getting Started With Windows 2000 window, click Exit.
4. Start Outlook. Microsoft Office XP will run its installation setup at this point but requires no input from you.
5. When the Outlook 2002 Startup Wizard starts, click Next twice.

Tip

Consult Windows Help to learn how to set up a new account if you are using a Windows operating system other than Windows 2000 Professional. In all Windows operating systems, creating a new Windows account and running Outlook in that account creates a separate Personal Folders (*outlook.pst*) file.

6. Select the server type for this account. If the new user is using a separate e-mail address with the same ISP account you use, select the same server type you use—typically POP3 or IMAP for Internet users. Click Next. ▶

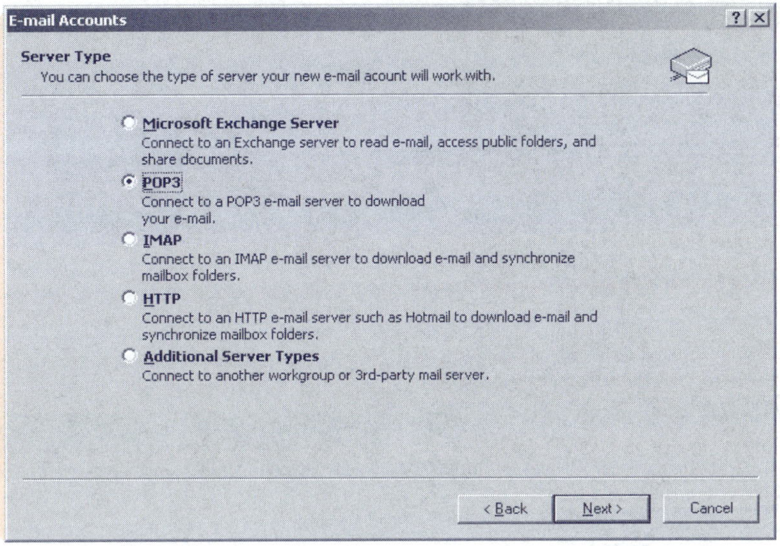

7. Type the user information (name and e-mail address), logon information (your ISP user name and password if the ISP connection is shared), and server information. If your ISP requires it, select the Log On Using Secure Password Authentication (SPA) check box.

8. Click Test Account Settings to make sure the information you entered is correct. If there are no errors in the Test Account Settings dialog box, click Close to close the Test Settings dialog box. ▶

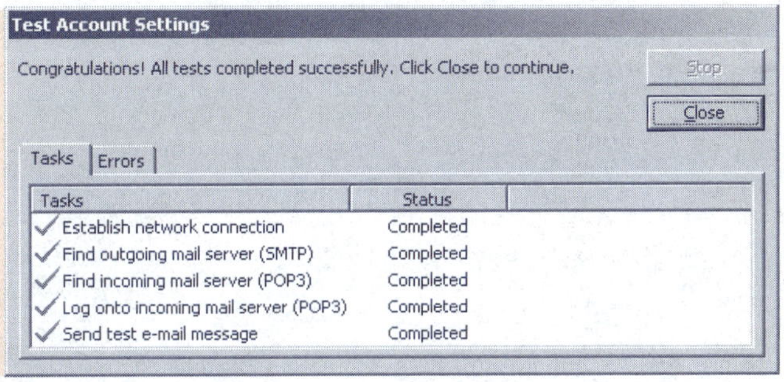

9. If there are errors in the Test Account Settings dialog box, reenter the information, and click Test Account Settings again; otherwise, click Next and then click Finish.

Tip

Users who log on to their own Windows accounts and then access Outlook have the password protection of their user accounts to keep others from logging on to their Outlook profiles. However, the *outlook.pst* file associated with the Outlook profile is still accessible unless it is password protected. (The file is stored in a hidden folder, but anyone can set Windows Explorer to view hidden files and easily find it.). See "Add Personal Folders File Security" earlier in this chapter to learn how to password-protect Personal Folders files.

Have you lost newsgroup messages that you've read recently?

yes → **Go to...** I've lost my newsgroup messages, page 214.

no

Are lines in your posted newsgroup messages cut short?

yes → **Go to...** The lines in my posted newsgroup messages are cut off, page 220.

no

Are there too many old newsgroup messages in your message list?

yes

no

Has Outlook Express picked up e-mail that you want to keep in Outlook?

yes → **Go to...** Outlook Express picked up e-mail that I need to save in Outlook, page 218.

no

Does Outlook Express pick up your e-mail when you read newsgroups?

yes

Newsgroups

Go to...

My newsgroup message list is too long, page 216.

Quick fix

Outlook Express is picking up e-mail when I read newsgroups

You open Outlook Express from Windows to check your newsgroups and you still have an e-mail account set up there. It's easy to fix this—just stop Outlook Express from checking for e-mail.

1. On the Tools menu, click Options.
2. On the General tab, clear the Send And Receive Messages At Startup check box and the Check for New Messages Every check box.
3. Click OK.

If your solution isn't here, see the general troubleshooting tips on page xvii.

I've lost my newsgroup messages

Source of the problem

You read several newsgroup messages last week, and when you tried to reread a few of them today, you couldn't find them.

Either the messages are hidden by a filter, or they've been deleted. If they've been hidden by a filter, you can remove the filter. If they've been deleted, you can get them back only by downloading the whole list from the newsgroup again. Then you can make sure messages aren't automatically deleted in the future.

How to fix it

Remove filters

1. In Outlook Express, open the folder for the newsgroup whose messages you want to find.
2. On the View menu, point to Current View, and then click Show All Messages. ▶

   If your missing messages don't reappear, they've been deleted from your local computer, and you will have to download all the messages from the newsgroup to find the missing ones again.

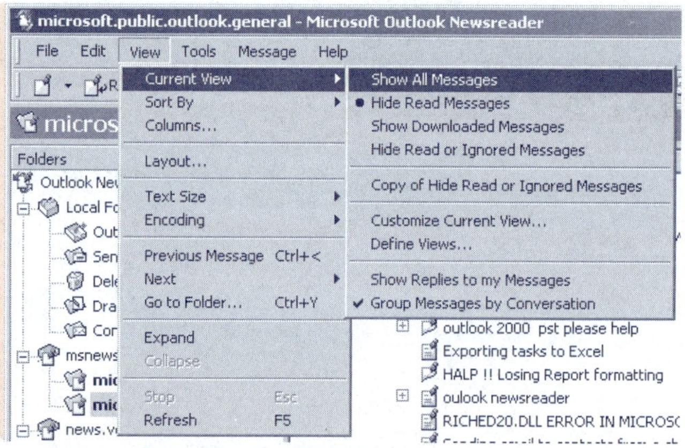

Stop deleting messages

1. On the Outlook Express Tools menu, click Options, and in the Options dialog box, click the Maintenance tab.
2. Clear the Delete Read Message Bodies In Newsgroups check box so that your read messages won't be deleted when you quit Outlook Express. ▶
3. To stop or delay automatic cleanup, clear the Delete News Messages check box, or change the number of days Outlook Express should wait before deleting news messages.
4. Click OK to close the Options dialog box.

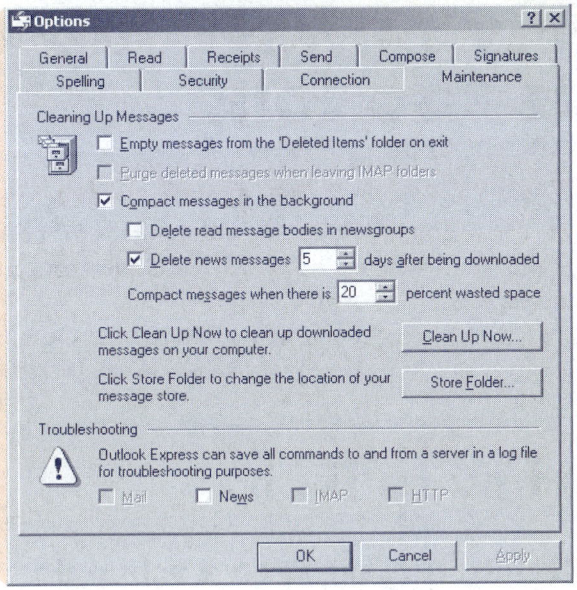

My newsgroup message list is too long

Source of the problem

Your newsgroup headers list has hundreds of messages and message headers in it, and it's no longer useful. But when you try to delete old messages and headers the way you do with your old e-mail messages, they don't go away!

There are a couple of ways to tell the Outlook Express newsreader to reduce the length of the list for you: automatically delete old messages on a time schedule, or clean out the list right now.

How to fix it

Delete messages on a schedule

1. On the Outlook Express Tools menu, click Options, and in the Options dialog box, click the Maintenance tab.
2. Select the Delete Read Message Bodies In Newsgroups check box so that messages you've read will be deleted when you quit Outlook Express. ▶
3. Select the Delete News Messages check box so that messages you've downloaded will be automatically deleted the specified number of days after you downloaded them.
4. Click OK.

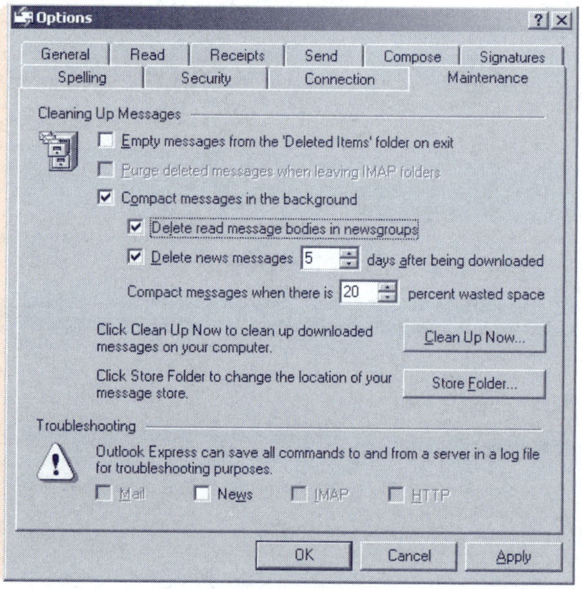

Delete all messages (or messages and headers) right now

1. On the Outlook Express Tools menu, click Options, and in the Options dialog box, click the Maintenance tab.
2. Click the Clean Up Now button.
3. In the Local File Cleanup dialog box, click the Browse button. ▶
4. In the Outlook Express dialog box, click either a news server or a specific newsgroup. (If you click a news server, all the newsgroups you're subscribed to on that news server will be cleaned up.) Click OK. ▶
5. In the Local File Clean Up dialog box, make sure the news server or newsgroup name appears in the Local File(s) For box, and then either click the Delete button to delete all messages and headers, or click the Remove Messages button to delete downloaded messages but leave the headers. ▶
6. When asked whether you're sure you want to delete all locally cached messages, click Yes.
7. Click Close, and then click OK to close each open dialog box.

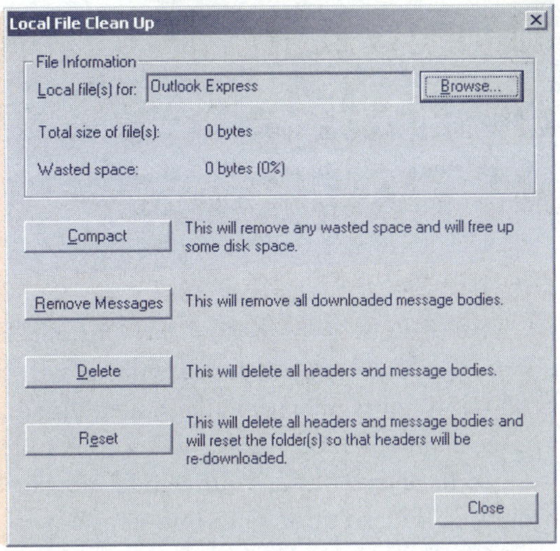

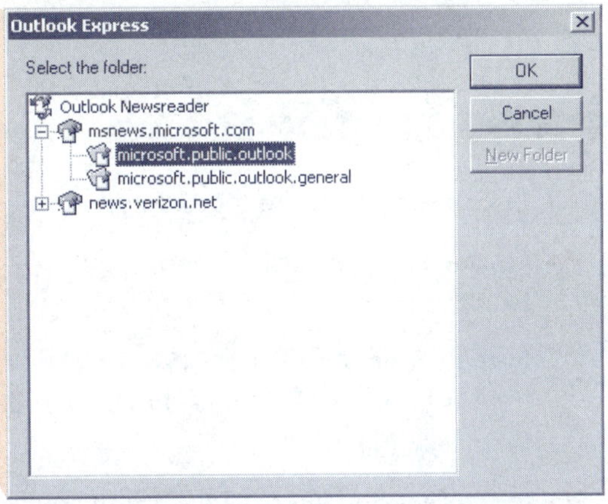

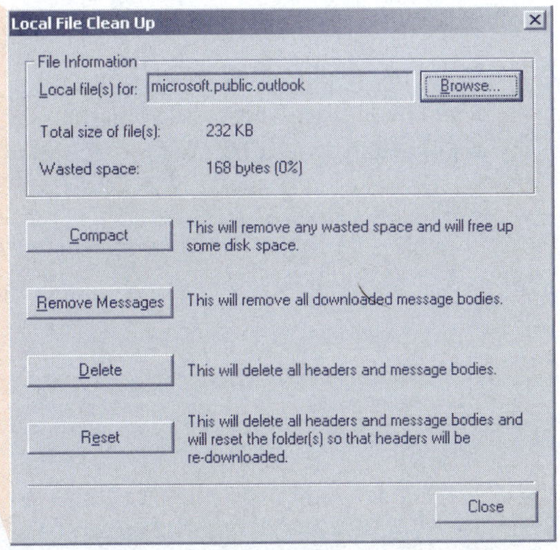

Outlook Express picked up e-mail that I need to save in Outlook

Source of the problem

You visited a newsgroup using the Outlook Express newsreader, and while you were online with the newsgroup, Outlook Express unexpectedly picked up your waiting e-mail. You normally pick up your e-mail with Outlook, and you don't want to have to look for your e-mail messages in two different programs. The solution is to import the messages into Outlook from Outlook Express.

Tip

To avoid this problem in the future, instead of opening Outlook Express directly, on the View menu, point to Go To, and then click News to open the Outlook Express newsreader.

How to fix it

1. In Outlook, open the Inbox folder.
2. On the File menu, click Import And Export.
3. In the Import And Export Wizard, click Import Internet Mail And Addresses, and then click Next.
4. In the Outlook Import Tool dialog box, click Outlook Express 4.x, 5.
5. Select the Import Mail check box, and clear the Import Address Book and Import Rules check boxes.
6. Click Finish.

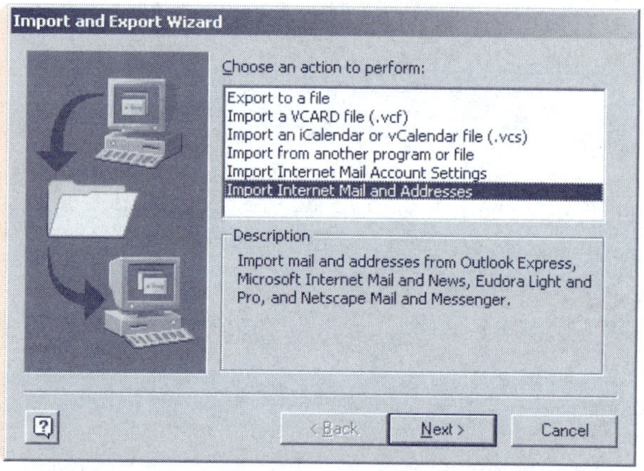

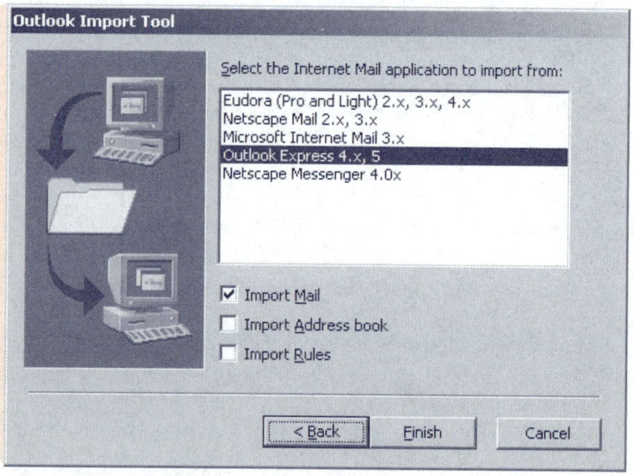

In the Import Summary dialog box, click OK. (If you click Save In Inbox, an extra message appears in your Inbox that tells you how many messages were imported.)

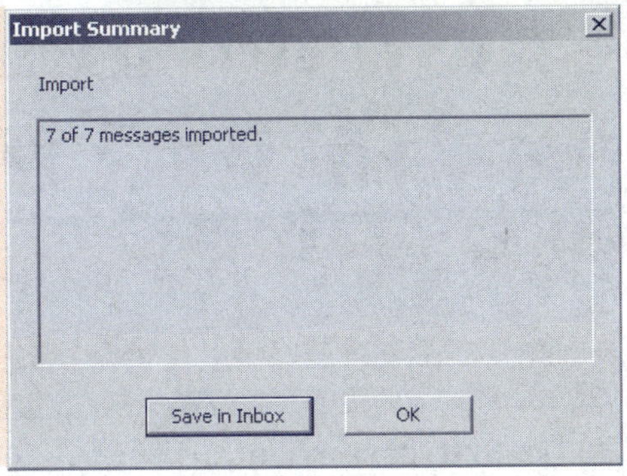

Copies of the messages in all your Outlook Express e-mail folders are imported into the corresponding folder or subfolder in Outlook, or into the Inbox if there's no corresponding subfolder in Outlook.

More about importing mail from Outlook Express

If you have more than one user account in Outlook Express, only the messages in the most recently opened user account's e-mail folders are imported. If you want to import messages from a specific Outlook Express user account, open Outlook Express from that user account before you import the messages into Outlook. It doesn't matter whether Outlook Express is open or closed during the import process.

Any messages that were sent to you in Rich Text format will have their original Rich Text formatting restored when you open them in Outlook—even though, when you open the same message in Outlook Express, the formatting is ignored and you see the message in plain text.

Tip

If you want to avoid copying duplicates of these messages into Outlook in the future, open Outlook Express, and delete the messages you just imported.

The lines in my posted newsgroup messages are cut off

Source of the problem

You posted a message to a newsgroup. Later, when you read your posted message, you found that the last word in every line of your message had been cut off!

By default, the Outlook Express newsreader sets the line length of plain text messages at 76 characters per line, but you can change that limit to a shorter or longer line length. Some news servers don't display more than 80 characters per line, and if your line length has been set to more than 80 characters, the extra characters are cut off.

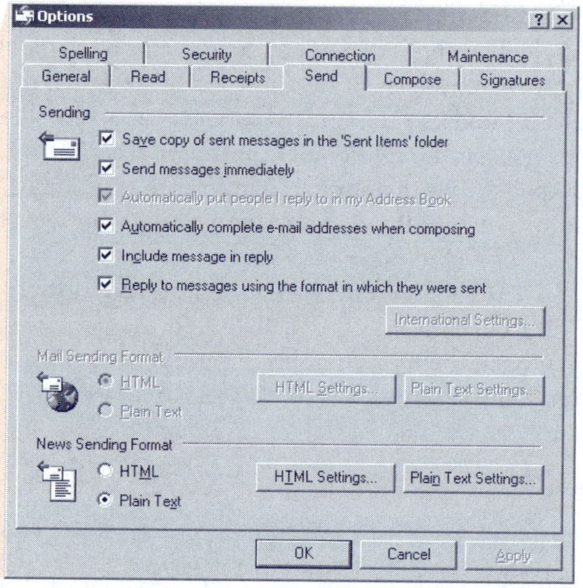

How to fix it

1. On the Outlook Express Tools menu, click Options, and in the Options dialog box, click the Send tab.
2. In the News Sending Format area, click the Plain Text Settings button. ▶
3. In the Plain Text Settings dialog box, in the Automatically Wrap Text At box, type the number of characters at which you want the lines of your message to wrap. ▶
4. Click OK to close each of the dialog boxes.

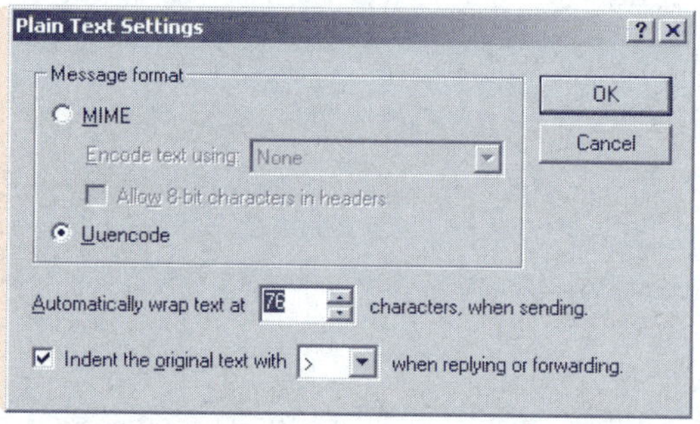

Newsgroups

Is your Outlook Bar missing?

yes

Quick fix

My Outlook Bar is missing You were clicking around in Outlook, experimenting with changing your layout and views and you lost your Outlook Bar. It's a snap to get it back. Just click the View menu, and then click Outlook Bar, and you'll see it instantly reappear.

no

Are your Outlook Bar shortcuts working?

yes

Is your Outlook Bar missing a shortcut to a subfolder?

yes

no

Are you missing an Outlook Bar group?

yes

no

Go to...
My Outlook Bar shortcuts stopped working, page 224.

Quick fix

My Outlook Bar is missing a shortcut to a folder In Outlook, all of your Outlook folders are listed in the Folder List. You can easily create an Outlook Bar shortcut for an Outlook folder.

1. On the View menu, click Folder List.
2. In the Folder List, display the folder (or subfolder) for which you want to create a shortcut.
3. Right-click the folder, and click Add To Outlook Bar on the shortcut menu.

Go to...

One of my Outlook Bar groups is missing, page 226.

If your solution isn't here, see the general trouble-shooting tips on page xvii.

My Outlook Bar shortcuts stopped working

Source of the problem

You started Outlook, and when you clicked a shortcut on your Outlook Bar, nothing happened.

The Outlook Bar file is probably corrupted, but you can fix it by rebuilding the Outlook Bar. (Unfortunately, rebuilding the Outlook Bar returns it to its default state, and all your custom shortcuts are removed.)

How to fix it

1. Quit Outlook.
2. Click the Windows Start button, point to Search, and then click For Files And Folders.
3. In the Search For Files Or Folders Named box, type *outlook.exe*.
4. Be sure your main hard disk (probably C) is in the Look In box, and then click Search Now. ▶

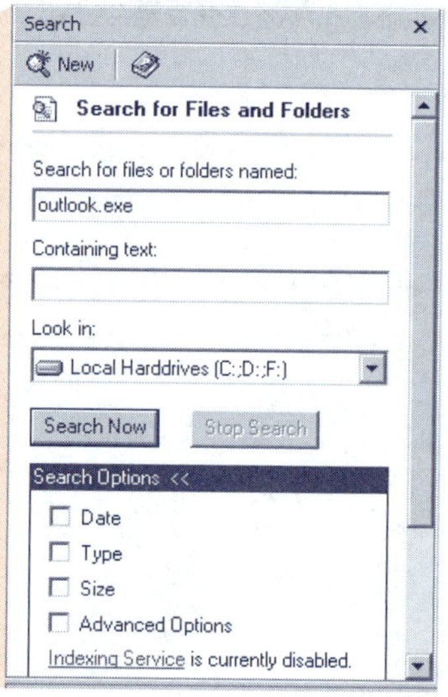

5. When Windows locates the file and stops searching, write down the path to the file. (You will need to type it in the next step.) The default path is "C:\Program Files\Microsoft Office\Office10\outlook.exe" (including the quotes).
6. Close the Search Results window.
7. Click Start, and then click Run.
8. In the Open box, type the complete path that you noted in step 5, including the file name and the quotes.

9. Following the closing quotation mark, type a single space, and then type */ResetOutlookBar*.

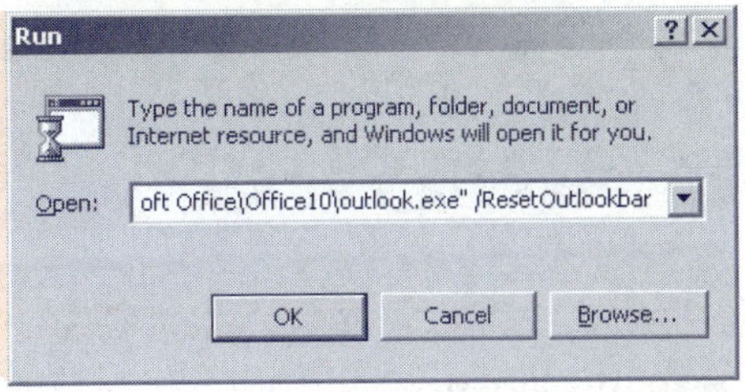

10. Click OK.

If this doesn't fix your Outlook Bar, follow the procedure again, but in step 9, type */CleanViews* instead of */ResetOutlookBar*. The CleanViews procedure restores the default views as well as the default Outlook Bar (which means you'll probably lose your customized views as well as your shortcuts).

Tip

Be sure to type the single space between the file name and the forward slash, and to enclose the path in quotation marks, as shown.

One of my Outlook Bar groups is missing

Source of the problem

In your colleague's copy of Outlook 2002, the Outlook Bar has a group named Other Shortcuts. This Outlook Bar group has shortcut icons that open lists of folders and files on the hard disk, rather than Outlook data. This Outlook Bar group seems very useful, but you can't find it in your copy of Outlook.

If you installed Outlook 2002 by itself, rather than as a part of the Office XP suite, the Other Shortcuts group might not have been created. Or, someone might have been practicing creating and deleting Outlook Bar groups and deleted your Other Shortcuts group. But that's okay—you can create a new group and name it Other Shortcuts or any name you like.

How to fix it

First, add a new group to the Outlook Bar. Then add shortcuts to the new group.

Add a new group to the Outlook Bar

1. Right-click the Outlook Bar, and click Add New Group.
2. Type the name you want (*Other Shortcuts* or another name). The name you type replaces the highlighted name "new group."

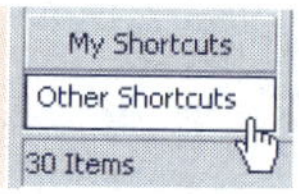

3. Press Enter.

Add shortcuts to the new group

1. On the Outlook Bar, click the new group's button to open the new group, which is empty.
2. Right-click the Outlook Bar for the new group, and click Outlook Bar Shortcut on the shortcut menu.
3. In the Add To Outlook Bar dialog box, click the down arrow to the right of the Look In box, and click File System in the drop-down list.

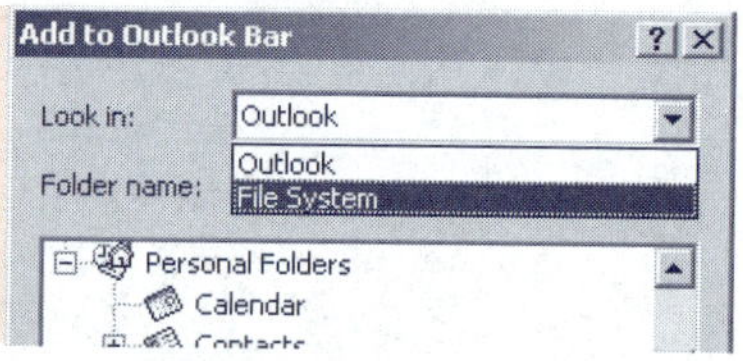

4. Click My Computer in the list box, and then click OK. ▶

The My Computer shortcut is added to your Outlook Bar. You can now click the My Computer icon on the Outlook Bar and navigate from there to any folder or file on your hard disk.

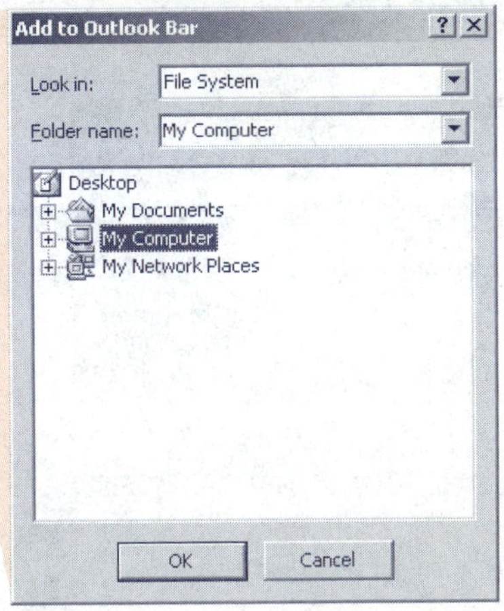

5. Repeat steps 1 through 4 to add shortcuts to folders and subfolders on your hard disk. In step 4, click the small plus sign next to My Computer to open the list of drives in the computer, and then click the small plus sign next to a drive to open the list of folders on that drive. Keep opening folders and subfolders until you find the subfolder you want to add to your Outlook Bar. Click the subfolder name, and then click OK. ▶

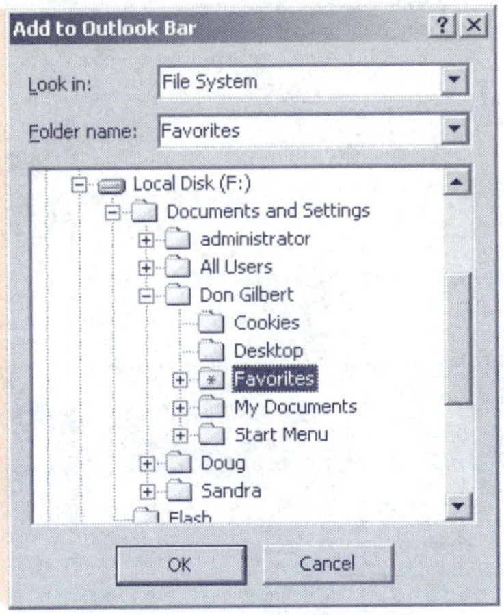

Tip

To add a shortcut to a file to your Outlook Bar, click Folder Shortcut on the Outlook Bar to display the list of subfolders and files in that folder. Navigate through the file structure in the Outlook window until you locate the file for which you want to create a shortcut. Then drag the file's icon from the list to the Outlook Bar.

Does the Calendar print private items that you don't want printed?

yes

no

Does your printer fail to print all the Calendar pages?

yes

no

Is text in a printed calendar week or month cut short?

yes

Go to...

The text in my printed calendar is cut short, page 232.

no

In a printed month, can you print just the dates that you want?

yes

Can you print a list of your contacts?

yes

no

no

Go to...

Outlook prints more dates on the page than I want, page 236.

Quick fix

I can print only single contacts instead of a list There are two reasons why this might happen: in the Print dialog box, the Memo Style is selected; or, a single contact is selected, and in the Print dialog box, the Only Selected Items option is selected. In the Print dialog box, be sure that your selections under both Print Style and Print Range match what you select or display in the Contacts window.

Quick fix

I don't want private items printed In the Print dialog box, select the Hide Details Of Private Appointments check box. Any appointment or event in which you selected the Private check box will be printed as "Private Appointment."

Go to...
My printer doesn't print all the pages of my Calendar, page 230.

Can you print a Contacts Phone list that includes addresses?

yes → Can you print a list of just specific contacts?

no →

Go to...
I need to print a phone list that includes addresses, page 235.

no →

Quick fix

I can't print a list of specific contacts Filter your view to show only those items that you want to print, and in the Print dialog box, click the All Items option. You can also use the Shift or Ctrl key to select the specific contacts you want to include in the printed list, and in the Print dialog box, select the Only Selected Items option.

If your solution isn't here, see the general troubleshooting tips on page xvii.

My printer doesn't print all the pages of my calendar

Source of the problem

You set up your calendar to display six months of appointments. You send it to the printer, which prints one or maybe two pages, and then quits. Your printer has plenty of paper, so what's the problem?

There are two possibilities: Your printer doesn't have enough memory to print what you want, or you need to set the complete date range for printing.

How to fix it

Printer memory

If you choose to print a special page size, such as one of the Franklin Day Planner or Day Runner styles, some printers don't have the memory to print complete pages. They print as much as they can and then quit. (You get an "Overrun" error message from some printers.)

To find out whether printer memory is the problem, try printing your pages using a very simple page size, such as Letter or Letter Half.

1. On the File menu, point to Page Setup, and then click the print style you want.
2. In the Page Setup dialog box, click the Paper tab. In the Page area, click one of the sizes at the top of the Size list. ▶
3. Click the Print button.
4. In the Print dialog box, click OK.

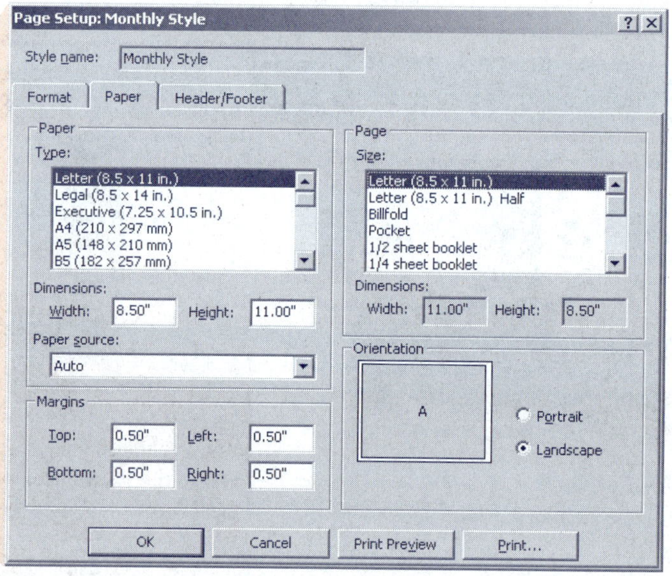

If the simpler page size prints without problems, you can either stick with simpler pages, try printing to a different printer, or get more memory for the printer you are having trouble with.

Date range

Another reason your printer might be not be printing all the pages you want is that the wrong print range (the date range in the calendar) is set in the Print dialog box. If you want to print monthly calendar pages for the entire year 2001, for example, you need to specify the entire range of months.

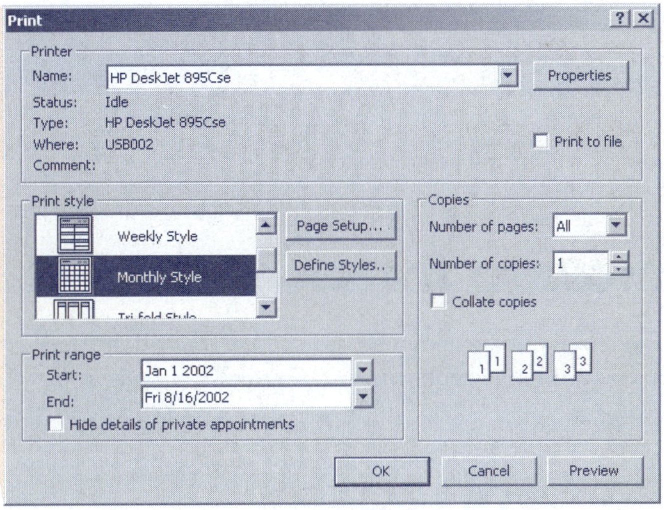

1. On the File menu, click Print.
2. In the Print dialog box, in the Print Range area, click the down arrow to the right of the Start box, and click the date on which you want the printed calendar to start. (If the Start date is far in the future, it might be faster to type the date—for example, *Jan 1 2002*.)
3. Use the same technique to set the date in the End box. For example, if you want to print calendar pages for the entire year, in the End box, type *Dec 31 2002*.
4. Click the Preview button to check your pages before you print them.
5. On the Print Preview window's toolbar, click the Multiple Pages button to see all the pages.

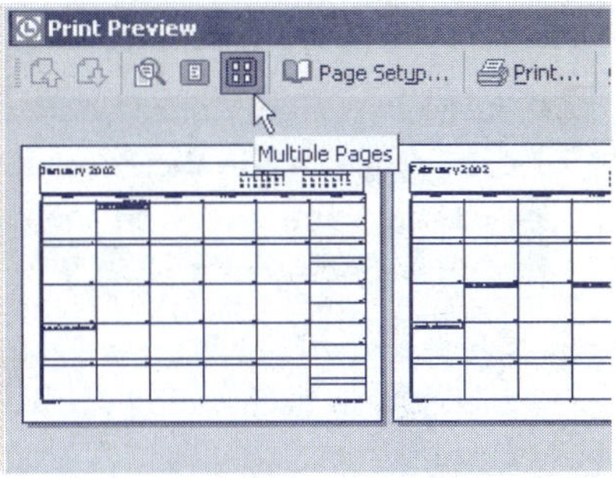

6. If you're ready to print the pages, on the Print Preview window's toolbar, click the Print button, and then in the Print dialog box, click OK.
7. If you need to make more layout changes, such as removing the TaskPad and Notes areas, on the Print Preview window's toolbar, click the Page Setup button. Make your changes in the Page Setup dialog box, click the Print button, and then in the Print dialog box, click OK.

Tip

To print a completely empty calendar, create a new Calendar subfolder, and print the new calendar without creating any appointments or events in it.

The text in my printed calendar is cut short

Source of the problem

After you print your calendar pages, you notice that the last few characters or words in some of your appointment entries are cut off. The problem arises because Outlook can print only as much text as will fit in each date's box.

How to fix it

There are three techniques you can try that might fix this problem. You can decrease the font size in the printed page, print from a view with AutoPreview turned on, or print the calendar larger on the page.

Decrease the font size

1. On the File menu, point to Page Setup, and click the style you want to print.
2. In the Page Setup dialog box, click the Format tab. In the Fonts area, click the Font button to the right of the Appointments box.
3. Click a new Font Size, and then click OK in each dialog box to close it.

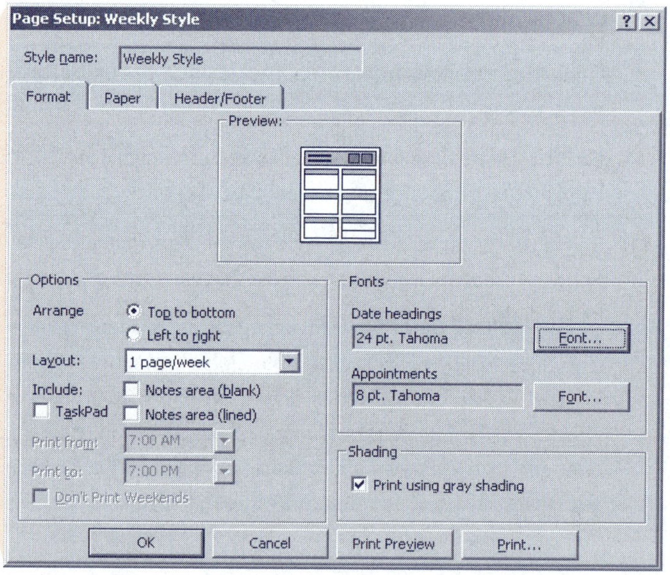

The smallest font size you can select is 8 point, but you can force your printer to use a smaller font size by typing the number you want in the Size box. A font size of 5 or 6 points is awfully small, but it might work for you. If it doesn't, try one of the other two techniques.

Turn on AutoPreview

If AutoPreview is turned on in your display view, the Notes in each appointment entry are printed on calendar pages.

1. On the View menu, point to Current View, and click Day/Week/Month View With AutoPreview.
2. On the File menu, click Print.
3. In the Print dialog box, in the Print Style area, make sure Daily Style is selected so that the complete text of each entry, with notes, will be printed.

If your notes for a particular appointment are very long, you might need to make that appointment larger in the Daily view (that is, increase the duration of the appointment) so that all the Notes in the entry can be displayed on the printed page.

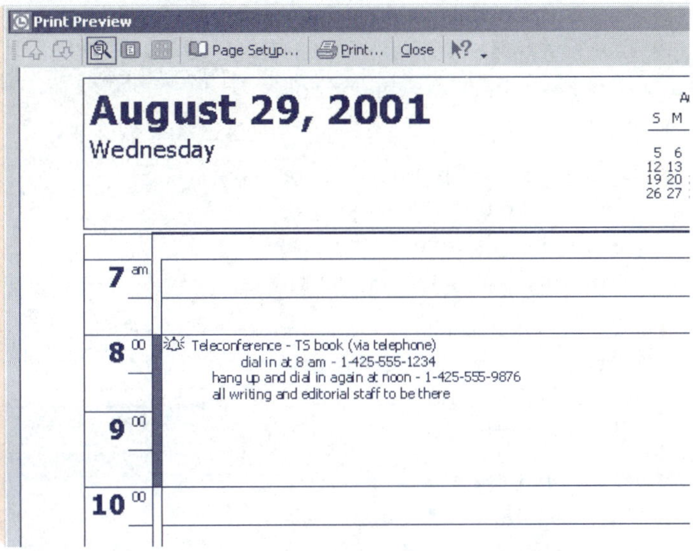

Tip

Whether your display is daily, weekly, or monthly, with AutoPreview view, you see all the appointment notes when you position your mouse pointer over an entry.

If this solution didn't solve your problem, go to the next page.

The text in my printed calendar is cut short

(continued from page 233)

Print the calendar larger

If you choose a larger print style and remove extraneous elements such as the TaskPad and Notes areas, the calendar will print larger on the page and each date box will be capable of holding more text.

1. In the Page Setup dialog box, on the Paper tab, click a larger page size and an orientation that makes best use of the page space.

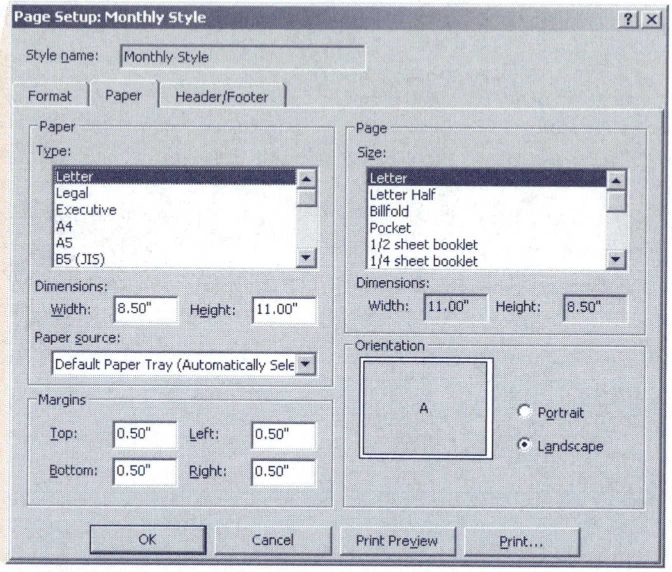

2. On the Format tab, in the Options area, clear the TaskPad, Notes Area (Blank), and Notes Area (Lined) check boxes.

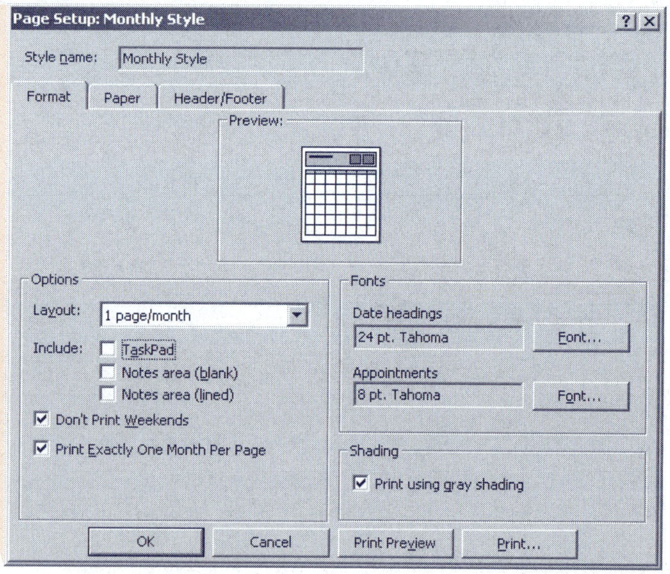

3. If you don't need to print weekend appointments, you can make more room for weekday appointments by selecting the Don't Print Weekends check box.
4. Click the Print Preview button to see whether these changes helped and whether you can make any more changes. For example, you can change the page margins on the Paper tab in the Page Setup dialog box, and you can reduce the size of the page header by deleting words in the Header boxes on the Header/Footer tab of the Page Setup dialog box.

I need to print a phone list that includes addresses

Source of the problem

You can quickly print a built-in telephone list of your contacts by choosing the Phone Directory Style in the Print dialog box. But the Phone Directory Style lists only phone numbers, and you can't alter the fields in that print style. You can, however, create your own phone list style that includes addresses.

How to fix it

1. In the Contacts folder, set up your Card view to show only the fields you want to print (names, addresses, and phone numbers).
2. On the File menu, click Print.
3. In the Print dialog box, in the Print Style area, click Card Style.
4. Click the Preview button to preview your phone list.
5. If the preview looks good, click the Print button, and in the Print dialog box, click OK.

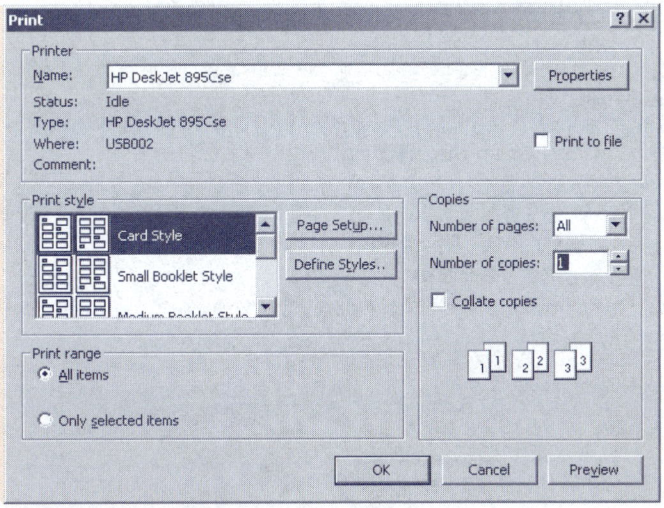

The printout is similar to the Phone Directory style, but it includes all the information displayed in your custom Card view.

Tip

To change the fields in your Card view, right-click an empty space in the Contacts window, and click Show Fields on the shortcut menu. In the Show Fields dialog box, in the Available Fields list, double-click the fields you want to include, and in the Show Fields In This Order list, double-click the fields you want to remove. Then click OK.

Outlook prints more dates on the page than I want

Source of the problem

You print a calendar month, and on your printed page, all the date squares on the page have dates in them (including the last few dates of the previous month and the first few dates of the following month). For clarity and simplicity, you want a page that shows only the dates for that one month.

How to fix it

Monthly style prints all the dates in a calendar month block, but you can direct Outlook to print only the dates within a single month. For example, instead of printing the month of November 2001 as October 29 through December 2, which fills all the squares on the page with dates, Outlook can be set up to print just the dates November 1 through November 30 and leave the remaining squares blank. ▶

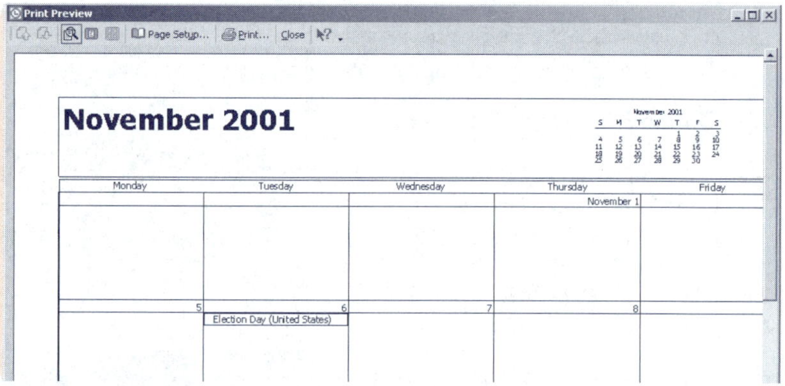

1. On the File menu, click Print.
2. In the Print dialog box, in the Print Range area, set the Start and End dates for your printed pages, and then click the Page Setup button.

3. In the Page Setup dialog box, select the Print Exactly One Month Per Page check box. ►

4. Click the Print Preview button to make sure the pages look the way you want them to before you print them.

5. Click the Print button, and in the Print dialog box, click OK.

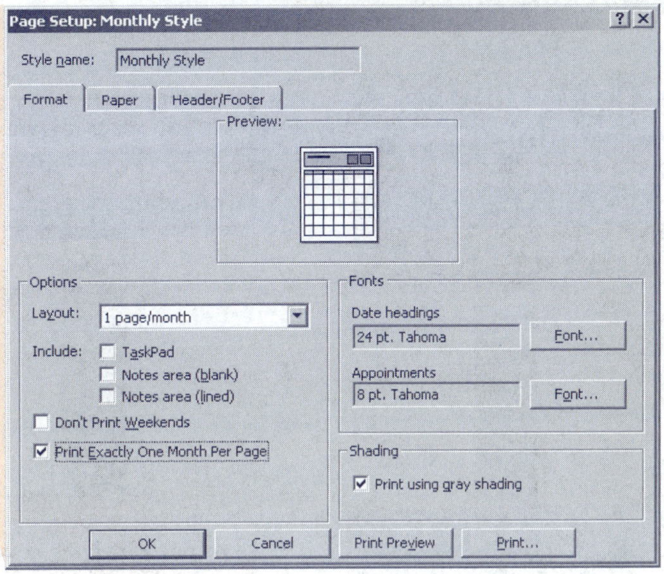

Is Outlook handling read receipts and requests correctly?

yes

Are you receiving the read receipts you requested from your recipients?

yes

no

no

Go to...

Outlook isn't handling my read receipts and requests correctly, page 240.

Quick fix

I'm not receiving read receipts from everyone You might not receive read receipts from your correspondents, depending on what e-mail programs your recipients use and how they have their responses set up. Some e-mail programs can't respond to read receipt requests at all. Correspondents who use e-mail programs that can respond to read receipts requests usually have the option of either ignoring read receipt requests altogether or responding to the requests selectively. It's not a good idea to send read receipt requests to everyone by default, because some people think it's rude. A better idea is to send read receipt requests individually to colleagues who expect them (or at least don't mind them).

Read receipts

When you test read receipts by sending yourself a message, do they work correctly?

no

Go to...

When I test read receipts, they don't work correctly, page 242.

If your solution isn't here, see the general troubleshooting tips on page xvii.

Outlook isn't handling my read receipts and requests correctly

Source of the problem

You are receiving a lot of read receipt requests, and it's getting annoying—you feel as if all these people are checking up on you. But you have specific senders (such as your supervisor) whose read receipt messages necessitate responses from you, and you don't know how to set things up so that you can respond to those people without having to respond to every one.

Or perhaps you are in the habit of requesting read receipts for every message you send and you have just gotten an irritated message from a new client asking you to please stop sending read receipt requests to him. You need to be able to change your read receipt request procedures immediately.

How to fix it

1. On the Tools menu, click Options, and in the Options dialog box, click the Preferences tab.
2. Click the E-mail Options button, and in the E-mail Options dialog box, click the Tracking Options button. ▶
3. To ignore all requests, select the Never Send A Response option.

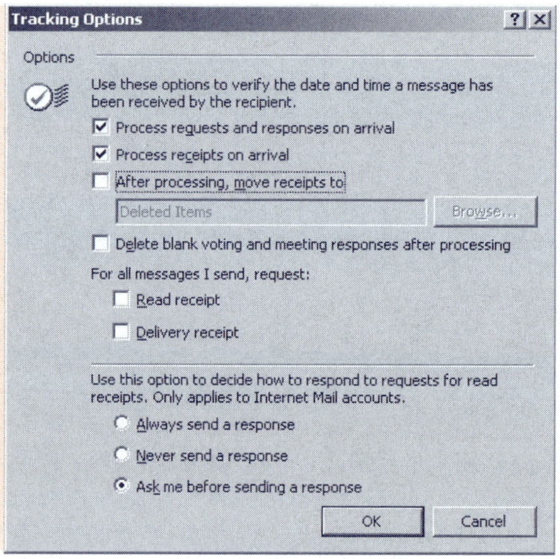

4. To respond to requests individually, select the Ask Me Before Sending A Response option.

5. To have Outlook automatically respond to every request, select the Always Send A Response option.

6. To request a read receipt with every message, select the Read Receipt check box.

7. To request a read receipt for an individual message, in the message form, click the Options button. In the Message Options dialog box, select the Request A Read Receipt For This Message check box, and then click Close.

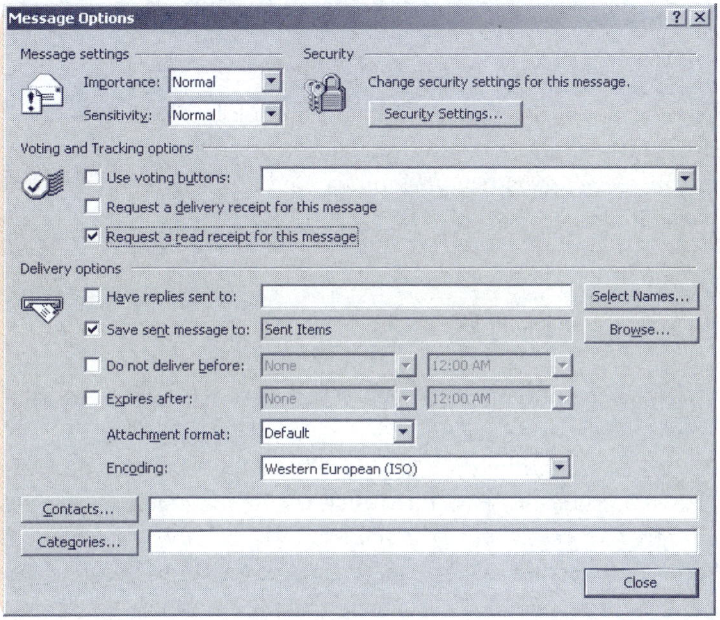

When I test read receipts, they don't work correctly

Source of the problem

You decide to test read receipts in Outlook by sending yourself a message that requests a read receipt. After you send and receive the message, you discover that no read receipt for your self-test message appears in your Inbox, and no tracking tab appears in the sent message in the Sent Items folder.

How to fix it

You've tested only half the procedure—the half in which you, the sender, send the message with a request for a read receipt.

The second half of the procedure happens after you, the recipient, open the message. The next time you send e-mail (or click the Send/Receive button), the read receipt is sent and is subsequently received by you, the sender. The time this takes depends on your ISP's e-mail servers, so you might need to click Send/Receive a few times before the read receipt is delivered. When you, the sender, receive the read receipt, you'll eventually see the tracking tab appear in the sent message in the Sent Items folder. (You can hasten this process by opening the read receipt in your Inbox.)

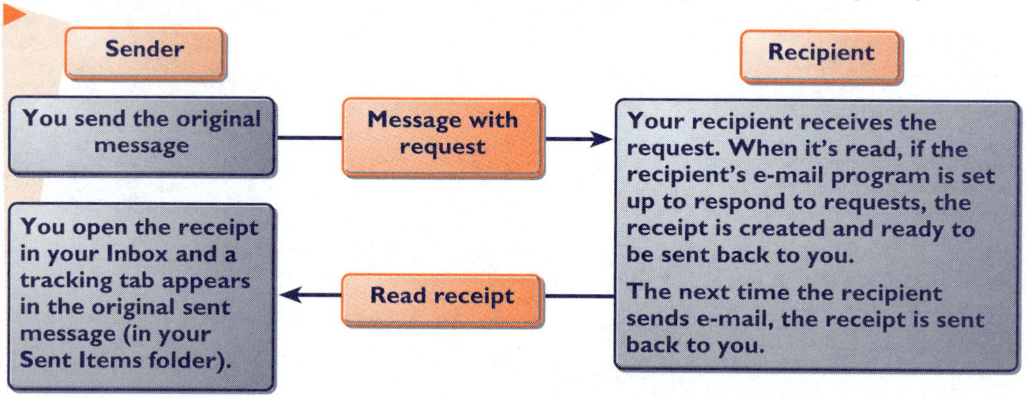

Read receipts

Is Outlook running?

yes

Is the appointment or task with the failed reminder saved in a subfolder instead of in the main Calendar or Task folder?

yes

Go to...
Reminders in my Calendar and Tasks subfolders don't work, page 246.

no

Are you creating appointments and tasks in the correct folder?

yes

no

After working through the previous solutions, are your reminders still not working?

yes

Quick fix

I don't know how to fix my Reminders file If all else fails, try repairing your Reminders file.

1. Quit Outlook.
2. Click Start, point to Run, and then type outlook /cleanreminders in the Open list box (be sure you type a space between outlook and the slash).
3. Click OK.

no

Quick fix

Reminders don't appear when Outlook isn't running If Outlook is not running, none of your reminders will appear. Next time you turn Outlook on, all of your overdue reminders will pile up on your Windows desktop.

To make sure your reminders appear, keep Outlook running, minimized or in the background, all the time.

Reminders

Quick fix

I don't know where to create appointments and tasks that will generate a reminder When using Outlook with a Microsoft Exchange Server or when you have another personal folders file open, more than one Calendar or Tasks folder might appear in your Folder List. However, you won't get reminders for any tasks or appointments that exist outside the Personal Folders file or network mailbox that receives your e-mail (and you will be warned of this when you save an appointment or task in one of these places). For example, if your e-mail is delivered to a network mailbox and you create an appointment in your Personal Folders Calendar folder, you won't receive a reminder. To fix this, move your tasks and appointments to the Personal Folders file containing the Inbox that receives your messages.

First determine where your e-mail messages are received.

1. On the Tools menu, click E-mail Accounts.
2. Select View Or Change Existing E-mail Accounts, and click Next. The Deliver New E-mail To The Following Location box appears where your e-mail is delivered and where reminders are triggered.
3. Click Finish.

If your solution isn't here, check these related chapters:

- Calendar, appointments, page 14
- Tasks and TaskPad, page 278

Or see the general trouble-shooting tips on page xvii.

Reminders in my Calendar and Tasks subfolders don't work

Source of the problem

You've created all your personal appointments—to get your hair cut, to go to the dentist, and so forth—in a Calendar subfolder, and even though you tried to set reminders for the appointments, none of them show up in the Calendar. This problem occurs because reminders work only from within your main Calendar and Tasks folders—not from the subfolders.

How to fix it

If you create a new appointment or task in a Calendar or Tasks subfolder instead of the main Calendar or Tasks folder, you will get an error message when you click Save And Close, and you won't get a reminder. ▶

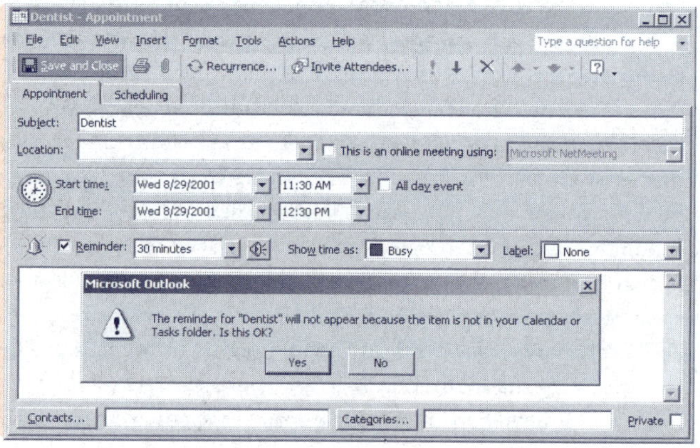

If you click No in the error message box, the appointment or task won't be saved, and the appointment's or task's dialog box remains open, but if you click Yes, the appointment or task will be saved, but you won't get a reminder. (Don't let the reminder icon in the appointment fool you—the reminder won't work.)

If you absolutely need to be reminded about an appointment or a task, make sure you save it in your main Calendar or Tasks folder.

Tip

If the appointment or task is private, select the Private check box in the lower-right corner of the dialog box to hide the item from all eyes but yours.

More about reminders

To change the default reminder times for either Calendar or Tasks, on the Tools menu, click Options, and make the changes on the Preferences tab of the Options dialog box.

If all your reminders appear too late to get you out of the office in time to make the appointments, you can reset your default reminder time to something much earlier—perhaps two hours. If a specific appointment requires a different reminder time—for example, 15 minutes or five hours—you can change the reminder time in the individual Appointment or Task form.

Reminders

Would you like a reminder to get in touch with a certain contact on a particular morning next month? You can flag a Contact form for follow-up and be reminded at the date and time you set.

1. Open the Contact form.
2. On the Actions menu, click Follow Up.

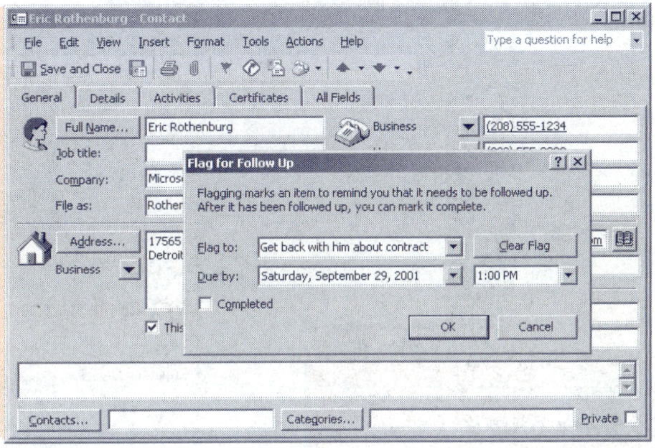

3. In the Flag For Follow Up dialog box, click the down arrow to the right of the Flag To box, and click the note content you want to include on the flag. You can also type a flag note to yourself.
4. Click the down arrow to the right of the Due By box, and then click the calendar date on which you want to be reminded. That date and a time appear in the Due By box.
5. In the box to the right of the Due By box, click the down arrow, and then click the time you prefer. For example, if you want to be reminded at 9:00 that morning, click 9:00 A.M.
6. Click OK.

If Outlook is running at the reminder time, you get a reminder to contact that person.

Does your computer make any sounds at all?

yes → Do you want to turn your reminder sounds on or off?

- yes →
- no → Do you want to turn the action feedback sounds on or off?
  - yes →
  - no → Do you want to turn the new mail notification sounds on or off?
    - yes → **Go to...** **My new mail notification sounds aren't doing what I want, page 254.**
    - no → Do you want to turn your modem's dialing sounds on or off?
      - yes →

no →

Quick fix

My computer is not making any sounds Be sure your computer's volume control is not muted—double-click the speaker icon on the right side of the taskbar, and check that the Mute All check box under Volume Control is cleared.

Sounds

Go to...
My reminder sounds aren't doing what I want, page 250.

Go to...
My action feedback sounds aren't doing what I want, page 252.

Go to...
My modem dialing noises aren't doing what I want, page 253.

If your solution isn't here, see the general troubleshooting tips on page xvii.

My reminder sounds aren't doing what I want

Source of the problem

The Calendar and Task reminder sounds in Outlook are supposed to alert you to an appointment or task that's due. If you're not being alerted by a sound (and you want to be), there are two places where the sounds might have been turned off. It could be that the reminder sound is turned off for all tasks, meetings, and events, even though the visual reminder appears, or you might not have Calendar reminders turned on by default, which means you need to remember to turn on each appointment's reminder when you create it.

How to fix it

1. On the Tools menu, click Options.
2. On the Other tab of the Options dialog box, click the Advanced Options button.
3. In the Advanced Options dialog box, click the Reminder Options button.
4. In the Reminder Options dialog box, select the Play Reminder Sound check box to turn reminder sounds on; or clear the check box to turn reminder sounds off.

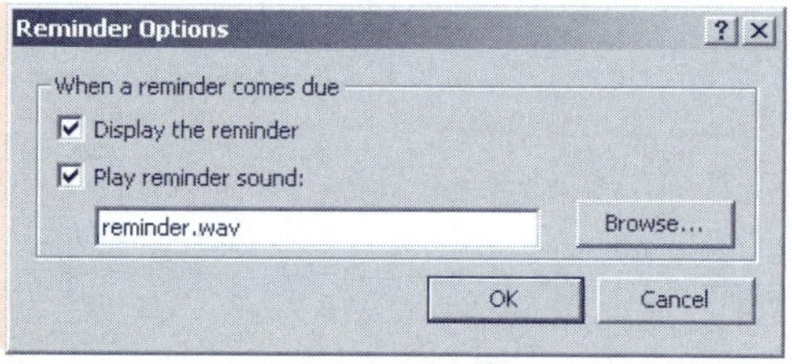

5. Click OK twice to return to the Options dialog box.

6. On the Preferences tab, in the Calendar area, select the Default Reminder check box to turn Calendar reminders on by default. Clear the check box if you want to set reminders only on specific appointments when you create them.

7. Click OK to close the Options dialog box.

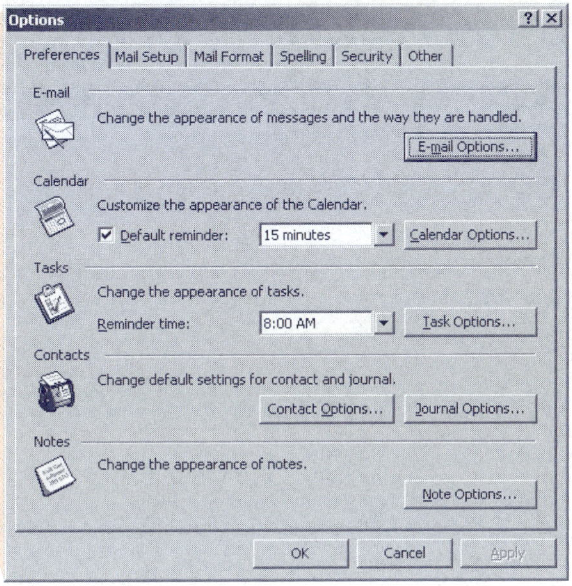

My action feedback sounds aren't doing what I want

Source of the problem

When you perform an action in Outlook, such as starting a program, deleting a message, or pressing the wrong key, the action makes a sound by default. If action sounds annoy you, you can turn them off. If someone turned them off and you want to hear them, you can turn them back on.

How to fix it

1. On the Tools menu, click Options.
2. On the Other tab of the Options dialog box, click the Advanced Options button.
3. In the General Settings area, select or clear the Provide Feedback With Sound check box.
4. Click OK to close each dialog box.

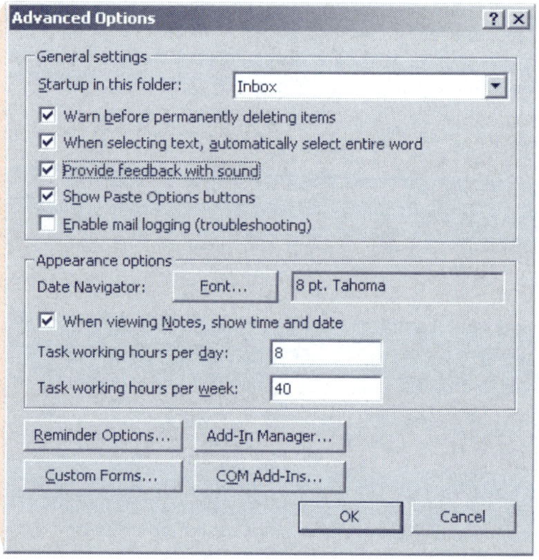

Tip

After you select the Provide Feedback With Sound check box and click OK, you might see a message telling you to download Office Sounds from the Microsoft Office Update Web site. Go ahead and download them if you like sounds on your computer—you might find them more interesting than the default Windows sounds, and they're free.

Tip

If you have a volume control on the Windows taskbar, click it once, and check whether the Mute check box is selected (for silence) or cleared (for sound).

My modem dialing noises aren't doing what I want

Source of the problem

When you first install and configure a modem, it's nice to hear the dialing noises and the modem static so that you know everything's working the way it should. But those noises can be really irritating after a while. You can turn them off, adjust the volume, or even turn them back on if you later find you need the reassurance of those noises. (If you get your e-mail messages through a Microsoft Exchange Server, cable, or DSL connection, modem noises won't be a problem.)

How to fix it

1. On the Tools menu, click E-mail Accounts.
2. In the E-mail Accounts wizard, select View Or Change Existing E-mail Accounts, and click Next.
3. Select your ISP account, and then click the Change button.
4. Click the More Settings button.
5. On the Connection tab of the Internet E-mail Settings dialog box, click Properties.
6. On the General tab of the connection's Properties dialog box, click Configure.
7. At the bottom of the dialog box, clear the Enable Modem Speaker check box.
8. Click OK three times to close all open dialog boxes, and then click Next in the E-mail Accounts Wizard.
9. Click Finish.

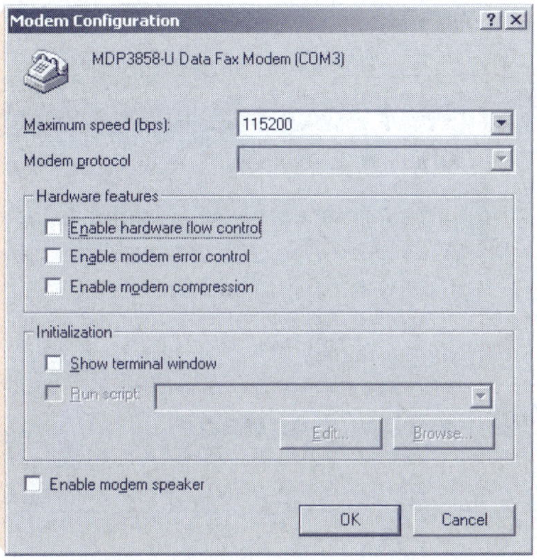

My new mail notification sounds aren't doing what I want

Source of the problem

New mail notification sounds are on by default. Some people find the sounds annoying because they interrupt their train of thought when new messages arrive. On the other hand, other people have communications that are time-critical, and they need to know the moment a new message arrives. Whether it's silence or sounds you need, if your new mail sounds aren't doing what you want, you can fix them.

How to fix it

1. On the Tools menu, click Options.
2. In the Options dialog box, click the Preferences tab.
3. Click the E-mail Options button.
4. In the E-mail Options dialog box, click the Advanced E-mail Options button.
5. In the Advanced E-mail Options dialog box, in the When New Items Arrive area, select (or clear) the Play A Sound check box. ▶
6. Click OK to close each open dialog box.

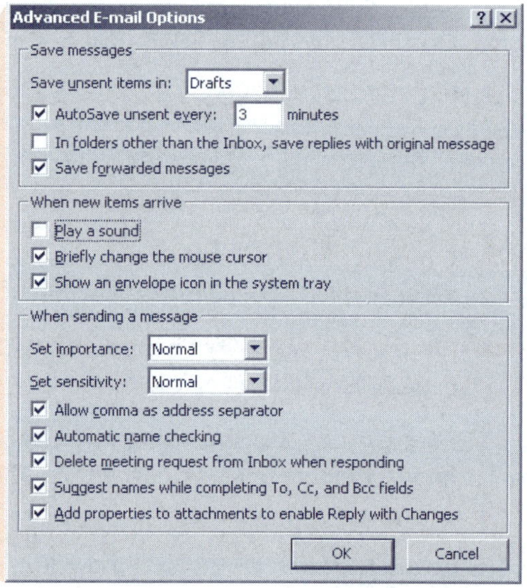

More about sounds

You can change the sound files for various computer events (computer actions that make noises). Sounds accompany events and alerts in Windows and in other programs, such as Excel, Word, and your anti-virus program.

To change a sound, click the Windows Start button, point to Settings, and then click Control Panel. In Windows 2000, double-click the Sounds And Multimedia icon to open the Sounds And Multimedia Properties dialog box.

Click an event in the Sound Events list box, click the down arrow to the right of the Name box, and click the name of a sound file for that event in the drop-down list. To preview the sound, click it, and then click the arrow button to the right of the Name box. ▶

To locate other sounds (such as the Microsoft Office sounds, which you can download from the Microsoft Web site), click the Browse button and look for *.wav* files in other folders. In the Browse for <Event> dialog box (where <Event> is the event to which you're attaching the sound), you can preview and select other sounds for your events.

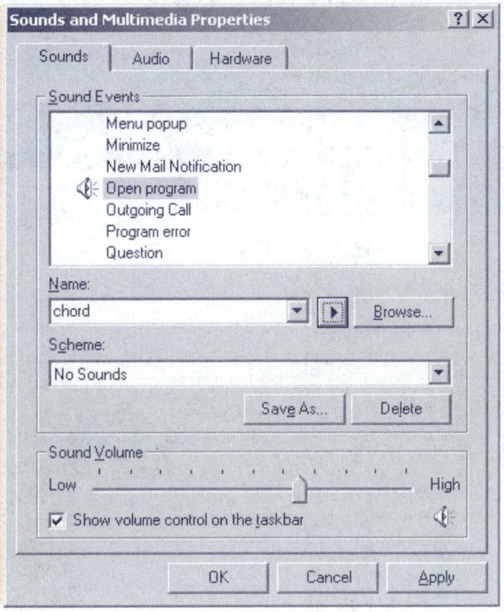

Note

If you're not using Windows 2000, you might see a Sounds icon instead of the Sounds And Multimedia icon in the Control Panel. In the Sounds Properties dialog box, there will be a right-pointing arrow next to the Preview box—click a sound file, and then click the arrow to preview the sound.

Does Outlook have problems when it starts?

yes

no

Does Outlook open with the wrong folder displayed?

yes

Quick fix

Outlook opens with the wrong folder displayed Specify which folder you want open when Outlook starts.

1. On the Tools menu, click Options.
2. On the Other tab of the Options dialog box, click the Advanced options button.
3. In the Startup In This Folder box, click the folder you want displayed when Outlook starts.

no

Do you want Outlook to start minimized?

yes

no

Do you want Outlook to start automatically when you start Windows?

yes

Go to...

Outlook doesn't start automatically, page 259.

Does Outlook stop responding after it starts?

yes — **Go to...** **Outlook starts, and then stops responding, page 258.**

no

Did you receive a message when you ran Outlook asking if you want to run in safe mode?

yes — **Go to...** **A message asks whether I want to start Outlook in safe mode, page 260.**

Quick fix

I don't know how to make Outlook start minimized This setting must be changed in the shortcut you normally use to start Outlook. The shortcut can be on your desktop, or it can be in the Windows startup folder. In either case, you have to make this change in a shortcut, not in the original Outlook icon on your desktop.

1. Right-click the Outlook shortcut, and click Properties on the shortcut menu. If you don't see the Properties command on the shortcut menu, you're clicking the main Outlook icon instead of a shortcut icon. In this case, click Create Shortcut on the shortcut menu, then right-click the shortcut icon, and click Properties.
2. In the Shortcut To Properties dialog box, on the Shortcut tab, in the Run list box, click Minimized.
3. Click OK.

If your solution isn't here, see the general troubleshooting tips on page xvii.

Outlook starts, and then stops responding

Source of the problem

When you start Outlook, usually the first thing you see is your Inbox with the first message displayed in the preview pane. This time, you started Outlook in your regular way, and Outlook stopped responding (it "hung") in the middle of startup.

This can happen if the first message in your list (the message Outlook is attempting to display in the preview pane) is corrupted and can't be displayed. So how do you get rid of that corrupted e-mail message if Outlook won't respond to your commands?

How to fix it

You need to start Outlook using the */NoPreview* switch, which starts Outlook without displaying the preview pane, and then delete the first message without opening it.

1. Click the Windows Start button, and then click Run.
2. In the Open box, type *outlook /nopreview*. (Make sure there is a space following *outlook*.)
3. Click OK. Outlook starts without opening the preview pane.
4. Delete the first message in the Inbox.

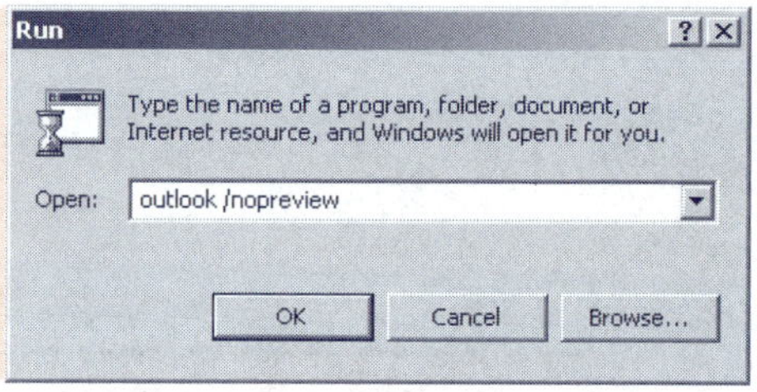

Starting Outlook with the */NoPreview* switch disables the preview pane completely. To make the Preview Pane command (on the View menu) available again, quit all copies of Outlook that are open, and then restart Outlook as you usually would (without using the */NoPreview* switch).

Tip

If Outlook isn't found when you click OK, in the Run dialog box, click the Browse button, then browse to your outlook.exe file. (The default path is "C:\Program Files\Microsoft Office\Office\Office10\outlook.exe", including the quotes.) Then type a space followed by */NoPreview*.

Outlook doesn't start automatically

Source of the problem

Every day when you turn on your computer, the first thing you do is pick up your e-mail. You are a very efficient person, and having to perform that same double-click every morning seems inefficient. Wouldn't it be great if your e-mail program could start when you turn on your computer? Well, it can—and it *is* more efficient.

How to fix it

1. Right-click the Outlook icon on your desktop, and click Create Shortcut on the shortcut menu.
2. Right-click the new shortcut, and click Copy on the shortcut menu.
3. Right-click the Windows Start button, and click Explore on the shortcut menu. The Windows Explorer window opens. Click the small plus sign next to the Start Menu folder, and then click the small plus sign next to the Programs folder.
4. Click the StartUp folder icon.
5. Right-click the right pane in the Explorer window, and then click Paste Shortcut on the shortcut menu. ▶
6. Close the Explorer window.

From now on, whenever you start Windows or log on to your account, Outlook will start automatically.

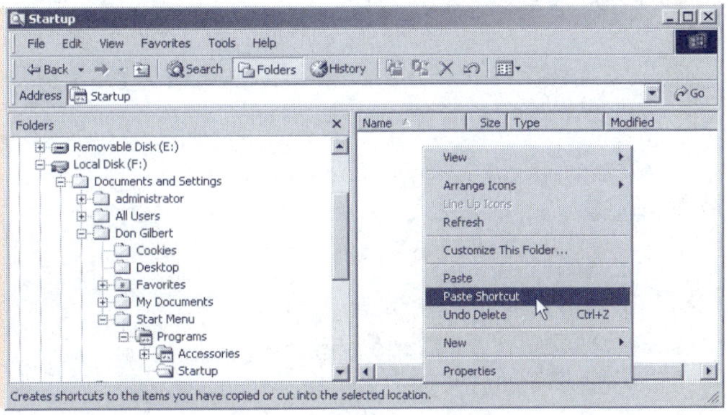

Tip

You don't need the new shortcut on your desktop after you've completed these steps. Right-click the shortcut, and click Delete on the shortcut menu. When you're asked whether you're sure you want to send the shortcut to the Recycle Bin, click Yes.

A message asks whether I want to start Outlook in safe mode

Source of the problem

You started Outlook, and the following message appeared:

> "Outlook failed to start correctly last time. Starting Outlook in safe mode will help you correct or isolate a startup problem in order to successfully start the program. Some functionality may be disabled in this mode. Do you want to start Outlook in safe mode?"

Now you're wondering what to do.

If you click Yes, Outlook starts in safe mode and turns off some components, including all add-in extensions and any other components that it identifies as being bad. Then, when you restart Outlook normally, some components remain turned off (those that Outlook has identified as causing problems), and all others go back to the state they were in before you ran Outlook in safe mode. If Outlook runs normally after you have run it in safe mode, you can assume the culprit is one of the components that Outlook turned off and left turned off. However, if Outlook still fails to run, it's likely that another component, such as an add-in that Outlook turned back on when you started it in normal mode, is causing the problem.

How to fix it

First you need to see if Outlook can spot the component that's the troublemaker.

1. If the error message box is not on your screen, hold down the Ctrl key, and click the Launch Outlook icon on the Windows taskbar; or double-click the Outlook shortcut on the Desktop.
2. In the message box that appears, click Yes to start Outlook in safe mode. ▶

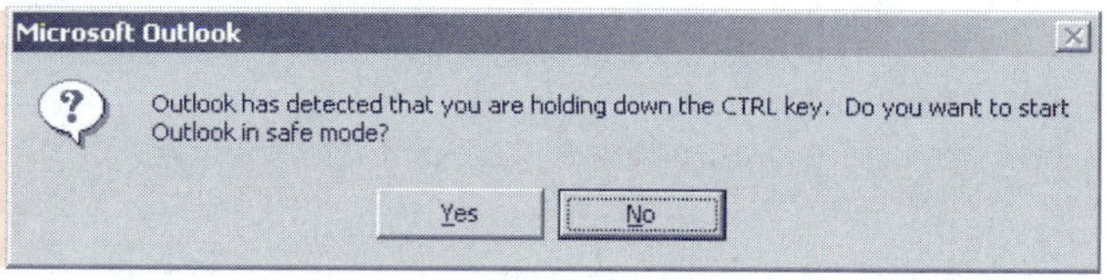

3. On the Help menu, click About Microsoft Outlook.
4. In the About Microsoft Outlook dialog box, click the Disabled Items button.
5. If you see any components listed in the Disabled Items dialog box, turn one component back on, and restart Outlook as you normally would. Repeat this step with each disabled component. When you find a component that causes Outlook to display the error message when you try to start it, you've found your bad component.

6. Start Outlook in safe mode to disable the component again, and this time, leave it disabled.

If no components appear in the Disabled Items dialog box, try looking for a bad or corrupted add-in that Outlook didn't spot. Because all add-ins are turned off by default when Outlook runs in safe mode, Outlook will run in safe mode without error, but you won't know which of the disabled add-ins caused the problem. And when Outlook runs normally again, it returns the add-ins to their normal state, so if a bad add-in that escaped Outlook's attention is turned back on, it will cause you grief the next time you run Outlook.

You can methodically test each add-in by running Outlook in safe mode, turning off the add-in, and then running Outlook normally again. If Outlook runs correctly, you've found the bad add-in. If not, start Outlook in safe mode, and disable the next add-in.

Tip

When the Add-In Manager dialog box first opens, you'll notice that all extension check boxes are cleared because Outlook is in safe mode. Don't let that fool you—unless you make changes to this list, the next time you run Outlook normally, all add-ins will return to their previous status.

1. Press the Ctrl key, and start Outlook in safe mode.
2. On the Tools menu, click Options.
3. On the Other tab of the Options dialog box, click Advanced Options.
4. In the Advanced Options dialog box, click Add-In Manager.
5. In the Add-In Manager dialog box, select every extension check box, and then clear the extension check box for the component most likely to be causing a failure (perhaps the one you've most recently added). If you can't decide which one to test, just try going in order, from top to bottom.

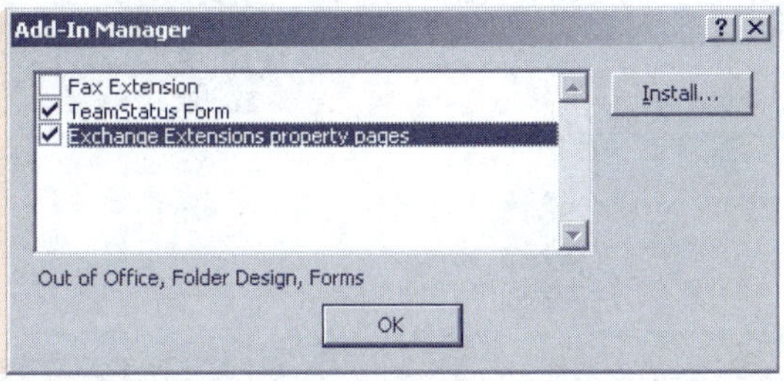

6. Click OK three times to close all dialog boxes.
7. Quit Outlook, and then restart it in normal mode.
8. If Outlook starts without problems, you've turned off the corrupted add-in. Otherwise, perform all of the previous steps again, but test a different add-in in step 5. Repeat this procedure until you either find the corrupt add-in or have turned off all add-ins (in which case, you at least know that it's not an add-in causing the problem).

Are you having problems synchronizing your offline folders?

yes → Are you trying to find the synchronization log?

- yes →
- no → **Go to...** My offline folders aren't synchronizing correctly, page 264.

no ↓

Are you not given a choice to work online or offline?

yes → **Go to...** I'm never prompted whether to work online or offline, page 269.

no ↓

Is your offline storage file growing too large?

yes →

no ↓

Do you want to set up Outlook to work offline?

yes → **Go to...** I don't know how to work offline with Microsoft Exchange Server, page 270.

no ↓

Do you just want to pick up e-mail when you're offline and not synchronize?

yes → **Go to...** I don't know how to set up and use Remote Mail, page 274.

Quick fix

I can't find the synchronization log When you synchronize your offline folder with Microsoft Exchange mailbox, an error occurs. You see in the Outlook Send/Receive Progress dialog box that a synchronization log is being saved but you don't know where it is.

1. In the Folder List, click Deleted Items.
2. Double-click the latest item with Synchronization log in the title.

Go to...
My offline storage file is becoming too large, page 277.

If your solution isn't here, check these related chapters:

- E-mail, connecting, page 80
- E-mail, receiving, page 104

Or see the general troubleshooting tips on page xvii.

My offline folders aren't synchronizing correctly

Source of the problem

You use Outlook on a corporate network that uses Microsoft Exchange Server as its e-mail server. You know Outlook is set up to use and synchronize offline folders, but lately it seems as if your synchronization is not working correctly.

There are several possible reasons why your offline folders might not be synchronizing. The best way to figure out what's wrong is to start with the easiest solution and work through different solutions until the problem is fixed.

How to fix it

Work through the troubleshooting procedures in this solution one by one to see whether you can find and fix the problem yourself. If synchronization still doesn't work after you have tried all the procedures, see your network administrator.

Account and delivery settings

1. On the Tools menu, click E-mail Accounts.
2. In the E-mail Accounts Wizard, make sure the View Or Change Existing E-mail Accounts option is selected, and click Next.
3. In the Outlook Processes These Accounts In The Following Order area, be sure that Microsoft Exchange Server is listed.
4. In the Deliver New E-mail To The Following Location box, be sure you see Mailbox – <*your account*>.
5. Click Finish when you've verified the settings.

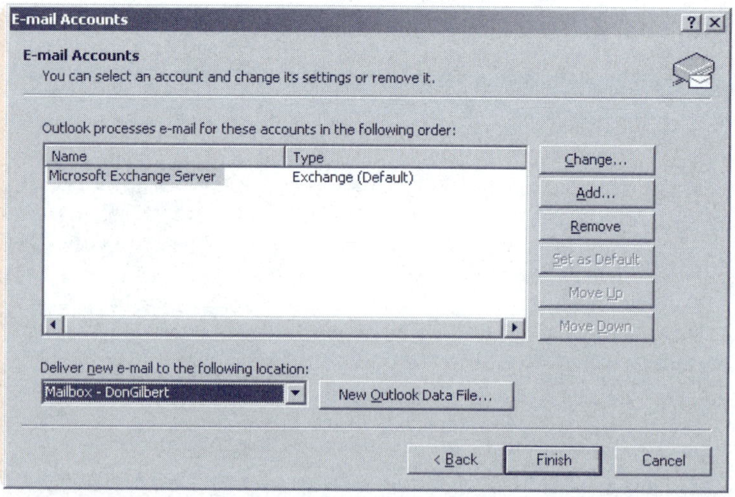

If your profile doesn't include Microsoft Exchange Server, or your e-mail is not delivered to the correct mailbox, make these changes and see whether your synchronization problems are solved. If not, move on to the next procedure in this solution.

Automatic synchronization settings

By default, the All Accounts group will synchronize your folders when you are online; when you are offline, it will synchronize when you click Send/Receive. Even if you've set up a dedicated Send/Receive group, try using the All Accounts group to synchronize both when you click Send/Receive and when you quit Outlook while online, and see if that fixes your problem.

1. On the Tools menu, point to Send/Receive Settings, and click Define Send/Receive Groups.
2. In the Send/Receive Groups dialog box, make sure All Accounts is selected.
3. Make sure the Include This Group In Send/Receive check box is selected in both the When Outlook Is Online and When Outlook Is Offline areas.
4. In the When Outlook Is Online area, select the Perform An Automatic Send/Receive When Exiting check box. ▶

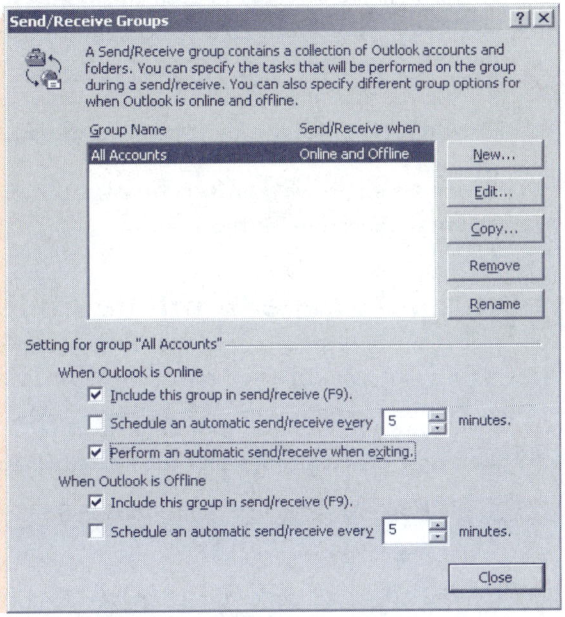

5. Click the Edit button.

This solution is continued on the next page.

My offline folders aren't synchronizing correctly

(continued from page 265)

6. In the Send/Receive Settings dialog box, select the Microsoft Exchange Server account in the Accounts column, and make sure the folders you want synchronized are selected in the Check Folders To Send/Receive box.
7. Click OK, and then click Close.
8. Click the Send/Receive button (or press F9).

If this doesn't solve your synchronization problem, move on to the next procedure in the solution.

Tip

To perform this procedure, you must have Windows Explorer set to display hidden files, folders, and file extensions. In Windows Explorer, on the Tools menu, click Folder Options. On the View tab of the Folder Options dialog box, in the Advanced Settings box, select the Show Hidden Files And Folders option, clear the Hide File Extensions For Known File Types check box, and then click OK.

Potential damage to offline folders

Your problem might be a damaged offline folder (*.ost*) file. To fix a damaged file, you replace it with a new one.

1. Right-click the Outlook Today icon on the Outlook Bar, and click Properties on the shortcut menu.
2. In the Mailbox – <*your account*> dialog box, click the Advanced button.
3. On the Advanced tab of the Microsoft Exchange Server dialog box, click the Offline Folder File Settings button.

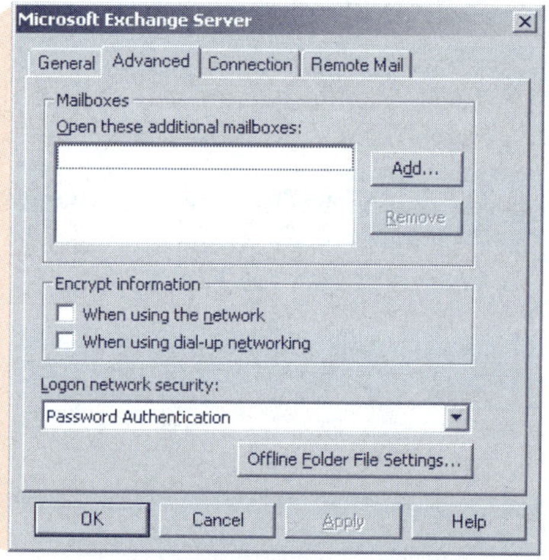

4. In the Offline Folder File Settings dialog box, look at the name and location of the *outlook.ost* file in the File box, and write it down. (Click the File box, and use the arrow keys to scroll back and forth to see the entire path.)

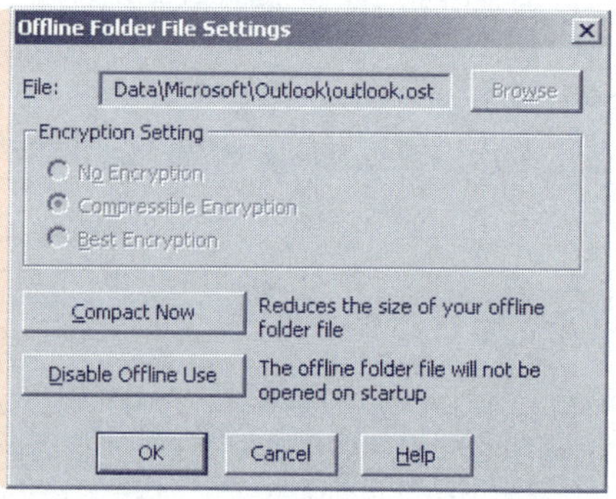

5. Click Cancel three times to close all open dialog boxes.
6. Quit Outlook.
7. In Windows Explorer, navigate to the location of the *outlook.ost* file.
8. Right-click the *outlook.ost* file icon, and click Rename on the shortcut menu.

9. Replace the extension *.ost* with *.old*, and press Enter.

10. Start Outlook.

11. On the Tools menu, point to Send/Receive, and click Send and Receive All.

Synchronizing all folders (as in step 9) creates a new offline folder (*.ost*) file. You won't lose or damage any information doing this, because your offline folder file is just a replica of the information that's stored in your Exchange Server mailbox. If synchronization doesn't work and you want your offline files back, rename the *outlook.old* file to outlook.ost.

If this procedure fixes your synchronization problems, great—stop here. If not, move on to the last procedure in the solution.

Tip

If you want to clean up your hard disk, feel free to delete the old offline folder file (the one with the *.old* extension).

Potential damage to Exchange Server support files

If you still can't synchronize your offline files, you might be working with damaged Microsoft Exchange Server support files. To fix this problem, remove your Exchange Server support files and replace the deleted files with fresh Outlook files by reinstalling Office XP.

1. Click the Windows Start button, point to Search, and click For Files Or Folders. (Point to Find In, and click Files Or Folders if you don't see Search on the menu.)

2. Type *em*32.dll* in the Search For Files Or Folders Named box, and make sure the Look In box contains the drive where you installed Outlook.

3. Click Search Now. Windows should find the files *emsabp32.dll*, *emsmdb32.dll*, *emsui32.dll*, and *emablt32.dll*.

4. Rename each file by replacing the *.dll* extension with *.old*.

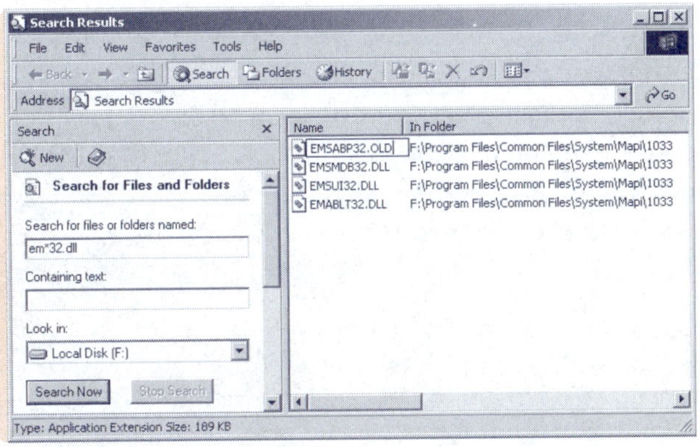

Tip

To rename a file, either right-click the file, and click Rename on the shortcut menu, or click the file name twice (not a double-click).

This solution is continued on the next page.

My offline folders aren't synchronizing correctly

(continued from page 267)

When you rename a file with a new extension, your programs won't be able to find and use that file, but the file will still be in your system. If you need to reinstall the file, all you have to do is replace the original extension in the file name.

1. Click the Windows Start button, point to Settings, and click Control Panel.
2. In the Control Panel, double-click the Add/Remove Programs icon.
3. In the Add/Remove Programs dialog box, on the Install/Uninstall tab, click the name of the Microsoft Office suite you've installed (such as Microsoft Office XP Professional), and click Change.

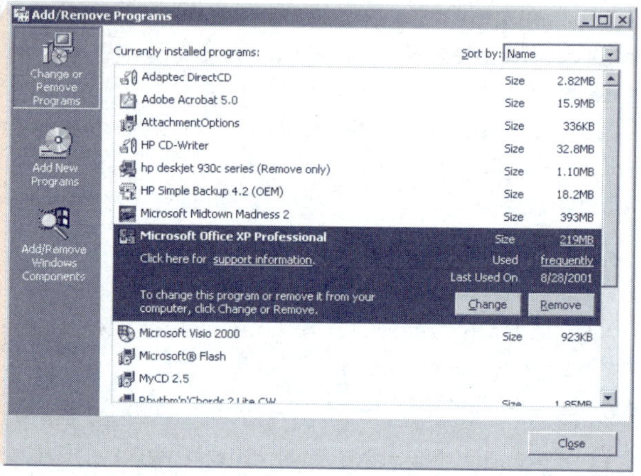

4. In the Microsoft Office XP Setup Wizard, select the Repair Office option, and click Next.
5. Select the Reinstall Office option, and then click Install.

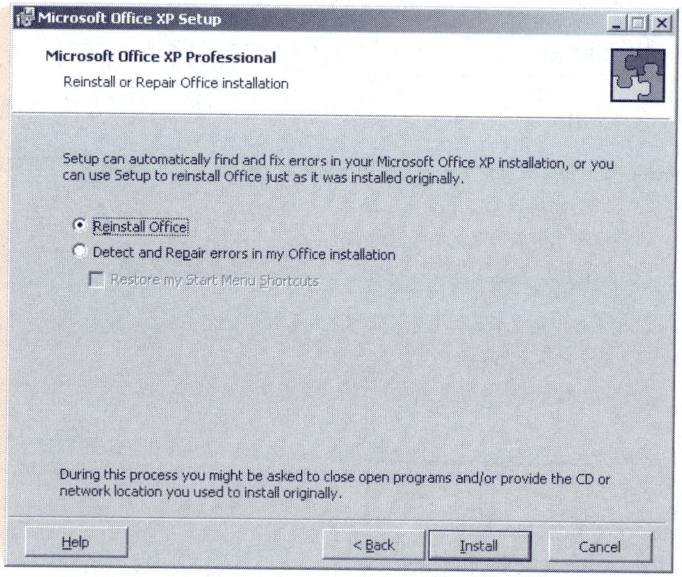

If this procedure fixes your synchronization problems, terrific. If it doesn't, contact your network administrator. Your synchronization problem might be something your network administrator needs to fix.

I'm never prompted whether to work online or offline

Source of the problem

You use a portable computer and use Outlook to connect to your Exchange Server from various locations. But for some reason you're never prompted when you start Outlook whether or not you want to work offline. This was an option when you first set up the capability to work offline, but if you declined it (or if the prompt used to appear, but you can't remember how you turned it off), it's easy to make the prompt appear and get back in control.

Tip

This procedure assumes you're set up to work offline. See "I don't know how to work offline with Microsoft Exchange Server" later in this chapter if you aren't set up to work offline (or if you're not sure whether you are or not).

How to fix it

1. On the Tools menu, click E-mail Options.
2. In the E-mail Accounts Wizard, make sure the View Or Change Existing E-mail Accounts option is selected, and click Next.
3. Make sure Microsoft Exchange Server is selected, and click the Change button.
4. Click the More Settings button.
5. On the General tab of the Microsoft Exchange Server dialog box, in the When Starting area, select the Manually Control Connection State option.
6. Make sure the Choose The Connection Type When Starting check box is selected.
7. Click OK.
8. Click Next, and then click Finish. The next time you run Outlook, you'll see a dialog box asking you how you want to connect.

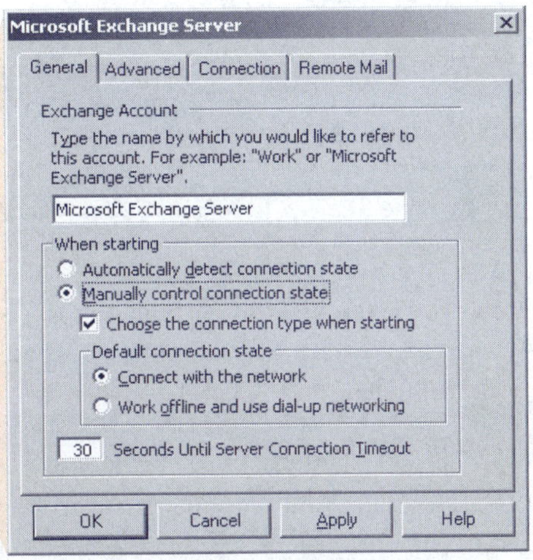

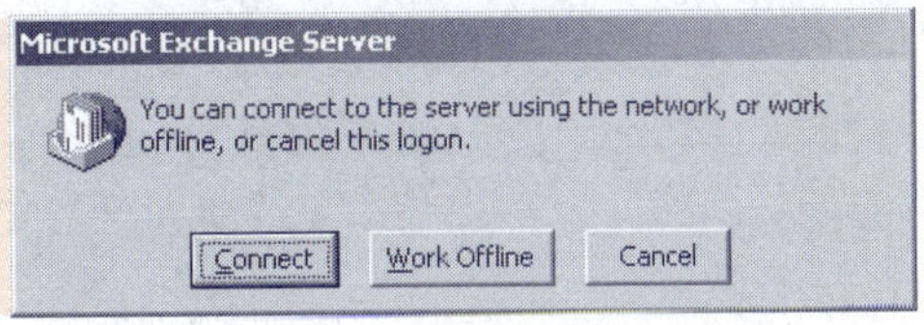

I don't know how to work offline with Microsoft Exchange Server

Source of the problem

Your computer is set up with a corporate account that uses Microsoft Exchange Server, but you'd like to take the computer, your e-mail, and your other Outlook data home or to another office for a while. Outlook can easily be configured to work from files downloaded from Microsoft Exchange Server and stored on your computer in a file called an offline storage file. When you move data back and forth between your mailbox and your offline storage file, it's called synchronizing. And you can pick exactly which folders you want to synchronize so you take only what you need.

> **Tip**
>
> If your computer is set up to work offline but you're not being prompted about working online or offline when you start Outlook, you can set Outlook to let you make that decision. See "I'm never prompted whether to work online or offline" earlier in this chapter.

How to fix it

1. On the File menu, click Work Offline. If the Work Offline command doesn't appear on the menu, your computer is already configured to work offline.
2. In the Set Up To Work Offline folder, click OK. ▶

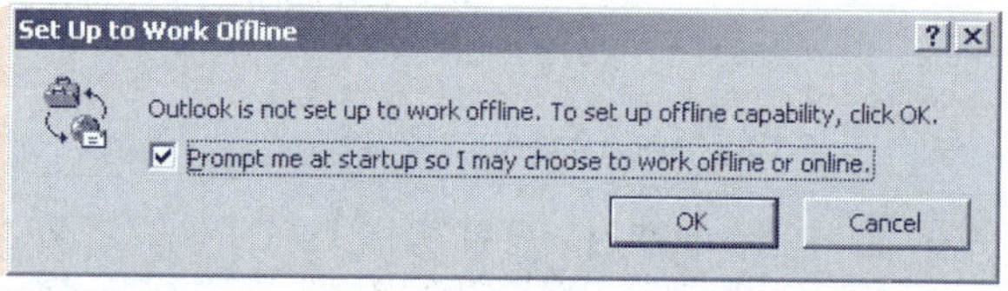

3. You'll see a message telling you that Outlook has completed setup for offline use. Click Yes. ▶

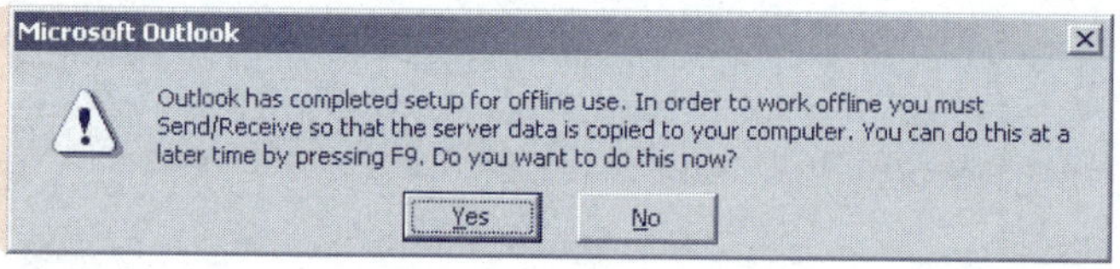

That's all there is to setting up the offline storage file. The next time you log on to Outlook, you'll be asked whether you want to work online or offline. If you choose offline, you'll connect to your mail server and synchronize only when you click the Send/Receive button on the toolbar.

More about setting up offline folders

Although Outlook provides you with a set of default folders to synchronize in the All Accounts group, you can tailor this list so that you synchronize only the ones you want. For example, you might not want to synchronize the Sent Items and Deleted Items folders to shorten your synchronization time.

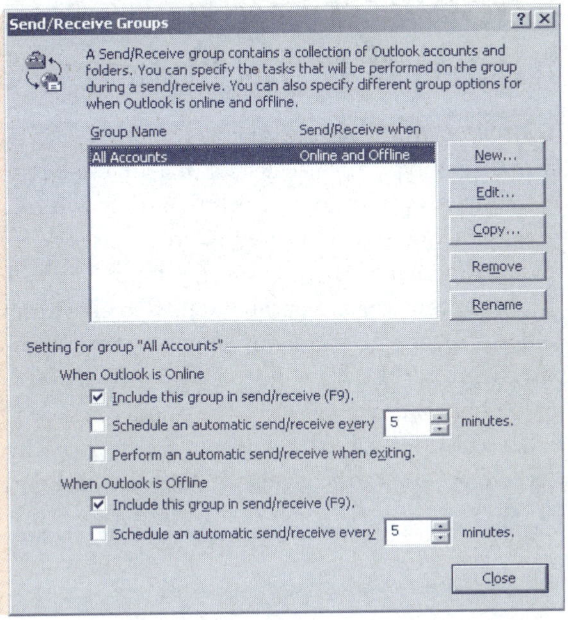

1. On the Tools menu, point to Send/Receive Settings, and click Define Send/Receive Groups.
2. In the Send/Receive Groups dialog box, select All Accounts, and click the Edit button.
3. In the Send/Receive Settings – All Accounts dialog box, clear the check boxes for the folders that you don't want to synchronize, or select those that you do.
4. Click OK, and then click Close to close each open dialog box.

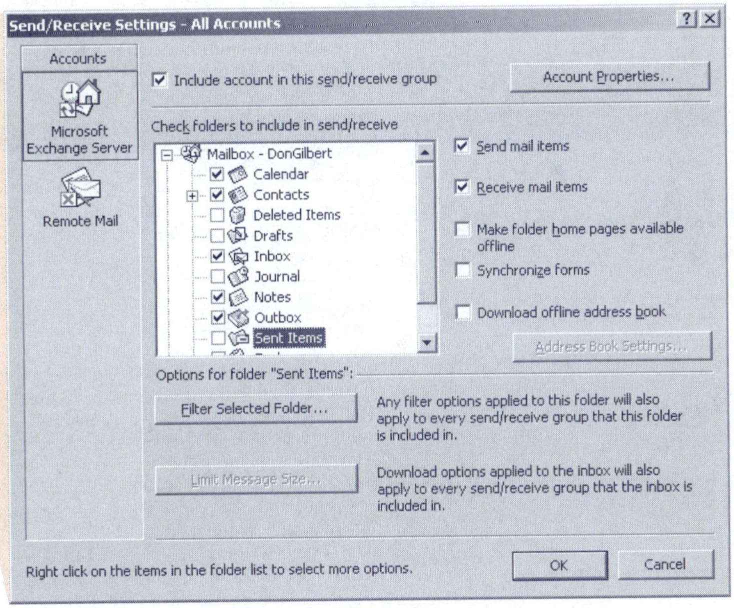

Note

Synchronized folders stay in the offline storage file, so the folders you grabbed at the office will remain on your computer—this speeds synchronization the next time.

This solution is continued on the next page.

I don't know how to work offline with Microsoft Exchange Server

(continued from page 271)

If you typically use a slow dial-up connection to connect to your mailbox and pick up your e-mail when you're away from the office, you might want to synchronize all your folders while you're at work and connected to your network. Then you can synchronize a smaller number of folders—perhaps just your Inbox—when you're away from the office.

You can create a unique Send/Receive account to synchronize only some of your Outlook folders. On the Tools menu, point to Send/Receive Settings, click Define Send/Receive Groups, and then click the New button. Type the name of your group in the Send/Receive Group Name dialog box, and click OK. In the Send/Receive Settings dialog box, you can then set up folders as described for the All Accounts group. When you want to synchronize using your new Send/Receive group, on the Tools menu, point to Send/Receive, and click the name of the group.

ynchronizing data

I don't know how to set up and use Remote Mail

Source of the problem

You use Outlook on a Microsoft Exchange Server network at work and have configured it to work offline. But when you're on the road and you connect to pick up your e-mail, you don't want to synchronize your offline storage file every time. (Synchronizations can sometimes take a surprisingly long time—usually when you have very little time to spare.)

If you're at a location, such as an airport, where you need to limit connection time, the quickest way to check your e-mail is to use Remote Mail, which downloads only the e-mail from your Inbox and doesn't synchronize. For an even shorter connection time, you can download only headers so that you can decide which messages you want to take the time to download later. You can even filter the e-mail messages downloaded—for example, messages from specific users you need to communicate with and not those from anyone else.

How to fix it

Set up your Remote Mail account

1. On the Tools menu, point to Send/Receive Settings, and click Define Send/Receive Groups.
2. In the Send/Receive Groups dialog box, click New.
3. In the Send/Receive Group Name dialog box, delete the default name provided, type a name you'll remember for accessing Remote Mail, such as *My Remote Mail*, and then click OK.

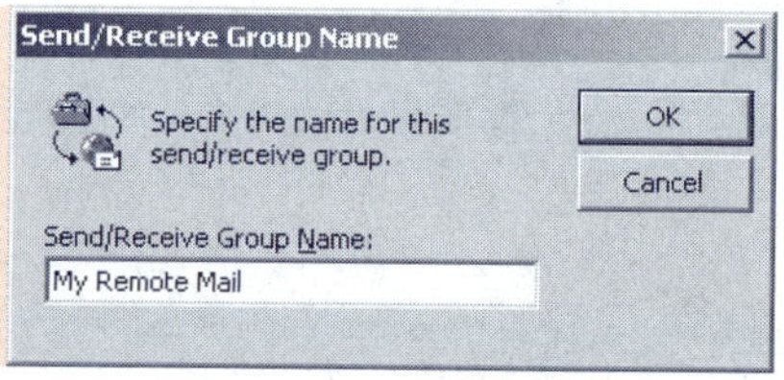

4. In the Send/Receive Settings dialog box, in the Accounts list on the left, click Remote Mail.

5. At the top of the Send/Receive Settings – <*group name*> dialog box, select the Include Account In This Send/Receive Group check box.

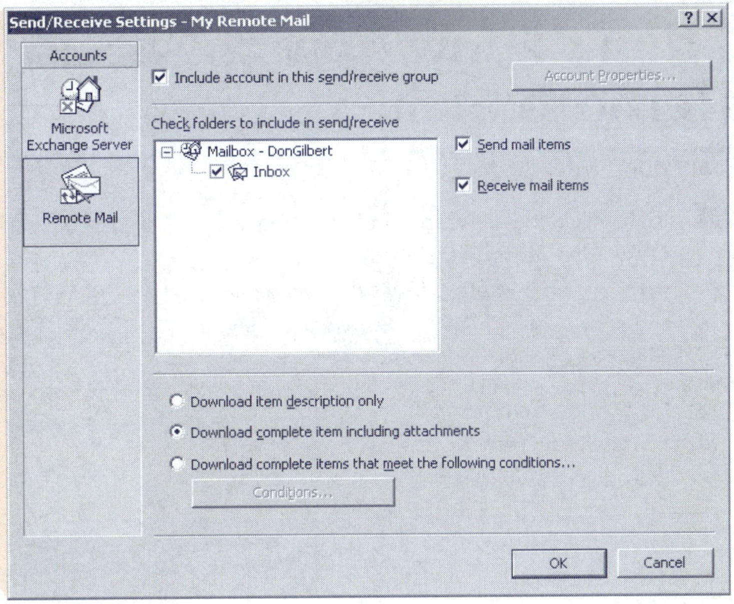

6. If you want only the headers downloaded, select the Download Item Description Only option. If you want to filter the e-mail, select the Download Complete Items That Meet The Following Conditions option, click Conditions, set the conditions of e-mail to download in the Filter dialog box, and click OK. (Click the Help button in the Filter dialog box if you need information on any of the options.)

7. Click OK, and then click Close to close each open dialog box.

Retrieving messages using Remote Mail

If Remote Mail is set up to download e-mail messages, retrieve your e-mail by pointing to Send/Receive on the Tools menu and clicking the name of your Remote Mail account—My Remote Mail, in this example.

If Remote Mail is set up to download only message headers, retrieving your e-mail involves a few more steps.

1. On the Tools menu, point to Send/Receive, and click the name of your Remote Mail account.

2. Look over the downloaded headers, and then select the ones for the messages you want to download.

Tip

You can download only headers even if Remote Mail is set up to download entire messages. On the Tools menu, point to Send/Receive, point to Work With Headers, and then click Download Headers. However, with this technique, synchronization is minimal.

This solution is continued on the next page.

I don't know how to set up and use Remote Mail

(continued from page 275)

3. Right-click the selection, and click Mark To Download Message(s) on the shortcut menu. (If you want to leave the message on the server, click Mark to Download Message Copy.) ▶

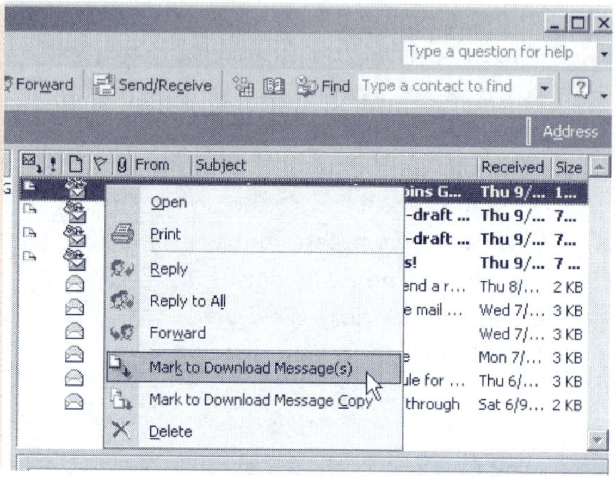

4. Click your Remote Mail account name (as in step 1) to retrieve the messages you selected to download.

My offline storage file is becoming too large

Source of the problem

In your previous version of Outlook, the contents of folders you stopped synchronizing were removed from your offline storage (*.ost*) file; but since upgrading to Outlook 2002, you've noticed that all information is maintained when you're no longer synchronizing them. This behavior is actually considered a benefit, because it provides access to more information when you are offline and takes less synchronization time over slow connections. However, it also means your *.ost* file continues to grow as you synchronize more folders because synchronized folders are never removed. Fortunately, you can easily remove any folder from offline storage that you no longer synchronize. First you need to make sure that the folder will not be synchronized; then you can clear its contents.

How to fix it

1. In the Folder List, click the folder from which you want to remove content.
2. On the Tools menu, point to Send/Receive Settings, and make sure the Make This Folder Available Offline option is turned off (no check mark appears next to it).
3. Right-click the folder and click Properties on the shortcut menu.
4. On the General tab of the folder's Properties dialog box, click the Clear Offline Items button.
5. Click OK twice to close the message box that appears and the Properties dialog box.

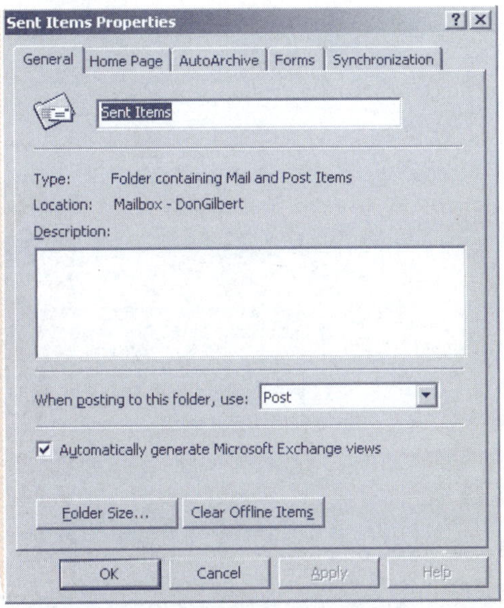

Tip

You can easily synchronize any folder you've cleared by pointing to Send/Receive Settings on the Tools menu and clicking Make This Folder Available Offline, and then clicking the Send/Receive button to synchronize the folder.

Do the tasks lists in your main Tasks folder, TaskPad, and Outlook Today window match?

yes → Are the TaskPad field and task list missing?

yes →

no ↓

Does your TaskPad display the fields you want?

no ↓

Quick fix

My TaskPad isn't displaying the fields I want to see

1. Right-click the TaskPad's column headings, and click Field Chooser on the shortcut menu.
2. In the list box at the top of the Field Chooser, select a category of fields. The category All Task Fields contains all the appropriate fields for the TaskPad.
3. Drag a field name button from the Field Chooser to the TaskPad, and drop it on the row of TaskPad column headings.
4. Close the Field Chooser by clicking its close button.

no ↓

Go to...

The task lists in different parts of Outlook don't match, page 280.

Tasks and TaskPad

Go to...

The TaskPad field and task list are missing from the TaskPad, page 282.

Do you want to change the column labels in your TaskPad or Tasks folder?

yes

Quick fix

I want different column labels in the TaskPad or Task folder

1. Right-click the column label you don't like, and click Format Columns on the shortcut menu.
2. In the Format Columns dialog box, in the Label box, type the column label you would rather have.
3. Click OK.

If your solution isn't here, check these related chapters:

- Importing and Exporting, page 184
- Calendar layout, page 24

Or see the general troubleshooting tips on page xvii.

The task lists in different parts of Outlook don't match

Source of the problem

The task lists in your TaskPad, Outlook Today window, and main Tasks folder don't show the same set of tasks in the same way—you can see tasks in one place that don't show up in another. Don't panic! All these tasks lists are based on the same master list. If you see different lists, it's because you have different views and possibly different filters applied in those windows.

On the one hand, it's useful to be able to maintain different task lists in these different Tasks folders—for example, you might want to display only your most critical tasks in the TaskPad and Outlook Today task lists, but display all your tasks in the main Tasks folder. But on the other hand, it's disconcerting and misleading if you don't see the list you expect.

Tip

The Outlook Today window and TaskPad display tasks from only the main Tasks folder. They won't display tasks from any Tasks subfolders you create.

How to fix it

Each task list offers a slightly different set of built-in views and a slightly different technique for choosing the view you want.

Change the Tasks folder view

In the main Tasks folder and the Tasks subfolders you create, you can choose built-in views, customize existing views, and create new views.

1. On the View menu, point to Current View, and click a view in the list of those available. ▶

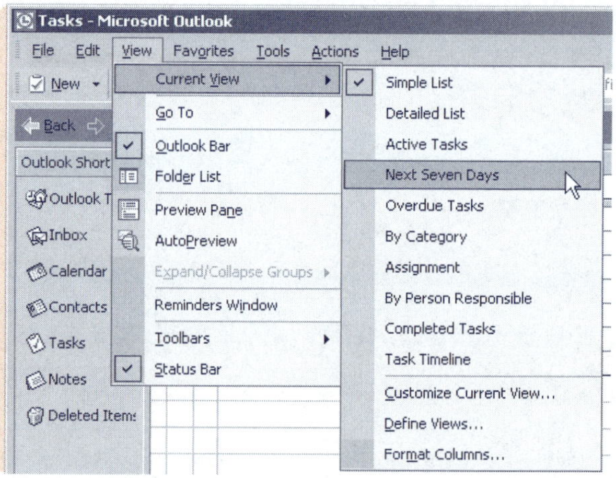

2. If you want to alter an existing view, click Customize Current View instead. In the View Summary dialog box, make changes to the view that's currently displayed.
3. If you want to create a new custom view, click Define Views. In the Define Views dialog box, click the New button, type a name for the new view, click Table, and then build your new view in the View Summary dialog box.

Change the TaskPad view

In the TaskPad, you can select from among only a handful of built-in views.

1. Open the Calendar, and be sure the TaskPad is displayed.
2. On the View menu, point to TaskPad View, and click a built-in view. ▶

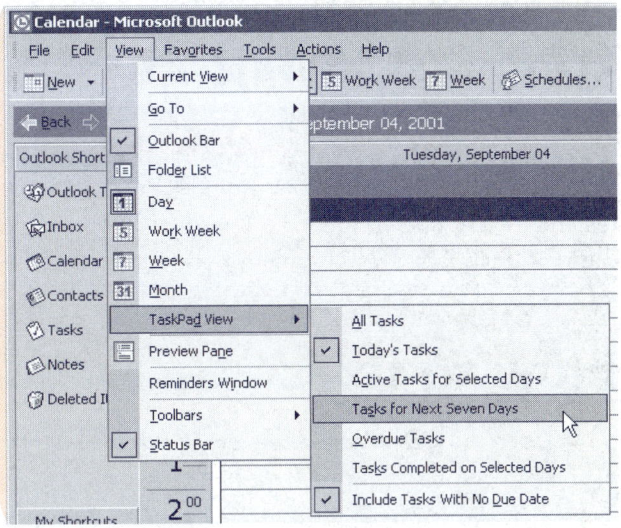

Change the Outlook Today task view

The Outlook Today window can display the task list in only a handful of built-in views.

1. Open the Outlook Today window.
2. Click the Customize Outlook Today button. ▶
3. In the Tasks area of the Customize Outlook Today window, select the options you want to use for the Outlook Today tasks list.
4. Click the Save Changes button. ▶

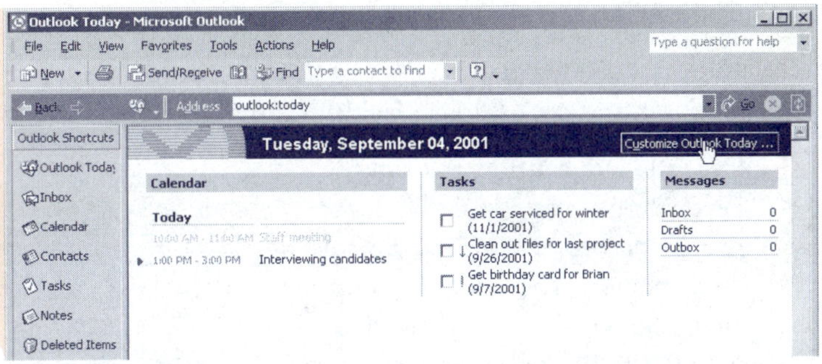

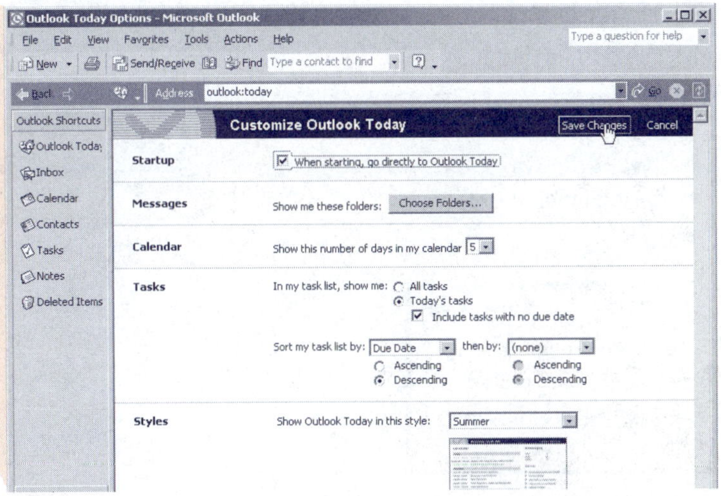

The Outlook Today window appears with your new tasks view displayed.

The TaskPad field and task list are missing from the TaskPad

Source of the problem

You've been clicking and dragging in the Calendar, learning how to change and customize your Calendar view, and you've inadvertently lost your task list by dragging the field out of the row of TaskPad field labels. No problem—it's easy to replace the missing field.

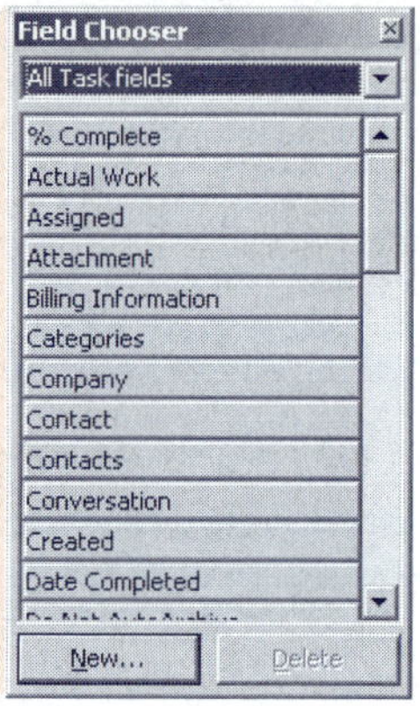

How to fix it

1. Open the Calendar in Daily or Weekly view so that the TaskPad is displayed.
2. Right-click any of the TaskPad's column headings, and then click Field Chooser on the shortcut menu.
3. Click the down arrow to the right of the box at the top of the Field Chooser, and click All Task Fields in the drop-down list.
4. Drag the Subject button from the Field Chooser to the TaskPad, and drop it on the row of TaskPad column headings. Then drag the button along the row of column headings until the red arrows point to the spot where you want to insert the field name.
5. Close the Field Chooser by clicking its Close button. Now your TaskPad looks the way it did when you first installed Outlook.

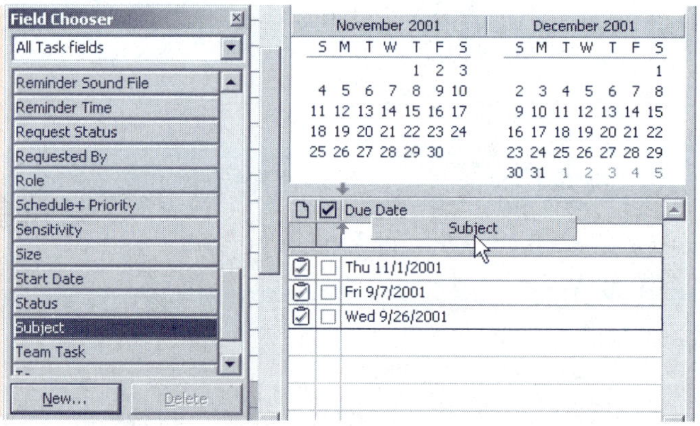

Tip

The trick here is the field label, *TaskPad*. It's really the Subject field, with an altered label.

More about Tasks folder view

Task items usually need notes in the Notes field, such as a phone number or an order quantity, to remind you of exactly what that task entails. You can use the Field Chooser to display the Notes field in your Tasks window, but the Notes field displays only four or five words. A more useful way to display notes is to turn on AutoPreview by right-clicking an empty space in the Tasks window and clicking AutoPreview on the shortcut menu. Every task that has notes associated with it will display up to three lines of notes in blue type in that task row.

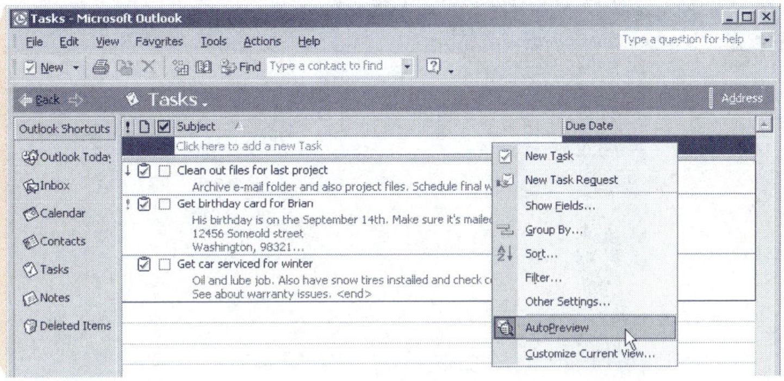

Are you deciding whether to upgrade to Outlook 2002?

yes

Are you unsure if features you currently use and require are supported in Outlook 2002?

yes

Go to...
I'm not sure whether I should upgrade to Outlook 2002, page 290.

no

Are you having problems getting your rules to work since you upgraded?

yes

no

Are you having trouble locating all the commands or features you used in previous versions of Outlook?

yes

Go to...
Some commands and features aren't where I expect them to be, page 286.

Upgrading

Quick fix

My rules don't work since I upgraded to Outlook 2002 The problem might be that you need to upgrade your rules. Upgrading your rules will make them incompatible with previous versions of Outlook, so don't do this unless you don't plan on reverting to an earlier version or your rules file is backed up.

1. On the Tools menu, click Rules Wizard.
2. In the Rules Wizard dialog box, click the Options button.
3. If the Upgrade Now button is available, click it. If it's not available, your rules have already been upgraded.

If your solution isn't here, see the general trouble-shooting tips on page xvii.

Some commands and features aren't where I expect them to be

Source of the problem

You've upgraded to Outlook 2002 from Outlook 2000. You like the new features, but you can't find some of the familiar features you used in the older version. Although user-interface improvements are common in new software versions, it can be frustrating to look for a familiar command and find that it's not there. Fortunately, with a few exceptions, most Outlook 2002 commands are in the same place as in previous versions. The most notable exceptions involve the Options dialog box, some e-mail commands, and the way Outlook now interfaces with Microsoft Exchange Server.

Tip

Some functionality available in Outlook 2000 is no longer supported in Outlook 2002. See "I'm not sure if I should upgrade to Outlook 2002" later in this chapter to see whether a feature you're looking for is simply not included in Outlook 2002.

How to fix it

Changes to the Options dialog box

The Options dialog box, which you access from the Tools menu, contains the largest number of features in one place in Outlook. Consequently, it has been affected the most by the upgrade:

- **Outlook 2000 Mail Format tab—Send Pictures From The Internet** In Outlook 2002, this check box has been removed from the Mail Format tab in the Options dialog box. However, it is still available for individual HTML e-mail messages when you are using Outlook's e-mail editor. On the message form's Format menu, click Send Pictures From The Internet.
- **Outlook 2000 Security tab—Zone box** Although not a missing or moved item, you should note that the Zone box in the Secure Content area defaults to Restricted Zone in Outlook 2002, which will cause certain elements on some Web pages not to work.

- **Outlook 2000 Advanced Tasks dialog box** The options in this Outlook 2000 dialog box (accessed by clicking the Advanced Options button on the Other tab and then clicking the Advanced Tasks button) are all accessed through the Task Options dialog box in Outlook 2002. On the Preferences tab, click the Task Options button.

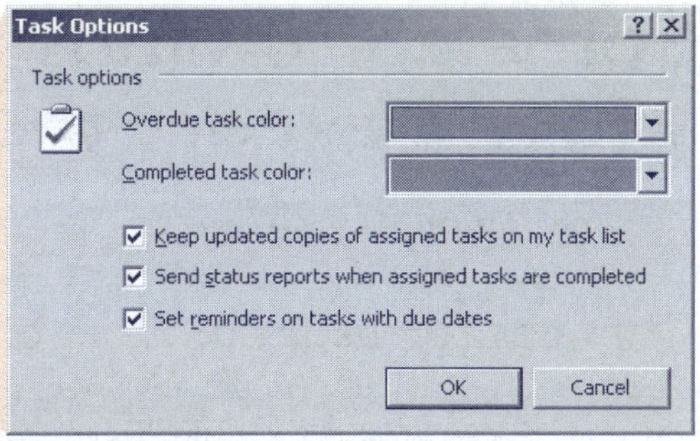

- **Outlook 2000 Other Tab—Preview Pane button** It's gone. You cannot change the font of the preview header in Outlook 2002.
- **Outlook 2000 Internet E-mail tab** This tab has been removed from Outlook 2002. The Internet E-mail sending format options are now accessed by clicking the Internet Format button on the Mail Format tab. The Dial-up connection options have been moved to the Mail Setup tab.

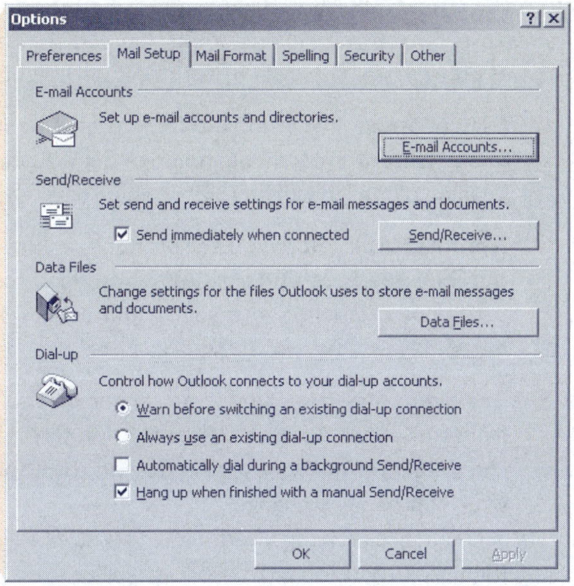

Changes to addressing e-mail messages

The method of addressing messages in Outlook 2002 is fairly consistent with previous versions, with only a couple of twists:

- **The Bcc and From fields** To add Bcc or From lines to your e-mail messages, click the down arrow to the right of the Options button, and then click the field you want to add to your message form in the drop-down list.

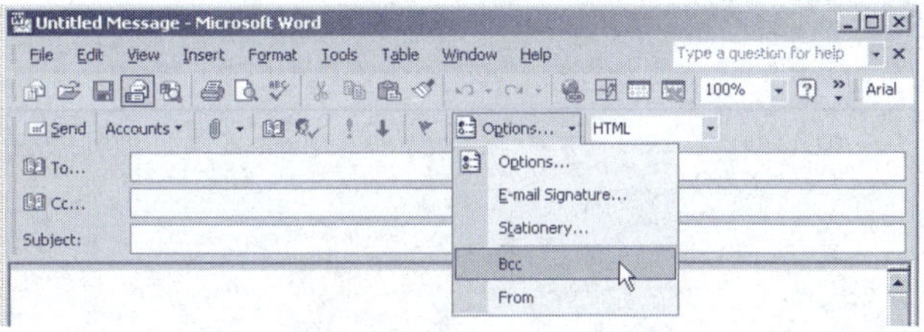

- **AutoName** The way Outlook looks up the e-mail addresses that you type has totally changed in Outlook 2002. For more details, see "My nicknames no longer distinguish between my contacts" on page 76.
- **Sorting names** When you open the Select Names dialog box (by clicking To in a message form, for example), you can no longer sort contact names by clicking on the column headers.

If this solution didn't solve your problem, go to the next page.

Some commands and features aren't where I expect them to be

(continued from page 287)

Changes for users of Corporate/Workgroup mode

The merging of what were previously separate Outlook modes into a single Outlook 2002 platform has the greatest impact on those using a Microsoft Exchange Server network and migrating from the Corporate/Workgroup mode of Outlook 2000. Although the changes in this area are too many to cover entirely in this book, here are the most common commands you might be looking for and pointers to the areas of Outlook 2002 where they are now handled:

- **Synchronize** In Outlook 2002, this command is no longer available directly from the Tools menu. On the Tools menu, point to Send/Receive Settings, and then click Define Send/Receive Groups to define offline folders and access synchronization options.
- **Remote Mail** After you set up Remote Mail in Outlook 2000, it was available as a submenu of the Tools menu. In Outlook 2002, you need to set up a Send/Receive Group for Remote Mail. See "I don't know how to set up and use Remote Mail" on page 274 to learn more about Remote Mail in Outlook 2002.
- **Services** This command is no longer on the Tools menu. Most of this information is accessed from the E-mail Accounts Wizard in Outlook 2002. For example, to access the Microsoft Exchange Server account properties, on the Tools menu, click E-mail Accounts, click Next, select your Microsoft Exchange account, click Change, and then click the More Settings button.

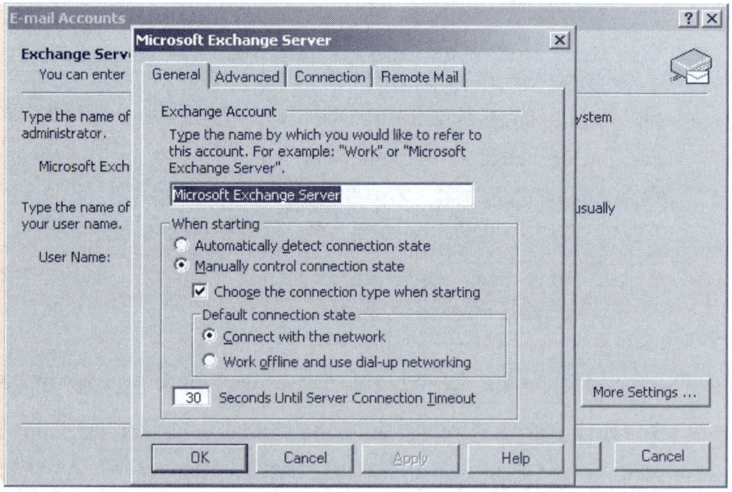

- **Mail Services tab of the Options dialog box** This tab is not part of the Options dialog box in Outlook 2002. To access the Startup settings, click the Windows Start menu, point to Settings, click Control Panel, double-click the Mail icon, and click the Show Profiles button. To access the offline folder options, on the Tools menu, point to Send/Receive Settings, and click Define Send/Receive Groups. Then select the account you want. In Outlook 2002, you automatically synchronize all folders when you click the Send/Receive button. But you can set up a Send/Receive group for use offline and then pick the folders you want to synchronize when you click Send/Receive for that group.

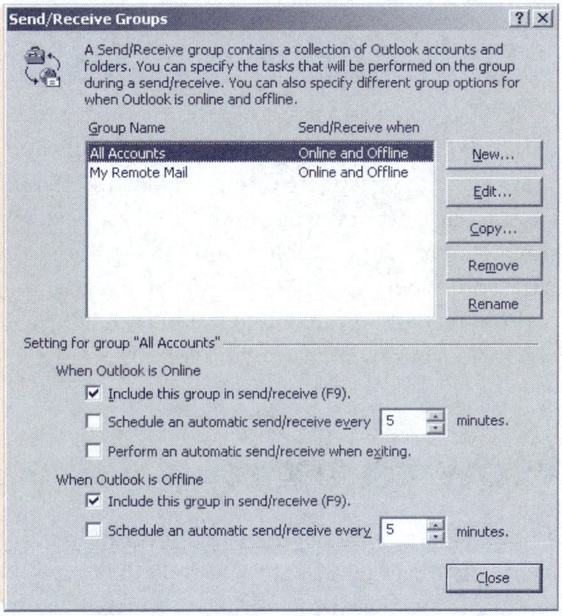

- **Preferences tab of the Options dialog box** In Outlook 2002, the Calendar Options dialog box, accessed by clicking the Calendar Options button, no longer includes the Use Microsoft Schedule+ As My Primary Calendar option or the Always Use Local Calendar option.

I'm not sure whether I should upgrade to Outlook 2002

Source of the problem

There are plenty of good reasons to upgrade to Outlook 2002, and you've read about many of them. But you also know that there are always some exceptions to the general rule of keeping up with upgrades, and you don't want any unpleasant surprises.

As with every software product, the designers of Outlook had to make some choices about what to support and what to drop. If you use one of the features in a previous version that isn't supported in Outlook 2002, you'll have to decide whether to change the way you do things or stay with your older version. Or, if you've already upgraded to Outlook 2002, maybe the missing feature is the source of a problem you've been having. So here's a list of what's been dropped so that you can make your own decision about upgrading.

How to fix it

These features are not supported in Outlook 2002. If you currently use any of the first four services, when you upgrade to Outlook 2002 you'll be notified during setup that these services will be removed if you elect to continue with the installation.

- **Fax services** Outlook 2002 does not support Microsoft Fax and WinFax Starter Edition (SE), which worked with earlier versions of Outlook. It does support Windows 2000 Fax, which is built into Windows 2000.
- **Net Folders** Outlook users who have only Internet e-mail access will need to find another means of sharing their data (perhaps a Web storage site) or stay with Outlook 2000.
- **Microsoft Mail** Outlook 2002 does not support Microsoft Mail and the workgroup post office that was part of older Windows versions.
- **CC:Mail** Microsoft dropped support for the translator service used to connect Outlook with CC:Mail.
- **Sharing the Address Book** In Outlook 2002, you can import the Windows Address Book to your Contacts folder, but changes you make to your contacts in Outlook 2002 are not copied back to the Address Book automatically. This makes it a little harder to use the same contact data for Outlook and other programs that use the Windows Address Book (such as Windows 2000 Fax). See "My Contacts list doesn't appear in the Windows 2000 Fax Wizard" on page 152 to learn how to move information between the Address Book and your Contacts folder.

Upgrading

Glossary

ActiveX *n.* A set of technologies that enables software components to interact with one another in a networked environment, regardless of the language in which the components were created. ActiveX, which was developed by Microsoft in the mid 1990s and is currently administered by the Open Group, is built on Microsoft's Component Object Model (COM). Currently, ActiveX is used primarily to develop interactive content for the World Wide Web although it can be used in desktop applications and other programs. ActiveX controls can be embedded in Web pages to produce animation and other multimedia effects, interactive objects, and sophisticated applications.

ActiveX control *n.* A reusable software component based on Microsoft's ActiveX technology that is used to add interactivity and more functionality, such as animation or a popup menu, to a Web page, applications, and software development tools. An ActiveX control can be written in any of a number of languages, including Java, C++, and Visual Basic.

add-in *n.* A component that adds functionality to Outlook. COM add-ins are executable (*.exe*) or Dynamic Link Library (*.dll*) files. Exchange Client add-in (*.ecf*) files can be used by Outlook programs that connect to a Microsoft Exchange Server.

adult mail *n.* An unsolicited e-mail message that typically contains an advertisement for a Web site or other business engaged in displaying material of a pornographic nature or otherwise targeted to adult viewers. *See* spam.

appointment *n.* A data type and form in Outlook, usually stored in the Calendar folder, which enables users to track meetings. From the appointment form, users can also perform related activities such as scheduling attendees, making notes about the meeting, and setting a reminder time.

archive *n.* **1.** A tape or disk containing files copied from another storage device and used as backup storage. **2.** A compressed file. **3.** A file directory on the Internet that is available by File Transfer Protocol (FTP) or an Internet directory established for dissemination of stored files.

Archive *vb.* **1.** To copy files onto a tape or disk for long-term storage. **2.** To compress a file.

AutoArchive **1.** *n.* An Outlook feature that automatically and at regular intervals moves items of a specified age from Outlook's main data store to a separate archive file. **2.** *vb.* To turn on the Outlook AutoArchive feature so that items are archived without requiring manual initiation.

AutoReply *vb.* To automatically send a reply message when receiving an e-mail message. AutoReply is a feature used in conjunction with the Out of Office Assistant, an Outlook extension available for Microsoft Exchange Server users. AutoReply responds to incoming e-mail messages with a preset message that typically indicates the recipient will not be reading the message soon.

backup *n.* A duplicate copy of a program, disk, or data, made either for archiving purposes or for "insurance" in case the active copy is damaged or destroyed. Some application programs automatically make backup copies of data files, maintaining both the current version and the preceding version on disk.

bcc *n.* Acronym for blind courtesy copy. A feature of e-mail programs that enables a user to send a copy of an e-mail message to a recipient without notifying other recipients that this was done. *Also called* blind carbon copy.

cable modem *n.* A modem that sends and receives data through a coaxial cable television network instead of telephone lines, as with a conventional modem. Cable modems, which have speeds of 500 kilobits per second (Kbps), can generally transmit data faster than current conventional modems. However, cable modems do not operate at the same rate upstream (when sending information) and downstream (when receiving information). Upstream rates vary from about 2 Mbps to 10 Mbps, downstream rates from about 10 Mbps to 36 Mbps.

Calendar *n.* An Outlook feature that graphically represents days, weeks, months, and years and is used for highlighting dates and scheduling appointments; also an Outlook folder containing Calendar data.

cc *n.* Acronym for courtesy copy. A directive to an e-mail program to send a complete copy of a given piece of mail to another individual. The use of cc e-mail addressing, as opposed to directly addressing the e-mail to a person, generally implies that the recipient is not required to take any action; the message is for informational purposes only. In a cc directive, the fact that this recipient received the e-mail is printed in the e-mail header and is thus known to all other recipients. *Also called* carbon copy.

COM *n.* Acronym for Component Object Model. A specification developed by Microsoft for building software components that can be assembled into programs or that add functionality to existing programs running on Microsoft Windows platforms.

COM components can be written in a variety of languages (although most are written in C++) and can be unplugged from a program at run time without having to recompile the program. COM is the foundation of the OLE (object linking and embedding), ActiveX, and DirectX specifications.

Contact *n.* **1.** An Outlook data type (form) that contains information about a person, typically including an e-mail address. The Outlook Contact form includes many fields for various types of information about the person and is stored in an appropriate Outlook folder such as the Contacts folder.

CSV *n.* Acronym for comma separated values. File name extensions are assigned to text files containing tabular data of the sort stored in database fields. As the name indicates, individual data entries are separated by commas.

custom field *n.* A field added to a form by a user to store information not included in the provided form.

dial-up connection *n.* Access to a data communications network through a public switched telecommunication network.

display name *n.* The name that appears in the General tab of a Contact form next to Display As. A contact's display name appears on the To, Cc, or Bcc line of any e-mail message that is sent to that person, or on the From line of any message received by that person. By default, Outlook creates a display name by using the full name followed by the e-mail address in parentheses, but this can be modified in the Contact form.

DSL *n.* Acronym for Digital Subscriber Line, a recently developed (late 1990s) digital communications technology that can provide high-speed transmissions over standard copper telephone wiring. DSL is often referred to as xDSL, where the *x* stands for one or two characters that define variations of the basic DSL technology, such as ADSL, HDSL, SDSL, and so on. Currently ADSL (Asymmetric DSL) is the form most often provided, and is commonly referred to simply as DSL.

e-mail *n.* **1.** Short for electronic mail. The exchange of text messages and computer files over a communications network, such as a local area network or the Internet, usually between computers or terminals. **2.** An electronic text message.

export *vb.* To make information available for another system or program by placing it in a file with a known format or structure.

fax *n.* Short for facsimile. The transmission of text or graphics over telephone lines in digitized form. Conventional fax machines scan an original document, transmit an image of the document as a bitmap, and reproduce the received image on a printer. Fax images can also be sent and received by computers equipped with fax hardware and software.

form *n.* A structured window, box, or other self-contained presentation element with predefined areas for entering or changing information. A form is a visual filter for the underlying data it is presenting, generally offering the advantages of better data organization and greater ease of viewing.

free/busy times *n.* Schedule information published by a people in a group and used to determine an available block of time for everyone in the group. Free/busy times are automatically generated and used by Outlook clients sharing a common Microsoft Exchange Server. For Internet-enabled Outlook users, free/busy times can also be published and read from a specified Web site or by using the Microsoft Office Internet Free/Busy Service.

FTP *n.* Acronym for File Transfer Protocol, a fast, application-level protocol widely used for copying files to and from remote computer systems on a network using TCP/IP, such as the Internet. This protocol also enables users to perform tasks such as listing files and directories on the remote system.

header *n.* The portion of an e-mail message containing the addresses and subject line.

HTML *n.* Acronym for Hypertext Markup Language. The markup language used for documents on the World Wide Web. HTML is an application of SGML (Standard Generalized Markup Language) that uses tags to mark elements such as text and graphics in a document. These tags indicate how Web browsers should display the elements to the user and how to respond to user actions such as activation of a link by means of a key press or mouse click.

HTTP *n.* Acronym for Hypertext Transfer Protocol. The protocol used to carry requests from a browser to a Web server and to transport pages from Web servers back to the requesting browser. Although HTTP is almost universally used on the Web, it is not an especially secure protocol.

hyperlink *n.* A connection between an element in a hypertext document, such as a word, phrase, symbol, or image, and another element in the document, another document, a file, or a script. The user activates the link by clicking on the linked element, which is usually underlined or in a color different from the rest of the document to indicate that the element is linked. Hyperlinks are indicated in a hypertext document through tags in markup languages such as SGML and HTML. These tags are generally not visible to the user. *Also called* hot link, hypertext link, link.

IMAP *n.* Acronym for Internet Message Access Protocol. A method for an e-mail program to gain access to e-mail and bulletin board messages stored on a mail server. Unlike POP3, a similar protocol, IMAP allows a user to retrieve messages efficiently from more than one computer.

import *vb.* To bring information from one system or program into another. The system or program receiving the data must support the internal format or structure of the data.

Inbox Repair Tool *n.* A Microsoft Office program, *scanpst.exe*, used to recover folders and items from a corrupted personal folders (*.pst*) file.

ISP *n.* Acronym for Internet service provider. A business that supplies Internet connectivity services to individuals, businesses, and other organizations. Some ISPs are large national or multinational corporations that offer access in many locations, while others are limited to a single city or region. *Also called* access provider, service provider.

Journal *n.* A Microsoft Outlook feature that automatically records actions associated with contacts and displays them in a timeline view.

junk mail *n.* Unsolicited e-mail, usually containing an advertisement, sent to a large number of people. Junk mail is often blocked by Internet service providers and can also be blocked from Outlook by adding the sender to the Junk senders list. *See* spam.

macro *n.* In applications, a set of keystrokes and instructions recorded and saved under a short key code or macro name. When the key code is typed or the macro name is entered, the program carries out the instructions of the macro. Users save time by creating a macro to replace an often-used and sometimes lengthy series of strokes with a shorter version.

mail merge *n.* A mass-mail facility that takes names, addresses, and sometimes pertinent facts about recipients and merges the information into a form letter or another basic document.

Microsoft Exchange Server administrator *n.* A person who manages a Microsoft Exchange Server network and who is responsible for maintaining the Microsoft Exchange software and handling the installation and configuration issues, among other problems, of users connected to the network.

Microsoft Knowledge Base *n.* A database created and maintained by Microsoft Technical Support that lists common software problems encountered by users of Microsoft products along with solutions for the problems. To access this database, go to *http://support.microsoft.com/directory/default.asp* and click Search Knowledge Base.

MIME *n.* Acronym for Multipurpose Internet Mail Extensions. A protocol widely used on the Internet that extends the SMTP (Simple Mail Transfer Protocol) to permit data, such as video, sound, and binary files, to be transmitted by Internet e-mail without having to be translated into ASCII format first. This is accomplished by the use of MIME types, which describe the contents of a document. A MIME-compliant application sending a file, such as some e-mail programs, assigns a MIME type to the file. The receiving application, which must also be MIME-compliant, refers to a standardized list of documents that are organized into MIME types and subtypes to interpret the content of the file. For instance, one MIME type is *text,* and it has a number of subtypes, including *plain* and *html.* A MIME type of *text/html* refers to a file that contains text written in HTML. MIME is part of HTTP, and both Web browsers and HTTP servers use MIME to interpret e-mail files they send and receive.

newsreader *n.* A Usenet client program that enables a user to subscribe to Usenet newsgroups, read articles, post follow-ups, reply by e-mail, and post articles. Many Web browsers also provide these functions. Outlook 2002 uses the Outlook Express newsreader that's part of the Internet Explorer Web browser software.

newsgroup *n.* A forum on the Internet for threaded discussions on a specified range of subjects. A newsgroup consists of articles and follow-up posts. An article and all its related follow-up posts constitute a thread. Each newsgroup has a name that consists of a series of words, separated by periods, indicating the newsgroup's subject in terms of increasingly narrow categories, such as rec.crafts.textiles.needlework. Some newsgroups can be read and posted to only on one site; others, such as those in the seven Usenet hierarchies or those in ClariNet, circulate throughout the Internet.

nickname *n.* An alternate name used to identify a contact, typically shorter than the contact's full name. The nickname can be entered on the Details tab of the Outlook Contact form.

note *n.* A form and data type in Outlook that enables users to keep relatively short text elements for temporary information or other data that they want to keep readily at hand.

offline storage file *(.ost)* *n.* A file containing Outlook data that can be accessed by Outlook while disconnected from the server.

overtype *n.* A text-entry mode in which newly typed characters replace existing characters under or to the left of the insertion point. *Also called* overwrite mode, typeover mode.

PAB *n.* Acronym for Personal Address Book, the Microsoft Exchange address book. Although the PAB can be maintained separately in Outlook 2002, it is recommended that it be converted to the Outlook Contacts folder.

password *n.* The string of characters entered by a user to verify his or her identity to the network. The system compares the code against a stored list of authorized passwords and users. If the code is legitimate, the system allows the user access at whatever security level has been approved for the owner of the password. Ideally, a password is a combination of text, numbers, and punctuation or other characters that cannot be guessed or easily cracked by intruders.

personal folders file *n.* A file with the extension of *.pst* that contains Outlook folders and items including e-mail, calendar data, and contacts. Outlook users who connect to a Microsoft Exchange Server do not have a personal folders file if all their data resides on the server.

plug-in *n.* A small software program that plugs into a larger application to provide added functionality. Most plug-ins are developed by software companies who have proprietary software in which the embedded files are created.

read receipt *n.* A notification automatically sent from the recipient of an e-mail message to the sender of the message when the message is received. A read receipt must be requested by the sender and is only sent by the recipient's mail program if it is compatible with this feature and if the recipient has not blocked the sending of this or all read receipts.

Registry or registry *n.* A central hierarchical database in Windows used to store information necessary to configure the system for one or more users, applications, and hardware devices. The Registry contains information that Windows continually references during operation, such as profiles for each user, the applications installed on the computer and the types of documents each can create, property sheet settings for folders and application icons, what hardware exists on the system, and which ports are being used. The Registry replaces most of the text-based *.ini* files used in Windows 3.*x* and MS-DOS configuration files, such as AUTOEXEC.BAT and CONFIG.SYS. Although the Registry is common to the several Windows platforms, there are some differences among them. *Also called* System Registry.

Reminder *n.* A feature of Outlook that notifies the user when an appointment is about to occur or a task is due. Reminders work only for appointments in the Calendar folder or tasks in the Tasks folder when the Reminder check box selected.

remote mail *n.* An Outlook feature available for any Microsoft Exchange Server user who wants to limit connection time when dialing in to retrieve e-mail by first downloading e-mail headers and then selecting specific complete e-mail messages to download. Remote mail works in conjunction with a Send/Receive group, the user's offline storage file, and the Work With Headers commands under Send/Receive on the Tools menu.

rich text format *n.* An adaptation of Document Content Architecture (DCA) that is used for transferring formatted text documents between applications, even applications running on different platforms, such as between IBM computers and compatibles and Macintosh computers.

Rules Wizard *n.* An Outlook feature that guides users through the process of creating e-mail rules.

Run dialog box *n.* The dialog box that appears when you click the Windows Start button and then click Run. It is typically used to run programs that do not appear as shortcuts on the Start menu or the Desktop.

script *n.* A program consisting of a set of instructions to an application or utility program. The instructions generally use the rules and syntax of the application or utility. On the World Wide Web, scripts are commonly used to customize or add interactivity to Web pages.

Send/Receive group *n.* An Outlook 2002 feature that enables users to define a set of criteria for sending or receiving e-mail from specific accounts. For example, a Send/Receive group might be created to minimize unnecessary transfers over slow or expensive connections by limiting downloaded messages to a certain size or by connecting only to e-mail accounts.

server *n.* **1.** On a local area network (LAN), a computer running administrative software that controls access to the network and its resources, such as printers and disk drives, and provides resources to computers functioning as workstations on the network. **2.** On the Internet or other network, a computer or program that responds to commands from a client. For example, a file server might contain an archive of data or program files; when a client submits a request for a file, the server transfers a copy of the file to the client.

signature *n.* A block of text that an e-mail client or a newsreader automatically places at the end of every message or article before the message or article is transmitted. Signature blocks typically contain the name, e-mail address, and affiliation of the person who created the message or article.

spam *n.* An unsolicited e-mail message sent to many recipients at one time, or a news article posted simultaneously to many newsgroups. Spam is the electronic equivalent of junk mail. In most cases, the content of a spam message or article is not relevant to the topic of the newsgroup or the interests of the recipient; spam is an abuse of the Internet in order to distribute a message (usually commercial) to a huge number of people at minimal cost.

subfolder *n.* A folder that exists within another folder and that can be opened only by first opening the outer folder.

synchronization *n.* In Outlook, the process of updating the offline storage file (*.ost*) with the Outlook data stored on a Microsoft Exchange server.

Task *n.* **1.** In Outlook, a data type and form that enables users to specify an item to be accomplished along with other information about the item, typically stored in the Outlook Tasks folder. **2.** A stand-alone application or a subprogram that is run as an independent entity.

TCP/IP *n.* Acronym for Transmission Control Protocol/Internet Protocol. A protocol suite (or set of protocols) developed by the Department of Defense for communications over interconnected, sometimes dissimilar, networks. It is built into the UNIX system and has become the de facto standard for data transmission over networks, including the Internet.

UNIX *n.* A multiuser, multitasking operating system. Originally developed by Ken Thompson and Dennis Ritchie at AT&T Bell Laboratories from 1969 through 1973 for use on minicomputers, UNIX has evolved into a complex, powerful operating system that, because it is written in the C language, is more portable—that is, less machine-specific—than many other operating systems. UNIX is widely used as a network operating system, especially in conjunction with the Internet.

URL (Universal Resource Locator) *n.* An address for a resource on the Internet. URLs are used by Web browsers to locate Internet resources. A URL specifies the protocol to be used in accessing the resource (such as *http:* for a World Wide Web page or *ftp:* for an FTP site), the name of the server on which the resource resides (such as *//www.whitehouse.gov*), and, optionally, the path to a resource (such as an HTML document or a file on that server).

Uuencode (UNIX to UNIX encode) *n.* A UNIX program that converts a binary file, in which all 8 bits of every byte are significant, into printable 7-bit ASCII characters without loss of information. This program (along with uudecode) allows binary data, such as images or executable code, to be disseminated through e-mail or newsgroups. A file thus encoded is one-third longer than the original.

Visual Basic for Applications (VBA) *n.* A macro-language version of Visual Basic that is used to program many Windows 9x applications and is included with several Microsoft applications.

virus *n.* An intrusive program that infects computer files by inserting copies of itself into those files. The copies are usually executed when the file is loaded into memory, allowing them to infect still other files, and so on. Viruses often have damaging side effects—sometimes intentionally, sometimes not. For example, some viruses can destroy a computer's hard disk or take up memory space that could otherwise be used by programs.

voting button *n.* A button control that is embedded in e-mail sent from one Outlook user to another, when both are clients of a Microsoft Exchange Server. The recipient responds to a question by clicking the button.

wizard *n.* An interactive help utility within an application that guides the user through each step of a particular task, such as starting a word processing document in the correct format for a business letter.

Quick fix index

Quick fix index

Index

A

D

E

I

J

L

M

R

S

About the authors

Don Gilbert

Don Gilbert has been writing about computer programs and operating systems for more than 16 years. As a technical writer at Microsoft for much of that time, Don gained technical experience of Microsoft products from the inside out by writing programming guides and documentation. In recent years, Don has shifted his focus to helping people who use, rather than write, software programs. He has authored one book for Microsoft Press on Windows 2000 Professional and has contributed to several other Microsoft Press books and projects, including the Web updates to the first edition of this book. When not researching, troubleshooting, or writing about computer problems, Don maintains what's left of his sanity playing piano and working in the garden.

Julia Kelly

Julia Kelly, cybergirl in cowspace, ex-jet jockey, and former mad scientist, has also done time as a hardware store cashier/barrista, theme park candy girl, veterinary cat holder, Caribbean pilot, graduate student, and teacher of diverse topics. She currently lives on her farm in north Idaho, where she writes books, teaches classes, builds databases, and shovels snow. When she's not at her computer, she's escaping from electrons in her pottery studio, barn, or garden.

Proof of Purchase

Use this page as proof of purchase if participating in a promotion or rebate offer on this title. Proof of purchase must be used in conjunction with other proof(s) of payment such as your dated sales receipt—see offer details.

Troubleshooting Microsoft® Outlook® 2002

0-7356-1487-3

____

CUSTOMER NAME

Microsoft Press, PO Box 97017, Redmond, WA 98073-9830